"I have served three congregations that offered mentoring programs for seminarians. Those programs varied from informal to highly structured. In all three churches, I came to understand that I was, happily, not the only mentor. Certain congregational members—some younger and some older—were often the most effective mentors to the seminarians who were passing through. How I wish I might have had this magnificent collection of essays, both to read myself and to pass around my congregations. Thompson and Murchison have gathered a wonderfully diverse assortment of wise mentors to reflect on what it means to be mentored and to mentor others faithfully."

— **Michael L. Lindvall**
The Brick Presbyterian Church, New York City

"I was surprised to realize this was the first book I have ever read about the power of mentoring. Yet I cannot imagine reading a better one. Thompson and Murchison have pulled together an amazingly rich, diverse collection of perspectives on the skills and gifts of both being a mentor and receiving that kind of guidance. The pages of my copy are now earmarked and underlined. I have no doubt I will keep coming back to it. While I was surprised that this was my first book to read about mentoring, I was not surprised that Thompson and Murchison were behind it. They have both been my mentors for a long time now. They practice what they preach."

— **Shannon Johnson Kershner**
Fourth Presbyterian Church, Chicago

Mentoring

Biblical, Theological,
and Practical Perspectives

Edited by

Dean K. Thompson and
D. Cameron Murchison

WILLIAM B. EERDMANS PUBLISHING COMPANY
GRAND RAPIDS, MICHIGAN

Wm. B. Eerdmans Publishing Co.
2140 Oak Industrial Drive N.E., Grand Rapids, Michigan 49505
www.eerdmans.com

27 26 25 24 23 22 21 20 19 18   1 2 3 4 5 6 7 8 9 10

ISBN 978-0-8028-7499-3

Library of Congress Cataloging-in-Publication Data

Names: Thompson, Dean K., editor.
Title: Mentoring : biblical, theological, and practical perspectives /
    edited by Dean K. Thompson and D. Cameron Murchison.
Description: Grand Rapids : Eerdmans Publishing Co., 2018. |
    Includes bibliographical references and index.
Identifiers: LCCN 2017042037 | ISBN 9780802874993 (pbk. : alk. paper)
Subjects: LCSH: Mentoring—Religious aspects—Christianity.
Classification: LCC BV4408.5 .M455 2018 | DDC 253—dc23
    LC record available at https://lccn.loc.gov/2017042037

To our mentors

Contents

Part 3: Diverse National and International
Communities of Mentoring

Part 4: Generational Mentoring

Foreword

Jill Duffield

I have a quilt that adorns the back of my sofa. Warm months render it simply decorative, but in colder seasons the blanket, stitched together by a group of church women I love, gets daily use. Over time, multiple washings have softened the fabric. The early stiffness is gone, and wrapping it around oneself feels easy and comforting. Instead of diminishing in value, the quilt gets better over time. The colors are varied, but complementary. Each square different, but connected. Sometimes I notice the intricate details, marvel at the small stitches, wonder which woman did which square. Other times I take in the whole, notice the patterns that emerge repeatedly, and recognize that without the batting and the large piece of cloth on the back, those parts that mostly go unseen, the whole thing would fall apart. The mantle not only gives the practical—warmth—but also provides a sense of care, a reminder of community, a means of making tangible the cloud of witnesses that surrounds us.

Reading this book, sometimes while wrapped in that quilt, provided a similar experience. The writers in this volume examine mentoring through many different lenses—theoretical, practical, biblical, academic, and anecdotal. There is a variety of tone and a depth and breadth of experience represented in the pages to follow. Hearing the questions posed, the stories recounted, the friendships cherished, makes for beautiful patterns that invite readers to consider their own mentors, mentees, and the importance of making space for these formative relationships. While each chapter, each square, is distinct and worthy of close exploration, the presence of the Holy Spirit, unseen but undeniable, sustains and illumines the entire volume.

There will be seasons when pulling this book from the shelf will be irresistible, the wisdom within required, because we never outgrow the need for mentors, and this volume, in its parts and entirety, is performative. It does the word it speaks. Certain phrases will stick like a burr to cotton batting and reveal themselves unexpectedly in our daily living. Over and over again, in prayer, in meetings, while writing, Katie Cannon's pointed question in her chapter on womanist mentoring came to my consciousness: "What is the work your soul must have?" Walter Brueggemann's chapter on mentoring in the Old Testament gave me this insight and marching order: "Remembered experience is mobilized as guidance for new circumstances." Thomas Long gave me a new way of understanding the power of preaching: "Courage modeled in the pulpit undergirds personal courage in those who hear." Preaching, too, is mentoring.

Both instructive and lovely, the wisdom of the communion of the saints, the insights of the great cloud of witnesses, given voice in these pages both comforts and challenges. Cristian De La Rosa's chapter on mentoring new generations of Latin@ leaders caused me to consider the dominant culture of meritocracy and its racism and the subsequent importance of understanding "this contextual reality in academic settings, with equivalents in religious settings." Rebekah Miles names "potential ethical landmine[s] in mentoring relationships," lifting up the need for boundaries, accountability, and autonomy. Douglas Ottati shares a personal story of a mentor whose question, "Do you want to be the sort of person other people can trust or not?" shaped his character. Mentors do not always tell us what we want to hear; they encourage us to grow and stretch. Trusting the one who sees in us the potential to be more than we currently are allows for the vulnerability and risk that enable change to happen.

The stories and thoughts expressed in these pages do not simply evoke admiration or affirmation, nods of recognition, or even the pleasant surprise of questioning a long-held assumption. These chapters invite a response. Like a good mentor, this book offers more than, in the words of Tom Currie's chapter on theological/pastoral perspectives on mentoring, "mastering a text or doing well in a course with a great teacher. Something else is going on . . . the joyful embrace of one's own vocation, even the happy discovery of the mysterious beauty and power of this particular calling." Reading this book was at times devotional, as the mysterious beauty and power of my particular calling was illumined.

We are given the gift of mentors, the communion of the saints, the great cloud of witnesses, not for our own sake alone, but for the sake of the world. The mantle is always getting larger, more squares added, different patterns emerging, the blessing encompassing an ever-expanding circle of disciples who are then sent to keep it growing. The stories, wisdom, and voices of the saints present and represented in this book not only envelop the reader with the love and call of Jesus Christ; they equip and inspire us to get off the sofa and extend that love to others. That, in its many varied and lovely forms, is the essence of Christian mentoring.

Introduction

Dean K. Thompson and D. Cameron Murchison

As we first pondered this project, we found ourselves voicing special gratitude for several significant mentors who had given us our respective foundations and wings. We also noted that we both have been blessed by the dear privilege of serving as mentors. The *mentoring windows* included in this volume touch on matters that are deeply formative and also bear the possibility of lifelong impact. Thus, in his profound analysis of Dietrich Bonhoeffer's *Letters and Papers from Prison*, Martin E. Marty affirms that "when peers meet and talk with each other, or when a generous mentor and an assertive student engage each other, something goes on that has the chance of altering world views."[1]

Some mentors seem best at content sharing and at suggesting how to accomplish things. Most but not all of our cherished mentors have been exceptional listeners. Many mentors have embodied a winsome blend of competence, confidence, and humility, which are also the marks of many outstanding leaders.

Mentees often go to mentors in order to authenticate, amend, and correct their thoughts on and approaches to life. The word *mentor* calls to mind the Greek word *meno*, meaning "to abide" or "to remain." The mentoring context frequently involves an intimate, committed, continuous, developmental, and reciprocal relationship. This relationship includes a reciprocal availability, where unforced influence and helpfulness take place. To have a mentor who abides and remains available in times of need and in situations of potential growth is to open oneself to life-shaping possibilities. Many of us and our institutions are fortunate to make ourselves available to mentoring

---

1. Martin E. Marty, *Dietrich Bonhoeffer's* Letters and Papers from Prison: *A Biography* (Princeton: Princeton University Press, 2011), 27.

relationships that abide. Moreover, these relationships are characterized by the aspects of reciprocity and accessibility, by accountability and engagement, by attentiveness and accommodation.

In *The Road to Character*, David Brooks makes several observations that touch on the ways in which mentoring can happen: "Example is the best teacher. Moral improvement occurs most reliably when the heart is warmed, when we come into contact with people we admire and love and we consciously and unconsciously bend our lives to mimic theirs."[2] This may explain why mentors can rarely be assigned randomly. There needs to be a relationship that evokes admiration and even love from those who would be mentored, so that they instinctively (consciously and unconsciously) yearn to have their lives mimic (imitate) such a trusted friend. From a Christian perspective, this may illustrate why Christ can be thought of as the primal mentor, classically expressed in the phrase *the imitation of Christ*.

Brooks adds: "We all need people to tell us when we are wrong, to advise us on how to do right, and to encourage, support, arouse, cooperate and inspire us along the way."[3] Thus, the encouragement that mentors provide is not inevitably congratulatory, but also includes correction and perhaps reproof. It intends to support and inspire. When Brooks observes that "we can immerse ourselves in the lives of outstanding people and try to understand the wisdom of the way they lived,"[4] he raises the intriguing possibility that we can be mentored by figures from the past or at a distance, as long as there is some way to immerse ourselves in their lives and to understand the wisdom of their living.

Our *mentoring windows* resonate with the ancient proverbial sage who taught that "iron sharpens iron, and one person sharpens the wits of another" (Prov. 27:17). They likewise resonate with the teaching wisdom of Stanley Hauerwas: "We need examples and masters. . . . If we are without either, the church cannot exist as a people who are pledged to be different from the world. The church has a stake in holding together our being and behaving in such a manner that our doing can only be a reflection of our character. . . . The ongoing history of the church requires persons—characters, if you will— who are capable of living appropriate to God's activity in the life and death of Jesus Christ."[5]

2. David Brooks, *The Road to Character* (New York: Random House, 2015), xv.

3. Brooks, *Road to Character*, 130.

4. Brooks, *Road to Character*, 15.

5. Quoted by Martin E. Marty, *Context*, February 1, 1986, 1.

Notwithstanding a considerable body of writing on mentoring, we have sensed a need for windows on mentoring that are biblically grounded, theologically informed, communally diverse, and generationally attentive. Thus, our gratitude is profound to all the colleagues who took up the challenge to help us see mentoring more clearly by writing chapters for this volume. We also want to offer words of thanks to Eerdmans Publishing Company for grace and support; to E. Carson Brisson, William P. Brown, Carlos F. Cardoza-Orlandi, Frances Taylor Gench, Justo Gonzalez, Clifton Kirkpatrick, Martin E. Marty, Patrick D. Miller, Joan Murchison, Rebecca Thompson, and Frank Yamada for helpful counsel; and to Ron Vinson for compiling the index.

As page proofs for this volume were being completed, word was received of the death of one of its contributors, David Bartlett. We are especially grateful for the typical, generous spirit that he brought to his chapter in this volume, and we believe it entirely fitting that one of his last published writings turned out to be about mentoring, which he so fully embodied.

PART I

Biblical Perspectives

CHAPTER 1

Mentoring in the Old Testament

Walter Brueggemann

Mentoring as an *idea* is a quite modern notion. The *practice* of mentoring, however, is quite old. It is as old as social relationships in which one person knows things that would help another person flourish with well-being and success. Characteristically (but not always) mentoring is a relationship between someone of an older generation with more experience providing guidance and counsel for someone in a younger generation.

The practice of mentoring, moreover, is an acknowledgment that this social relationship works amid the ambiguity of continuity and discontinuity. On the one hand, there is continuity, as the older person or both persons assume that wisdom and know-how from an earlier experience still pertains and is relevantly operative for the younger person. On the other hand the relationship assumes, when honest, an awareness of discontinuity, for circumstances and possibilities for the younger person are different; one cannot simply replicate or reiterate old wisdom without recognizing that a leap of imagination is required in order that the wisdom of older experience can be recalibrated for new circumstance. Thus the mentoring relationship depends for its effectiveness on both in honoring what has been learned from the past and in recognizing that "new occasions teach new duties."[1] In what follows I will consider several examples in the Old Testament of that venturesome process and the way in which remembered experience is mobilized as guidance for new circumstances.

---

1. James Russell Lowell, "The Present Crisis"; available at: https://www.poets.org/poets org/poem/present-crisis.

Wisdom Tradition

It is appropriate to begin our investigation of mentoring in the Old Testament with reference to the wisdom tradition and most particularly the book of Proverbs. The very term *wisdom* by which we designate the books of Proverbs, Job, and Ecclesiastes refers to the accumulated learning of the community over time that is passed from generation to generation. This accumulated learning has arisen from actual experience, observation, and discernment about how the world works, even though that empirical data has been variously stylized and reduced to standard (normative) articulation. Its rootage is quite practical.

The practicality of this accumulated tradition over time has two dimensions to it. On the one hand, it is quite pragmatic. The wise know what works and what fails to work toward success, security, wealth, or a good reputation. That is why there is advocacy concerning hard work, avoidance of debt, shunning of bad companions, and danger of wanton speech. On the other hand, the legacy of Proverbs is devoted to identifying modes of life and conduct that are in sync with the will of the Creator. As a result, wisdom teaching is labeled as "creation theology" because it is a reflection on how the world works as it has been ordered by the Creator God. While some interpreters attempt to distinguish between *pragmatic, secular learning* and *theological wisdom*, it is not possible in the ancient world to make such a distinction. What "works" is what is in sync with God's will for creation. That legacy of wisdom, based on experience and observation, is an offer to the younger generation. James Crenshaw observes that this treasury of experience was passed on with great authority to the next generation so that it remained important even when problematized: "This treasury from the past came with certain claims of authority and therefore placed new generations in a context of decision. . . . In a sense, the legacy from the past comprised faith reports, and devotion toward parents complicated matters enormously. The tendency was to accept these faith reports at face value, even when they contradicted the personal experience of later generations."[2]

Crenshaw further observes that the receiving voice of the younger generation is "the missing voice" in the tradition:[3] "The usual speakers in the Book of Proverbs are parents, both father and mother. They teach their children in

2. James L. Crenshaw, *Education in Ancient Israel: Across the Deadening Silence* (New York: Doubleday, 1998), 125.

3. Crenshaw, *Education in Ancient Israel*, 187.

the privacy of the home. . . . To shape character in the youth, parents rely on insights accumulated over years of experience by the community at large. These fresh discoveries, stated in succinct form, are presented as statements demanding assent because they represent a consensus. Such sayings need not be argued or defended; they just are."[4] Thus it is plausible to think that the mentoring of the wisdom tradition was one-directional; except that the poem of Job bears witness to critical restlessness with such an authoritative tradition so that, as the book of Job has it, a radically different articulation was required in order to resonate with lived experience.

The stylized mentoring in the wisdom tradition is from father to son, so that we get a chorus of "Listen, my son": "In Proverbs, the father-to-son setting continues through chapters 1–9 and is assumed occasionally elsewhere in the book. . . . Twice, the father associates his teaching with that of the youth's mother (1:8 and 6:20), but she never speaks directly to the son."[5] There is no doubt that this teaching is highly stylized, but surely it reflects the patriarchal setting of the tradition.

An important exception to masculine figures of speech in the book of Proverbs are the words of "King Lemuel," who repeats "an oracle that his mother taught him" (31:1). This mentoring took place in the royal household, but it might be the admonition that any mother would give to a son, a warning about dangerous sex and the risks of alcohol. Beyond that, the mother summons her royal son to exercise royal authority in a particular direction:

> Speak out for those who cannot speak,
>   for the rights of all the destitute.
> Speak out, judge righteously,
>   defend the rights of the poor and needy. (Prov. 31:8–9)

Christine Roy Yoder comments on this counsel: "The mother implores Lemuel to do his job, to enact and protect just laws and judgments and to advocate for the poor, whose lack of voice and powerlessness she captures with the expressions 'mute' and 'those passing away.' When people cannot speak—*especially* when they cannot—the king must speak for them."[6] In this wisdom tradition, for the most part there is no comeback from those who are addressed,

---

4. Crenshaw, *Education in Ancient Israel*, 133.

5. Christine Roy Yoder, *Proverbs*, Abingdon Old Testament Commentaries (Nashville: Abingdon, 2009), 13.

6. Yoder, *Proverbs*, 292.

an indication that the tradition of accumulated wisdom has great authority. It is evident, moreover, that it is all about sons, without reference to daughters, what one would expect in a patriarchal setting. Indeed the reorientation from patriarchy to an inclusive "sons and daughters" is itself an example, in our own time, of the way in which mentoring requires discontinuity and a leap of imagination to new social reality.

Early Narratives

From the early narrative materials of the Old Testament, I review three instances of mentoring, recognizing that the textual evidence is terse; it requires and permits extensive unpacking according to our theme.[7]

Jethro-Moses (Exodus 18)

In the wake of the exodus and the crisis of food and water in the wilderness, Moses was left with the task of consolidating the erstwhile slave community into a sustainable institutional form. Fortunately his father-in-law, Jethro, came to his rescue and mentored Moses on the management of that onerous process. The meeting between Jethro and Moses is highly stylized and couched in phrasings of theological awareness. Moses greets Jethro in solemn deference, and they exchange greetings of mutual concern (Exod. 18:7). Moses bears witness to Jethro concerning the exodus deliverance, and Jethro responds in kind (18:8–12).

Then the narrative moves beyond conventional formula to practical matters. Jethro observes Moses functioning as judge and administrator of the people. Before he mentors Moses, he must be sure he has rightly sized up the situation. The exchange between them radically alters Moses's assumptions and actions:

- Jethro questions Moses in a way that has a note of reprimand: "What is this that you are doing for the people? Why do you sit alone, while all the people stand around you from morning until evening?" (18:14).
- Moses explains that he is acting responsibly (18:15–16a).

---

7. By "early narrative materials" I refer to the time that the text purports to narrate. I raise no critical question here concerning the historical origin of the text.

- Jethro, in a more extended speech, offers Moses specific advice: "I will give you counsel" (18:19).

Moses had not asked for such counsel and likely would have continued his burdensome task without critical reflection. Jethro intrudes into Moses's busyness with a series of imperative recommendations:

> You should represent the people before God,
> and you should bring their cases before God;
> teach them the statutes and instructions
> and make known to them the way they are to go. . . .
> You should also look for able men . . .
> set such men over them. (18:19–21)

Jethro concludes: "Let them sit as judges for the people at all times; let them bring every important case to you, but decide every minor case themselves. So it will be easier for you, and they will bear the burden with you. If you do this, and God so commands you, then you will be able to endure, and all these people will go to their home in peace" (18:22–23).

Jethro proposes a new judicial structure that will ease Moses's work and urges Moses to focus on his most important tasks. Moses heeds Jethro's counsel and undertakes new practices whereby he shares responsibility (18:24–25). Jethro's uninvited wisdom rescues Moses from his overcommitment to his work and reminds Moses that he needs help and that alternatives are available. Jethro is a model mentor who identifies the crisis, suggests a solution, and permits greater effectiveness by Moses with less personal cost. Well done!

Moses-Joshua (Numbers 27:18–23)

There is no doubt that the tradition intends to exhibit Joshua as the successor to Moses and is at some pains to establish his authority in that role. Joshua functions in the narrative as an aide to Moses, who assists him in his various tasks, notably as military leader (Exod. 17:9–14; 24:13; 33:11; Num. 11:28). It is clear that Joshua, in his role as aide to Moses, is being instructed and groomed to assume leadership.

The most interesting part of their relationship is the way in which Moses takes care to fully authorize Joshua to carry on his work:

- He changes Joshua's name, thus giving him a new identity in the tradition (Num. 13:16).
- He authorizes him to be shepherd of the sheep by laying hands on him (Num. 27:18–23; see Deut. 34:9). The latter text notes that Joshua is "full of the spirit of wisdom," surely a result of having been with Moses for so long.

The specificity of mentoring is evident in two accent points. On the one hand, Moses "charges" Joshua with a mission to complete the transition into the new land: "Be strong and bold, for you shall bring the Israelites into the land that I promised them; I will be with you" (Deut. 31:23). On the other hand, when Joshua tries to stop the prophesying in the camp, Moses reprimands him: "Are you jealous for my sake? Would that all the LORD's people were prophets, and that the LORD would put his spirit on them!" (Num. 11:29).

The entire narrative process shows the way in which Joshua is prepared for leadership. By their companionship in which he is the compliant junior partner, Joshua is inculcated into Moses's vision of what can be done and must be done. Moses is effectively shaping him for the hard work that is to come.

Eli-Samuel (1 Samuel 3:1–18)

This narrative is well known. The young Samuel is "under care" to the decrepit priest Eli. Sleeping in the temple, Samuel is three times addressed by YHWH but, young as he is, he does not know it. It remains for the aged Eli to recognize what is going on, so that he instructs Samuel on how to receive the address from God. In our church reading, we regularly read through only 1 Samuel 3:10, the result being a lovely little romantic tale. The sharp edge of the text, however, is after this verse. Faithful to the advice of Eli, Samuel listens for the divine word that is given as prophetic oracle (3:11–14). It is astonishing that, in the very temple over which Eli presides, God declares that God will terminate the priestly house of Eli: "For I have told him that I am about to punish his house forever, for the iniquity that he knew, because his sons were blaspheming God, and he did not restrain them. Therefore I swear to the house of Eli that the iniquity of Eli's house shall not be expiated by sacrifice or offering forever" (3:13–14). It is no wonder that the young Samuel is "afraid to tell the vision to Eli" (3:15). Eli, however, is not corrupt as are his sons. He is a faithful priest who does not flinch from the divine declaration.

When Samuel reports the divine verdict against his house, Eli responds: "It is the LORD; let him do what seems good to him" (3:18).

This narrative has important aspects of mentoring. Samuel would not have received the divine word except for Eli's guidance. Beyond that, Eli and Samuel enjoy full confidence and trust in each other, so that Samuel can overcome his fear and tell Eli all. Eli, I suggest, is a model mentor. He understands that the child whom he mentors must grow decisively beyond him. He does not try to control or restrain Samuel, but fully accepts that Samuel must move into an arena that not only outruns Eli, but in fact turns in negativity against Eli. Good mentoring requires release of the one mentored to go beyond the horizon and interests of the mentor.

Prophetic Tradition

From the prophetic tradition, I comment on two instances of mentoring.

Elijah-Elisha (1 Kings 19:19–21)

The narrative encounter between Elijah and Elisha is terse. It is dominated by the threefold use of the term *follow*. In the first usage, Elisha proposes to follow Elijah. In the second use (translating a different Hebrew term), Elisha turns back from Elijah; and in the third usage he follows Elijah. He becomes Elijah's "aide," the same word used for Joshua. That is all. Elijah gives him no instruction or command. "Follow" surely means to be in the company and under the instruction of Elijah. The casting of his mantle over him, moreover, is an act of designation.

Their relationship, brief as it is, continues in the final scene of Elijah's life (2 Kings 2:1–12). In this narrative, Elisha promises three times:

I will not leave you. (2:2)

I will not leave you. (2:4)

I will not leave you. (2:6)

He is totally committed to Elijah. He then asks from Elijah "a double share of your spirit" (2:9). We are not told that he received it until the next paragraph, when his companions observed his mighty act and drew the conclusion: "The spirit of Elijah rests on Elisha" (2:15).

This is all accomplished in the narrative without any utterance by Elijah except for his quite enigmatic statement about bequeathing his spirit to Elisha. Clearly Elijah has mentored Elisha by his presence, his courage, and his performance. By being so closely committed to him, Elisha "inherits" his transformative capacity. The mentor has given his disciple a capacity to continue his subversive work, which is detailed in the narratives that follow.

Hulda-Josiah (2 Kings 22:14–20)

I am not sure this counts as mentoring, because the prophet Hulda never meets with Josiah. But she does address him. In the wake of finding the scroll in the temple, the closest advisors of King Josiah approach Hulda to consult with her. Second Kings 22:18 makes clear that they come to Hulda at the behest of the king. They wonder what to make of the onerous words of the scroll, presumably the disastrous curses for covenant disobedience in Deuteronomy 28, the book that is commonly identified as the scroll that had been found. Hulda's response to their inquiry is in two parts. First, in 2 Kings 22:15–17, she issues a characteristic prophetic speech of judgment. In 22:16 she confirms the threat of the scroll that there will be a coming disaster on Jerusalem and its inhabitants. In 22:17, introduced by "because," the death sentence of 22:16 is justified by an indictment for covenantal disobedience and the worship of other gods in defiance of the first command of Sinai. This oracle is surely a cliché of familiar prophetic rhetoric.

What surprises us and what may qualify as mentoring is that in 22:18–20 Hulda makes an exception to the speech of judgment and directly addresses the king himself, even though he has not come to see Hulda. This second part of her oracle has the same structure in reverse as the preceding, marked by "because ... therefore." The "because" of Josiah is that he has taken the scroll seriously and has effectively engaged in penitence and humbleness before its great threat (22:18–19). He has acted out his humbleness by tearing his clothes (22:11) and by weeping in sad repentance. That is, he does not respond to the scroll with royal imperviousness, but knows himself to be addressed. He is a true child of the Torah.

As a result Hulda can promise the king, with a "therefore," a peaceable death in which he will not have to witness the savage undoing of Jerusalem. The king will be immune to the threat of covenant curses evoked by disobedience to the Torah. That Josiah in fact died a violent death at the hand of his enemy (23:29–30) does not discredit the assurance offered at the time. Mentoring is not omniscient but makes the best judgment available at the time. It cannot control or predict the outcome of any choice, but invites the one mentored to take chances on the future on the basis of best choice.

In the case of Hulda and Josiah, there is no doubt that in framing the literature as it is, Hulda is a "plant" designed to voice the Deuteronomic urgency that Josiah is made to perform. That larger concern, however, does not detract from the narrated specificity of Hulda-to-Josiah. Her mentoring of the king is a reinforcement of Josiah's life choices. In 23:25 Josiah's life choice is given in a quite stylized generic way. In Jeremiah 22:15–16, by contrast, it is expressed with more specificity concerning "justice and righteousness" for the "poor and needy."

Royal Figures

The Hulda-Josiah narrative provides a fine segue to consider mentoring among royal figures. Here I cite three instances of such mentoring.

Hushai-Ahithophel-Absalom (2 Samuel 15–17)

In his rebellion against his father, David, Absalom has available two mentors, and he must choose between them. On the one hand, he has available the sobering mentoring of Ahithophel whose "wise" counsel is like "the oracle of God" (2 Sam. 16:23). Ahithophel advises Absalom to commit an overt act of defiance by publicly usurping the authority of his father by dramatically seizing his father's concubines. The alternative mentor is Hushai, who has been recruited by David to infiltrate Absalom's coup and subvert the more practical advice of Ahithophel (15:32–37). In contrast to the simple but strong stratagem of Ahithophel, Hushai, in a quite bombastic speech, counsels Absalom to huge military gestures that are quite impractical (17:7–13).

The narrative is arranged so that Absalom has to choose between the two counselors. In the end, "Absalom and all the men of Israel said, 'The counsel of Hushai the Archite is better than the counsel of Ahithophel.' For the LORD had ordained to defeat the good counsel of Ahithophel, so that the LORD might bring ruin on Absalom" (17:14).

Hushai has been mandated by David to "defeat for me the counsel of Ahithophel" (15:34). And so it happens. It is as though Absalom's judgment is impaired so that he cannot see how foolish is the advice of Hushai. Hushai counsels Absalom to make the wrong choice that leads to his wholesale defeat. Mentoring does not occur in contexts of simple innocence. Mentoring is most important in the midst of complexity when difficult choices have to be made. In this case, Absalom chooses, but chooses wrongly, perhaps because of being seduced by the sweeping rhetoric of Hushai.

In the end, however, the narrator lets us know what Absalom could not have known, that "the LORD had ordained" that Absalom would follow the wrong mentor. The term that the New Revised Standard Version renders "ordained" is *tsavah*, "to command." The narrator does not comment on this astonishing disclosure. The acknowledgment made in this verse is a recognition that historical choices are not clear and rational. They are rather complex, and the route to decision making is so hidden that room is allowed for the surreptitious working of God, even in ways that we do not recognize. This narrative voices an awareness that a choice of mentors and a decision about strategy are finally in the hands of God. The narrative, aware of the limits of human wisdom and human imagination, resituates all mentoring in a cloud of unknowing. The end of the narrative is an echo of the conviction that wisdom finally is not control; it is yielding to a cunning reality beyond our best wisdom:

> No wisdom, no understanding, no counsel,
>   can avail against the LORD.
> The horse is made ready for the day of battle,
>   but the victory belongs to the LORD. (Prov. 21:30–31)

Gerhard von Rad comments on these verses: "Its aim is, rather, to put a stop to the erroneous concept that a guarantee of success was to be found simply in practicing human wisdom and in making preparations. Man must always keep himself open to the activity of God, an activity that completely escapes all calculation, for between the putting into practice of the most reliable wisdom and that which then actually takes place, there always lies a great unknown."[8] Thus all mentoring is sharply relativized.

---

8. Gerhard von Rad, *Wisdom in Israel* (Nashville: Abingdon, 1972), 101.

David-Solomon (1 Kings 2:1–9)

There is no reason to suppose, in the scope of the royal narrative, that David had any ongoing connection of intimacy with his son and heir, Solomon. It is only on his deathbed that David offers counsel to his son. Indeed, it is his last act and last utterance in the narrative, after which his death is reported (1 Kings 2:10–12). The deathbed counsel of king to prince is like a last will and testament.

In 2:1–4 David gives counsel to Solomon that fully expresses Deuteronomic conviction: "Be strong, be courageous, and keep the charge of the LORD your God, walking in his ways and keeping his statutes, his commandments, his ordinances, and his testimonies, as it is written in the law of Moses, so that you may prosper in all that you do and wherever you turn" (2:2–3).

Everything depends on Torah obedience. The father counsels his son to "do the right thing." David himself has not been a spectacular Torah-keeper. In this scene, it is as though David undertakes deathbed repentance or reparation and gives covenantal advice to his son, even if that advice contradicts the ruthless way of his own life. Indeed, Nathan had accused David directly of violating Torah (2 Sam. 12:9). That violation, however, does not tell against mentoring. Many mentors have learned the hard way and give counsel to "do better than I have done."

That Torah-oriented Deuteronomic counsel, however, is juxtaposed directly in 1 Kings 2:5–9 by a very different counsel that sounds more authentically like what David might say. Now David expresses no piety, but offers the crassest kind of pragmatism in which he urges his son to protect himself and his coming rule by hard-nosed realism against those who had opposed the father and who constitute an ongoing threat to the son:

- Concerning Joab, his ruthless general who had done his dirty work, he is to be eliminated: "Act therefore according to your wisdom, but do not let his gray head go down to Sheol in peace" (2:6). David's horizon is here limited to "your wisdom," the same limited orientation with which David earlier assured Joab concerning the murder of Uriah: "Do not let this matter trouble you" (2 Sam. 11:25). Unfortunate translations have eliminated the intentional parallel between "your eyes" in 2 Samuel 11:25 and "YHWH's eyes" in 12:1.[9] This is wisdom with a very "low ceiling," limited to quite visible self-interest.

9. Many English translations render the first as "displease [*or* trouble] you" and the second as "displeased the LORD," thereby losing the contrast between "your eyes" and "YHWH's eyes."

- Concerning Barzillai, David counsels generosity as a payback for previous hospitality and support offered by Barzillai (1 Kings 2:7). Perhaps this counsel is designed to soften the brutality of his extended advice to his son, or to exhibit royal generosity in the midst of royal violence.
- Concerning Shimei, a continuing advocate of the rival rule of Saul's family, David urges brutal retaliation (2:8–9). As with Joab, David urges Solomon to act "according to your wisdom." Clearly David's notion of wisdom amounts to calculating self-protection and self-advancement, a kind of political shrewdness that contradicts the long-term intent of Torah wisdom. This recommendation to kill Shimei is David's final utterance.

In the narrative that follows, Solomon readily follows through on David's mentoring and proceeds to eliminate his enemies. In a sequence not unlike the violent sequence in *The Godfather*, Solomon, via Benaiah his general, eliminates all of his rivals and would-be challengers: Adonijah (2:25), Joab (2:34), and Shimei (2:46). In the narrative report of implementation, the advice to "deal loyally" with Barzillai is not mentioned. Moreover, Abiathar, who did not make David's hit list, now appears in Solomon's narrative of execution. Solomon does not kill the priest "at this time," but clearly the royal threat lingers over Abiathar (2:26–27).

The juxtaposition of 2:1–4 and 2:5–9 is stunning; the editor, moreover, takes no trouble at all to comment on or to justify the contradiction. But mentoring can be like that, filled with contradictions as the mentor may send mixed messages reflective of both *noble ideals* and *ignoble self-interest*. In this case as in so many cases, the counsel of emotive self-interest prevails. Solomon became a Torah-keeper (3:12–13). That commitment, however, fades as Solomon goes farther down the road of self-aggrandizement with predatory tax policies, forced labor, economic greed, and compromising religious commitments. Perhaps he takes his father's ambiguous counsel as warrant for his own deeply compromised reign. The Deuteronomist belatedly hopes for better concerning Torah obedience (6:11–13; 9:4–5), but it is a disappointed hope.[10]

---

10. Walter Brueggemann, *Solomon: Israel's Ironic Icon of Human Achievement* (Columbia: University of South Carolina Press, 2005), 139–59.

Mordecai-Esther (Esther 4:10–17)

The Persian imperial household of Ahasuerus was an arena, like many such arenas, for hardball in which contending parties played for keeps. Early on, Queen Vashti is banished because she refused the summons of the king. Her successor, Esther, is fully aware of the risks of disobedience to the royal whim. With word of Haman's vendetta against the Jews, Mordecai, a big player in royal affairs, urges Queen Esther to make supplication to the king on behalf of the Jews. Tim Beal describes Esther's speech of refusal as a "long way of saying no" (Esther 4:10–11).[11] It is in this ominous circumstance that Mordecai mentors Esther to think beyond conventional royal protocol and to run risks commensurate with the danger to the Jews. She, however, will not be commanded by Mordecai, who seeks to mentor her to risky conduct.

In response to Esther's refusal, the counsel of Mordecai becomes more urgent and more demanding. He warns Esther that she will not in any case be safe because she refuses to act. Then he summons her afresh to risk: "For if you keep silence at such a time as this, relief and deliverance will rise for the Jews from another quarter, but you and your father's family will perish. Who knows? Perhaps you have come to royal dignity for just such a time as this" (4:14).

Esther's response is an acceptance of the challenge of Mordecai (4:16). After an extended pause for fasting, she is prepared to run the risk of confronting the king. By this remarkable exchange, Esther is transformed into an active agent. In 4:8 Mordecai seeks to command Esther. By 4:17 she will now command Mordecai. His role as her mentor is crucial to the narrative. His role shows the way in which mentoring may amount to a call beyond conventional prudence to take a leap of faith and to run great risks. Mentoring may be wise, but it is not always prudent. Sometimes it is a way to summon one to become a bold history maker. In what follows in the narrative, Esther does, in response to the challenge of Mordecai, play a decisive role in the history of her people and in the history of the empire. Mentoring in this case is the trigger that turns the course of history. Mordecai does not flinch from putting his prodigy at risk in the service of an urgent cause.

11. Timothy K. Beal, *The Book of Hiding: Gender, Ethnicity, Annihilation, and Esther,* Biblical Limits (New York: Routledge, 1997), 71.

Variety of Styles and Strategies

It is clear from these examples that mentoring allows for a great variety of styles and strategies. In each case, the mentor seeks to guide the advisee in a particular direction; in these cases, the mentoring advice is characteristically accepted.

It does not surprise that in this *Torah-dominated*, YHWH-focused tradition, much of the mentoring is an urging to stay faithful to YHWH and to YHWH's Torah. Such an urging, however, often has in purview a particular outcome. Thus:

- Moses charges Joshua that the land promised by YHWH may be received; he has YHWH declare: "Be strong and bold, for you shall bring the Israelites into the land that I promised them; I will be with you" (Deut. 31:23).
- Eli counsels Samuel to listen for YHWH's will, even if that divine word subsequently tells against Eli and his house: "Go, lie down; and if he calls you, you shall say, 'Speak, LORD, for your servant is listening.' . . . It is the LORD; let him do what seems good to him" (1 Sam. 3:9, 18).
- Elijah summons Elisha to follow and gives him, at the end, the power of his spirit: "You have asked a hard thing; yet, if you see me as I am being taken from you, it will be granted to you; if not, it will not" (2 Kings 2:10).
- Hulda commends Josiah because he has been humble and penitent. Hulda has the Lord say: "Because your heart was penitent, and you humbled yourself before the LORD, when you heard how I spoke against this place, and against its inhabitants, that they should become a desolation and a curse, and because you have torn your clothes and wept before me, I also have heard you, says the LORD" (2 Kings 22:19).

There is a commonality in these instances, for each mentor is singularly committed to the rule of YHWH and urges in each case trusting obedience to YHWH.

There are, however, important variations on our defining theme, so that mentoring may go in many specific directions:

- The advice of Jethro to Moses (which he heeded) is quite practical concerning the organizational development of his administration.
- The mentoring that David provides for Solomon is profoundly ambiguous. One has the impression that the real force of the words of father to son is a call to purge one's adversaries and so to eliminate their potential threat, all the Torah talk notwithstanding.

- Hushai's advice to Absalom is cynical and calculating. In fact Hushai has intentions that are wholly contrary to the good outcomes he ostensibly offers to Absalom.
- Mordecai's urging to Esther is a summons beyond conventional self-interest to risky action for a larger good.

In these latter four cases, appeal to YHWH is less than central:

- Jethro alludes to God (not YHWH!) in his rhetorical flourish, but that is clearly not essential to his guidance.
- David begins with an appeal to YHWH and to YHWH's Torah; such reference appears to be only pro forma in light of what follows.
- Hushai's imaginative counsel makes no reference to God, though we are able to know what Hushai does not know, that YHWH is deeply implicated in his manipulative mentoring words.
- The closest Mordecai comes to such divine reference is an allusion to "another quarter," which suggests that more is underway here than what Esther perceives (Esther 4:14).

Clearly mentoring readily moves back and forth between an acute theological sensibility and quite practical awareness of specific tasks that need to be accomplished.

Our beginning point in wisdom has an appropriate concluding counterpoint with reference to Deuteronomy, as Deuteronomy is likely much shaped by sapiential interpretive tradition.[12] *The commanding voice of Deuteronomy* clearly intends to recruit the next generation into the salvific memory and its durable requirements. Thus the mentoring advice of Deuteronomy is consistently to adhere to the Torah tradition as the singular path to life and well-being. Thus in Deuteronomy 6, following the Shema, Moses urges Israel: "Recite [God's commands] to your children and talk about them when you are at home and when you are away, when you lie down and when you arise. Bind them as a sign on your hand, fix them as an emblem on your forehead, and write them on the doorposts of your house and on your gates" (6:7–9).

Moses proposes saturation socialization.[13] In 6:20–25, moreover, the normative memory is to be told to the children in order that they should not fall

---

12. Moshe Weinfeld, *Deuteronomy and the Deuteronomic School* (Oxford: Clarendon, 1972).

13. Walter Brueggemann, *Biblical Perspectives on Evangelism: Living in a Three-Storied Universe* (Nashville: Abingdon, 1993), 94–128.

into indifferent amnesia. The counsel of Deuteronomy is to heed the Torah, which is Israel's true wisdom:

> See, just as the LORD my God has charged me, I now teach you statutes and ordinances for you to obey in the land that you are about to enter and occupy. You must observe them diligently, for this will show your wisdom and discernment to the peoples, who, when they hear all these statutes, will say, "Surely this great nation is a wise and discerning people!" For what other great nation has a god so near it as the LORD our God is whenever we call to him? And what other great nation has statutes and ordinances as just as this entire law that I am setting before you today? (4:5–8)

Michael Fishbane notices the intense urgency in the counsel of Deuteronomy. He concludes, albeit in a patriarchal mode: "The teaching of the fathers in Deuteronomy 6:20–25 is an attempt to involve their sons in the covenant community of the future, and undoubtedly reflects the sociological reality of the settlement in Canaan. The attempt by fathers to transform their uninvolved sons from '*dis*temporaries' to *con*temporaries, i.e., time-life sharers, is an issue of supreme and recurrent significance in the Bible."[14] Thus the mentoring process hopes for continuity in the practice of Torah-wisdom. As every wise mentor knows, however, the ones advised have freedom and may make leaps into newness that are remote and discontinuous from what the mentor has in mind, sometimes for evil, sometimes for good (Gen. 50:20).

14. Michael Fishbane, *Text and Texture: Close Readings of Selected Biblical Texts* (New York: Schocken, 1979), 81–82.

CHAPTER 2

Mentoring in the New Testament

David L. Bartlett

Not surprisingly there is no word in New Testament Greek that can readily be translated into the English word *mentor*. Therefore in order to study mentoring in the New Testament we need to look at terms and passages that shed light on a concept that is never itself employed in the New Testament.

All this is to say that no one in the New Testament can simply be identified as a mentor. However, as we shall see, there are places where Paul acts in ways close enough to our interest in mentoring that we can appropriately see him as a mentor to other early Christians.

It seems much less clear that Jesus can rightly be described as a mentor. On the one hand, the quest for Jesus the mentor sounds a little too much driven by our current agendas and theories of leadership, not all that different from the search for Jesus as CEO.[1] On the other hand, the concept of Jesus as mentor can seem a little tepid compared to the more common descriptions of him as Lord, Savior, Redeemer, King, and Master. No mentor worth his or her salt would aspire to any of those titles, and yet the New Testament unashamedly ascribes them all to Jesus. To put it too glibly, John's Gospel would have a very different christological climax if, when he saw the risen Lord, Thomas cried out, "My Mentor!" rather than what he does say: "My Lord and my God!" (John 20:28).

For these reasons this chapter will begin with Paul, then move to literature about Paul; and we will only then turn to the Gospels to see whether Jesus can help us understand mentoring or whether the term *mentor* can help us understand Jesus.

---

1. Laurie Beth Jones, *Jesus CEO: Using Ancient Wisdom for Visionary Leadership* (New York: Hyperion, 1995).

There is of course also good historical reason for proceeding in this way. Though the Gospels are the first New Testament books in the order of our canon, historically the earliest New Testament books are Paul's letters—with 1 Thessalonians being the earliest Christian writing we possess.

Paul and His Letters

If we look at Paul we can see how the relationship between mentor and mentee, or between teacher and pupil, or between apostle and congregation, emerged at the beginning of the Christian mission to the Gentiles, and from that study we may be able to discern some features of Paul's ministry that will help us raise the question of mentoring in the stories about Jesus.

Paul and His Companions

Like other letters of the time, Paul's letters always begin with the identification of the person sending the letter. Sometimes this self-identification includes others besides Paul: "Paul, an apostle of Christ Jesus by the will of God, and Timothy our brother" (2 Cor. 1:1); and "Paul, Silvanus, and Timothy, to the church of the Thessalonians" (1 Thess. 1:1).

We do not have a great deal of evidence of how Paul worked with Silvanus, Timothy, Titus, and others, but there is considerable evidence from the letters that Paul traveled with companions and included them in his ministry.[2]

We have some sense of what Paul expected from these companions. Certainly in some cases the companion was the scribe who actually wrote down the words of the letter. At the end of Galatians, Paul has taken the pen from whoever his scribe may be (we don't get a name this time) and says: "See what large letters I make when I am writing in my own hand!" (Gal. 6:11).

At other times the companion performs tasks assigned by Paul but also explicitly part of a common ministry. In 1 Thessalonians 3:1–3 Paul reminds the Thessalonians of the way in which Timothy has helped to fulfill Paul's own mission: "Therefore when we could bear it no longer, we decided to be left alone in Athens; and we sent Timothy, our brother and co-worker for God

---

2. The Pastoral Epistles, especially 2 Timothy, give rich description of this kind of relationship, but I think these are written some time after Paul's death (see discussion below).

in proclaiming the gospel of Christ, to strengthen and encourage you for the sake of your faith, so that no one would be shaken by these persecutions."

When Paul says that he "sent" Timothy we get the sense that as Paul is an ambassador for Christ, so Timothy is an ambassador for Paul. He ministers under Paul's authority, and he follows Paul's example in preaching, strengthening, and encouraging.

Though Paul does not use the Greek word that is the root for his own favorite title (*apostello*, "apostle") when he describes his work through Timothy, in 2 Corinthians he does use that term for Titus and an unnamed fellow believer: "Did I take advantage of you through any of those whom I *sent* to you? I urged Titus to go, and *sent* the brother with him. Titus did not take advantage of you, did he? Did we not consider ourselves with the same spirit? Did we not take the same steps?" (2 Cor. 12:17–18).

As the one sent by Paul, as the apostle's apostle, Titus shows three characteristics that indicate how Paul was a kind of mentor to him. First, he takes on something of Paul's authority. Second, he imitates Paul's behavior—he behaves with the same spirit. Third, he lives up to Paul's own high ethical standards by not taking any advantage of the Thessalonians.

In 2 Corinthians 8:16–24 Paul makes clear why he is sending Titus and the other believer to Corinth; they are to be his delegates in collecting an offering for the suffering believers in Jerusalem. Again Titus follows the pattern of his "mentor," Paul. God has "put in the heart of Titus the same eagerness for you that I myself have." Now a new theme emerges: as Titus's mentor, Paul has still not forced Titus to do anything: "He is going to you of his own accord." Again, while it is clear that Paul is the senior partner in this relationship, he refers to Titus as "my partner and co-worker in your service."

Though Paul has no term corresponding precisely to our term *mentor*, we can see in his relationship to his coworkers clues to what Christian mentoring might look like in our own time:

1. Paul's relationships are marked by mutuality and partnership.
2. Nonetheless, there is no doubt that Paul is the senior partner and that the mentee derives much of his authority from his relationship to Paul.
3. Mentees imitate the mentor, both in their integrity and in their zeal for the gospel and for the churches.

Paul and His Churches

There are two passages where Paul describes his relationship to the churches he has founded in ways that might be helpful as we think about Christian mentoring. Of course these texts do not describe a one-on-one relationship, but the relationship between a mentor and the community he mentors.

Philippians is the most affectionate of Paul's letters and describes a relationship between apostle and people that might provide some guidance for our thoughts on mentoring: "I thank my God every time I remember you, constantly praying with joy in every one of my prayers for all of you, because of your sharing in the gospel from the first day until now. I am confident of this, that the one who began a good work among you will bring it to completion by the day of Jesus Christ" (Phil. 1:3–6).

The word that the New Revised Standard Version translates as "sharing" is the Greek word *koinonia*, which can have a richer meaning than "sharing." In the context of the work of the ministry at Philippi the word can mean "partnership"—indicating that apostle and people are joined together in the common proclamation and work of the good news. Paul's apostleship is always only complete in his work with the churches he has founded.

The word could also be translated "fellowship"—the deep spiritual communion that apostle and church (mentor and mentee?) can share when they are engaged in common service.

For Christians this passage suggests that an essential mark of mentorship is prayer; no Christian who undertakes the care and growth of another can neglect the ministry of prayer, and none can serve without the prayer of the other. "Prayer partner" may be a kind of cliché of our church life, but it points to the reality of what any deep relationship in Christ must entail.

And the passage shows Paul's very deep hope for the congregation he has founded and nourished and prays for. It is hard to imagine any fruitful Christian relationship, including that of apostle and people—and we might expand this to include mentor and mentee—where either does not continue to hope for the other. The fulfillment of Paul's ministry is in the fullness of life of those he serves.

In 1 Thessalonians 2:7–8 Paul uses the image of a woman who is both nurse and mother to illuminate his relationship to the Thessalonian Christians: "But we were gentle among you, like a nurse tenderly caring for her own children. So deeply do we care for you that we are determined to share with you not only the gospel of God but also our own selves, because you have become very dear to us."

In his helpful commentary on the Thessalonian letters, Abraham Malherbe points out that Paul combines two images here—nurse and mother.[3] If a good nurse cares gently for someone else's children, how much more will she care lovingly for children of her own. That kind of deeply giving love and service is what marks Paul's relationship to the Thessalonians. In that sense he becomes mentor and more than mentor to them.

A Case Study: Philemon

In the Letter to Philemon we have a unique instance of Paul's relationship to a single member of one of his churches, Philemon. As we see how Paul deals with Philemon, we get a sense of what kind of wisdom we might find for mentoring from his example.

Philemon is a brief letter with a clear purpose, but some of the details of the story behind the letter are still somewhat unclear. Paul is in prison and has there met Onesimus. Onesimus is a slave who has run away from his owner, Philemon. Philemon is a member of one of the churches Paul has founded, probably in Colossae. He is clearly a leader of the church that meets in his house.

It is clear that Paul wants Philemon to welcome Onesimus back as a Christian brother, forgiving him for any perceived wrong. It is not clear whether Paul implicitly believes that Philemon should recognize his brotherhood with Onesimus by setting him free, or whether Paul asks only that he treat Onesimus with mercy and generosity.

In any case, we can see in the following features of the short letter some of the strategies Paul uses to try to persuade Philemon to open his heart to his departed slave.

First, and this may be more a matter of clever strategy than mentoring on Paul's part, Paul addresses the letter not only to Philemon but also to Apphia, probably Philemon's wife, and to Archippus, a friend, and then of course to the whole church. Second, Paul addresses Philemon as "friend and co-worker," acknowledging the kind of partnership that trusts Philemon but also entrusts him to Paul's guidance.

As with all of Paul's letters, except to the Galatians, Paul begins with a prayer of thanksgiving. The prayer mentions Paul's close ties to Philemon, but

3. Abraham Malherbe, *The Letters to the Thessalonians*, Anchor Bible 32 (New York: Doubleday, 2000), 146–47.

more than that, the prayer is a manifestation of those close ties. Philemon is one for whom Paul prays.

The reasons for Paul's gratitude point toward the request that he will make: "I pray that the sharing of your faith may become effective when you perceive all of the good that we may do for Christ. I have indeed received much joy and encouragement from your love, because the hearts of the saints have been refreshed through you my brother" (Philem. 6–7).

The New Revised Standard Version phrase *the sharing of your faith* translates the Greek word *koinonia* that we saw in Philippians 1. This sharing, this fellowship, this partnership includes fellowship with Christ, with Paul, with the community of Philemon's church. Paul will soon reveal that Onesimus is now also a believer, joined in that fellowship. Surely this partner who has refreshed the hearts of the saints will also refresh the heart of his returning slave.

The full reach of this *koinonia* becomes clear when Paul uses a variant of the same word again in Philemon 17: "So if you are really partnered/in fellowship with me, welcome Onesimus as you would welcome me" (my translation), that is as another member of that fellowship, as another partner. Now that Onesimus has become a Christian, he and Paul and Philemon are bound together in the same *koinonia*. Therefore Philemon will not be able to treat Onesimus in the old way: "That you might have him back forever, no longer as a slave but more than a slave, a beloved brother—especially to me but how much more to you, both in the flesh and in the Lord" (Philem. 15–16).

As he has in other passages Paul insists that his relationship to Philemon must be based in Philemon's good will and eagerness to serve the gospel. Paul does not intend to command or to coerce—a good reminder when we think of the richest kind of mentoring.

Paul does, however, invite Philemon to imitate Paul's own generous spirit in a reminder surely intended to provoke both guilt and compliance: "I, Paul, am writing this with my own hand.[4] I will repay [anything Onesimus owes you]. I say nothing about you owing me your own self" (Philem. 19).

Paul is the master of pretending not to say what he intends to say: "I will not boast, but if I would, here's what I'd say"; or: "I'm going to ask you a little favor, but I won't mention the big favor I did for you."

The paragraph reminds us a little of the parental email: "I'll understand

---

4. This is another place where Paul seems to take the pen from the scribe to emphasize his personal and emphatic commitment to what he says.

if you don't have time to do this for me. And I won't mention all that I've done for you." The mentor is a brother and a friend and a partner; he is also a parent slightly ready to be aggrieved and a senior partner, too.

In all these passages and in all these contexts Paul does not say what it means to be a mentor. But he shows us what it means to have friends, companions, and coworkers who look to him for wisdom. He shows us what it is to have churches that owe their life to him and still read his letters because he has influence, even authority, over them. He shows us what it is to draw on his relationship with Philemon to try to effect good for that other, newer brother—mentee?—Onesimus.

If we were to sum up Paul's clues for a strong mentorlike relationship they would include these:

- Acknowledge interdependence and partnership.
- Make that interdependence tangible through prayer for each other.
- Exhort without coercion.
- Set an example but without being obvious about it.
- Sustain the relationship through hope—for the other and for the unfolding goodness of God.

A Letter in Paul's Name

I am among those teachers of New Testament who believe that the three "Pastoral" Epistles—1 and 2 Timothy and Titus—were not written by Paul but were written in his name, at some time after his death. They were written by a follower of Paul who wanted to apply wisdom like Paul's to later situations in the churches. To put a complicated matter simply, the churches of the Pastoral Epistles seem to have moved toward more organized structure and more structured dogma than we find in the letters universally believed to be by Paul.

It is pertinent for the purposes of this chapter that each of those three letters claims to be a letter written by Paul to one of his younger companions; each looks very much like a letter that in our time a mentor might write to a beloved friend who looked to him or her for example and advice. So in these letters we either have someone acting like a mentor and doing so in Paul's name, applying what he thinks to be Pauline principles to later situations; or we have Paul late in his life giving wise advice as he prepares for his own death.

Of the three Pastoral Epistles, the letter that most clearly represents the wisdom of an elder Christian passed on to a younger is 2 Timothy. The letter is written in a form very much like the farewell speeches we find in the Old Testament (Jacob's blessing in Gen. 49:1–28; Moses's farewell in Deut. 33) and in some Jewish material written shortly before the New Testament (*Testament of the Twelve Patriarchs*).

In 2 Timothy 3–4 three themes point toward the author's understanding of what it might mean to be in partnership for the gospel, especially partnership between a more seasoned Christian and a younger one:

> Now you have observed my teaching, my conduct, my aim in life, my faith, my patience, my love, my steadfastness, my persecutions and suffering the things that happened to me in Antioch, Iconium, and Lystra. What persecutions I endured! Yet the Lord rescued me from all of them. Indeed, all who want to live a godly life in Christ Jesus will be persecuted. But wicked people and impostors will go from bad to worse, deceiving others and being deceived. But as for you, continue in what you have learned and firmly believed, knowing from whom you learned it, and how from childhood you have known the sacred writings that are able to instruct you for salvation through faith in Christ Jesus. All scripture is inspired by God and is useful for teaching, for reproof, for correction, and for training in righteousness, so that everyone who belongs to God may be proficient, equipped for every good work. (2 Tim. 3:10–17)

Paul urges Timothy to imitate him in two ways. First he urges him to remember and follow the teachings that Paul entrusted to him. Second and equally important, Paul urges Timothy to model his way of behavior after that of Paul—his aim in life, his patience, love, and steadfastness.

Like many an experienced teacher speaking to a younger pupil, or a parent speaking to a child, Paul encourages Timothy to live through the dangers and sufferings that he has to endure by reminding him that Paul himself lived through similar dangers. Anyone who has heard or given a parental lecture beginning with "I know just how you feel, because when I was your age I had plenty of problems, too" will recognize in this an attempt to build fellow feeling on the foundation of reminiscence. It is a familiar form of mentoring, whether or not it is a particularly effective one.

If, as I think, this is a letter written in Paul's name to a generation after Paul's death, the writer reminds this new generation of Christians that they are not the first to suffer for their faith.

In addition to calling for imitation and inspiring hope, 2 Timothy provides one more mode of mentoring—exhortation:

> In the presence of God and of Christ Jesus, who is to judge the living and the dead, and in view of his appearing and his kingdom, I solemnly urge you: proclaim the message; be persistent whether the time is favorable or unfavorable; convince, rebuke, and encourage, with the utmost patience in teaching. For the time is coming when people will not put up with sound doctrine, but having itching ears, they will accumulate for themselves teachers to suit their own desires, and will turn away from listening to the truth and wander away to myths. As for you, always be sober, endure suffering, do the work of an evangelist, carry out your ministry fully. (2 Tim. 4:1–5)

The reference to false doctrine and itching ears, to seductive teachers and mistaken myths, may be some clue to why the author felt the need to invoke Paul's authority (or why Paul felt he needed to reassert his authority) over some opponents. However, the actual features of these false teachings are entirely elusive.

What is not elusive is the strong emphasis on exhortation. Timothy and those like him are to continue teaching bravely, and as we have seen they are to hold fast to those truths whose validity is rooted in tradition—in Paul, but also in Paul's generation and the doctrines they have passed on. Paul is not Timothy's only mentor: his mother and grandmother were his first teachers (2 Tim. 1:5).

The final chapter of the letter draws explicitly on the power of remembrance to inspire courage and imitation: "As for me, I am already being poured out as a libation, and the time of my departure has come. I have fought the good fight, I have finished the race, I have kept the faith. From now on there is reserved for me the crown of righteousness, which the Lord, the righteous judge, will give me on that day, and not only to me but also to all who have longed for his appearing" (2 Tim. 4:6–8).

We saw in Philippians and 1 Thessalonians how much Paul grounds the call to imitation of his life and affirmation of his teaching in the hope he has for himself and for all believers. Here 2 Timothy grounds Timothy's hope and the hope of the reader in the promise that those who like Paul are steadfast and patient will like Paul receive the crown of righteousness. Insofar as this becomes a model for mentoring, the Christian mentor always relates to the other in hope.

Thus in 2 Timothy we get a portrait of the relationship of the older and wiser apostle to his younger and earnest student. The relationship between the two is built on imitation, exhortation, and hope.

An Aside: A Story about Paul

Before turning to the Gospels we look at the other place in the New Testament besides the letters where Paul has a leading role—the Acts of the Apostles. I am inclined to think that Luke and Acts were written about the same time as the Pastoral Epistles—toward the end of the first century—and so, like 2 Timothy, they may reflect a somewhat later picture of Paul than the undisputed letters do.[5]

When Paul writes of his own astonishing new faith in Jesus and his apostleship, he tends to move from Jesus to himself without any intervention from mentors, teachers, or exemplars: "But when God, who had set me apart before I was born and called me through his grace, was pleased to reveal his Son to [or in] me, so that I might proclaim him among the Gentiles, I did not confer with any human being" (Gal. 1:15-16). In the context of Galatians it is clear that Paul means especially that he did not confer with any of the apostles dwelling in Jerusalem, and there is a great deal of silence surrounding the whole account of his call.

Writing some years later, however, the author of Acts provides Paul with a link between the already active church and himself:

> Now there was a disciple in Damascus named Ananias. The Lord said to him in a vision, "Ananias." He answered, "Here I am, Lord." The Lord said to him, "Get up and go to the street called Straight, and at the house of Judas look for a man of Tarsus named Saul. At this moment he is praying, and he has seen in a vision a man named Ananias come in and lay his hands on him so that he might regain his sight." But Ananias answered, "Lord, I have heard from many about this man, how much evil he has done to your saints in Jerusalem; and here he has authority from the chief priests to bind all who invoke your name." But the Lord said to him, "Go, for he is an instrument whom I have chosen to bring my name before Gentiles and

---

5. My late friend (and mentor!) Jerome A. Quinn argues that the Pastorals may have been written by the author of Luke and Acts as the third volume in a study of the church from Jesus through Paul and beyond; see *The Letter to Titus*, Anchor Bible 35 (New York: Doubleday, 1990).

kings and before the people of Israel; I myself will show him how much he must suffer for the sake of my name." So Ananias went and entered the house. He laid his hands on Saul and said, "Brother Saul, the Lord Jesus, who appeared to you on your way here, has sent me so that you may regain your sight and be filled with the Holy Spirit." And immediately something like scales fell from his eyes, and his sight was restored. Then he got up and was baptized, and after taking some food, he regained his strength.

For several days he was with the disciples in Damascus. (Acts 9:10–19)

We have no idea what Ananias said to Paul in those days but we can guess that the first readers of Acts would have known that when Ananias helped Paul gain his sight he did so not only physically but metaphorically. And when he was with the disciples in Damascus surely Paul did some listening before he began (almost immediately) proclaiming. At the very least his own remarkable experience on the road had to be followed by his participation in community, by some sense of dependence on the others who had been Christians first.

In fact there are two places in Paul's writings where he makes clear that his gospel did not come to him entirely in a vision or a dream: "For I handed on to you as of first importance what I in turn had received: that Christ died for our sins in accordance with the scriptures, and that he was buried, and that he was raised on the third day in accordance with the scriptures" (1 Cor. 15:3–4). That little phrase *in turn* makes clear what we would surely have suspected, that this preacher had heard the word preached, that the apostle had had someone or some ones who were sent (the root meaning of the word *apostle*) to deliver to him the good news of Jesus Christ—that he, too, had been mentored.

Again earlier in 1 Corinthians, Paul speaks of a tradition he received, though here he designates the bearer of the tradition as Jesus: "For I received from the Lord what I also handed on to you, that the Lord Jesus on the night he was betrayed, took a loaf of bread" (11:23). Paul then goes on to recite the story of Jesus's last supper. There is no doubt that Christ the Lord was the ultimate source of this tradition. But we have the same story in very similar words in Matthew, Mark, and Luke, and there can be little doubt that Paul received the story through the remembering and proclaiming of those who had followed Jesus before him.

Paul is very reticent about acknowledging those who opened to him the gospel, but someone had mentored him before he could mentor Philemon and Timothy and all those others.

Jesus in the Gospels

I began this essay by suggesting that the term *mentor* reflects important contemporary concerns but has no exact parallel in any word of the Greek New Testament. I further suggested that for all its conceptual richness, the term seems to fall far short of what the Gospel writers declare of Jesus:

Truly this man was God's Son! (Mark 15:39)

All authority in heaven and on earth has been given to me. (Matt. 28:18)

Then he led them out as far as Bethany, and, lifting up his hands, he blessed them. While he was blessing them, he withdrew from them and was carried up into heaven. And they worshiped him. (Luke 24:50–52)

Thomas answered him, "My Lord and my God!" (John 20:28)

The reason that the Gospel writers (and Paul) wanted to name Jesus "Christ" and "Lord" and "Son of God" was that they believed in his resurrection from the dead. Because of the resurrection, whatever the closest Greek word to "mentor" may have been, it seemed a little thin. But so did "master" and "teacher" and "healer."

Without faith in the resurrection, first-century writers would have told a very different story about Jesus; more likely they would not have bothered to tell his story at all. Yet in the light of the resurrection it became useful to remember and understand the Lord as master and teacher and healer, too.

So our question becomes not whether "mentor" is an adequate title for the Jesus of the Gospels, because the answer is obviously that it is not. The question is: do any of the Gospel writers, acknowledging Jesus as Lord, still show in his story some features that might help us understand what it is to be a mentor?

Somewhat to my surprise as I pondered this question I discovered that the Gospel that most helpfully shows Jesus in ways that approach mentoring is the Gospel with the very highest Christology—the Gospel of John. This is evident in at least three passages.

In John 12:20–25 some Greeks come and ask the disciples about Jesus, and Jesus tells them this: "The hour has come for the Son of Man to be glorified. Very truly, I tell you, unless a grain of wheat falls into the earth and dies, it remains just a single grain; but if it dies, it bears much fruit. Those who love their life will lose it, and those who hate their life in this world will keep it for eternal life" (John 12:23–25).

When Jesus refers to "the Son of Man" he is referring to himself. In John, Jesus will be glorified, above all, in his crucifixion, when he begins to return to the Father from whom he came. For Jesus the only way to bear fruit, to lead people to eternal life, is to be willing to sacrifice his own life.

To many students of John's Gospel, it seems that one reason John wrote his Gospel was to encourage timid believers of his own time—especially members of the synagogue—to give up the comforts and securities of their present lives and to identify with the more marginalized and insecure Christian churches. In this chapter John takes that claim and moves it beyond the synagogue to include Gentile believers as well—and suggests that for all (both the Son of Man and all humankind) the way to eternal life leads through death, whether physical death or the death that means giving up the comforts and prerequisites upon which people have based their lives.[6]

In this passage, therefore, Jesus invites the Greeks, the disciples who overhear the conversation, and those who will hear this gospel to give up any practice or any community that stands between them and faithfulness to the gospel.

Though Jesus is much more than a mentor, he does act like a mentor here: he calls others to imitate him. Of course, with most mentors one hopes that imitation will be a road to satisfaction and success. With Jesus, imitation is the way to eternal life.

A similar ethic of imitation marks one implication of the story of Jesus's washing the disciples' feet in John 13. The disciples have gathered for a meal, and Jesus insists on acting like a servant by washing their feet; Peter perhaps misunderstands what it is to be Lord or even mentor in this situation and insists that he should wash Jesus's feet. Jesus, of course, persists and after the foot washing he says: "Do you know what I have done to you? You call me Teacher and Lord—and you are right, for that is what I am. So if I, your Lord and Teacher, have washed your feet, you also ought to wash one another's feet. For I have set an example, that you should also do as I have done to you" (John 13:12–15).

It may be, as some denominations practice regularly and most denominations practice occasionally, that Jesus here presents an ordinance, a rite of worship, to be followed in the years ahead. But more obviously and probably

---

6. For a more thorough discussion of this context for John's Gospel, see David L. Bartlett, *What's Good about This News?* (Louisville: Westminster John Knox, 2003), 99–110.

more importantly the washing of feet becomes a token, a sample, of the much larger practice of serving one another in love. As the mentor has done for us, we should do for one another.

Finally, a little later on in the night in which he was betrayed, Jesus presents a long farewell discourse to his disciples. Midway through the discourse he says this: "This is my commandment, that you love one another as I have loved you. No one has greater love than this, to lay down one's life for one's friends. You are my friends if you do what I command you. I do not call you servants any longer, because the servant does not know what the master is doing; but I have called you friends, because I have made known to you everything that I have heard from the Father" (John 15:12–15). Here several of the marks noted above for mentoring come together: exhortation, instruction, and call to imitation.

And then one thing more. For an astonishing moment the one who has been their Lord and Master acknowledges his companions as friends. In this passage is writ large the kind of relationship for which every mentee hopes and toward which every mentor should aim: Jesus and those who follow him are friends.

PART 2

Theological Perspectives

CHAPTER 3

Theological-Pastoral Perspectives on Mentoring

Thomas W. Currie

In the field of theology and pastoral ministry, the task of mentoring is impossible to describe apart from the life, death, and resurrection of Jesus Christ, who fills this task with its own substance and directs it to his own goal. Here, mentoring depends on the Mentor, the Teacher, the Rabbi who calls and trains and sends his disciples.

Perhaps this is obvious. Perhaps such a claim may seem no more than the voicing of a pious sentiment, a preliminary expectoration before going on to identify the requisite skills and dispositions of real mentoring. But here as in all things theological, the last thing is always what needs to be said first. Though a skill, even an art, mentoring as it is practiced in the work of theology and pastoral ministry has a particular focus and a definite end: life in Christ. Apart from his ministry, any theological talk of mentoring becomes formulaic and boring, the passing on of certain skills and techniques, perhaps admired for their efficiency and professionalism, but disconnected from the claims and the joys of his scandalous life and teaching. In theology and pastoral ministry, mentoring is for the sake of witnessing to Jesus Christ.

Not all disciples would understand themselves to be mentors, though all disciples do mentor in one way or another, and there are no mentors who are not first of all disciples. And since there are no self-made Christians, but only God-made and God-claimed ones, no one knows in himself or herself how to become a witness, how to follow, learn, grow, and serve.

Sanctification requires saints. And the progress of saints is rarely straightforward. Their mentoring of others, as well as their own apprenticeship in teaching and pastoring, can be dauntingly resistant to measurable progress. Claiming expertise here is a fool's game that only illustrates how little the gospel's story has been understood. Karl Barth notes with approval Friedrich

Schleiermacher's decision even in old age to affix next to his signature the abbreviation "*stud. theol.*," student of theology.[1]

And yet, precisely because theology and pastoral ministry are driven to begin again at the beginning in all their work, those who engage in these tasks soon learn not to be embarrassed by the poverty of their own resources, even taking delight in the gifts received in the company of saints who have found themselves on this way. As a result, the Christian life and particularly theological study and pastoral ministry are surprisingly full of mentors, not experts, but good companions on the road who have lived with the questions that discipleship inevitably raises and who have found treasure hidden and shared in some unlikely fields. If life in Christ is the substance and goal of theological and pastoral mentoring, then theologians and pastors should not be surprised that he sends mentors to those whom he has called, good teachers to help along the way. That is why the church is the real context of theological and pastoral mentoring. The kind of witness needed here is not the virtuoso but the fellow traveler, the one who walks alongside and accompanies those struggling to discern the way ahead. Mentoring in this context is rooted in life together that is characterized by asking, shaped by dependence upon another, finding its way forward by being drawn into a life not of its own making. Just so are theologians and pastors rendered open to being mentored, learning to ask questions they had not considered important before, even discovering questions that question their own firmly held certainties.

Before attempting to describe in more detail the mentoring task in this context, I should make two other general comments. The first is that the task of mentoring theologians and pastoral ministers requires an equal measure of humility and confidence. As Paul states to the Corinthians: "Be imitators of me, as I am of Christ" (1 Cor. 11:1). One wonders how many pastors or theologians would dare follow Paul in saying such a thing today. The invitation to "imitate me" lays one so open to ridicule that most of us are afraid to venture such. And after all, who among us could really imitate Christ? But here our cowardice convicts us and our humility proves utterly false. Paul's trust in the gospel's power to shine through the earthen vessel that he embodies illustrates the humble confidence or confident humility that is absolutely necessary for mentors in this field. To be a mentor here one must risk just such seemingly "unhumble" words, knowing that whatever the Christian life is, the theological task intends not greater timidity but scandalously large

---

1. Karl Barth, *Evangelical Theology: An Introduction* (New York: Holt, Rinehart & Winston, 1963), 172.

claims about what Christ has done and is doing even with the very earthen vessels he has chosen.

According to Eberhard Bethge, those who studied with Bonhoeffer at Finkenwalde and shared with him a common life were both impressed by and somewhat frightened of Bonhoeffer's disciplined self-confidence in laying out a course of study and prayer that forced them to "discover resources within themselves which they had never previously suspected."[2] Such mentoring is a bit scary, just as it is deeply encouraging. To "imitate me" entails, however, nothing less.

Which leads to this observation about "trembling" by Father Schmemann: "'The earth trembled. . . .' To feel that trembling in all things, in words, in nature, in ourselves, this is Christian life, or rather life itself given by Christ. As usual on this day, I remembered in the altar all those mentors who made me feel that trembling. My whole theology is about it. About joy that 'no man taketh from you' (John 16:22)."[3]

In theology, the mentoring task is neither tedious nor formulaic. The journey may well be hard and the lessons along the way difficult and even painfully instructive, but the work, the reality to which one learns to point, and the words one is given to voice are filled with joy. Not giddiness, not euphoria, not even happiness, but that trembling joy that is at the heart of him who has called theologians and pastors to witness to this strange new world that is God's kingdom.

Following

In the economy of the gospel, mentors are saints who have learned to follow. This truth runs counter to the culture's understanding of leadership, but it expresses eloquently and simply the way that is the Christian life. John Calvin insisted that "all right knowledge of God is born of obedience."[4] Obedience in twenty-first-century America may not strike many as the highest virtue but that very fact may testify more to the directionlessness of contemporary understandings of human freedom than to anything else. We are all follow-

2. Eberhard Bethge, *Dietrich Bonhoeffer*, trans. Eric Mosbacher et al., rev. Victoria J. Barnett (Minneapolis: Fortress, 2000), 430.

3. Alexander Schmemann, *The Journals of Father Alexander Schmemann, 1973–1983* (Crestwood, NY: St. Vladimir's Press, 2000), 83.

4. John Calvin, *The Institutes of the Christian Religion*, ed. John T. McNeill, trans. Ford Lewis Battles (Philadelphia: Westminster, 1960), 1.6.2, vol. 1, p. 72.

ers. The question is, whom or what do we follow? The Enlightenment's confidence in some pristine neutrality embodied in the "critical thinker" who follows no one but his or her own reason has dissolved into questions concerning which tradition informs our notions of rationality and critical thinking.[5] The obedience of which Calvin speaks involves a recognition that one's life is not one's own but belongs to one whom to know is to follow in a particular way, even to entering a tradition in the Pauline sense of receiving and handing on a gift that has been delivered into one's hands (1 Cor. 11:23). The call to discipleship has always been a call to "follow me" (Mark 2:14).

Even in Scripture, however, what it means to follow is not self-evident, much less a matter of romantic self-discovery. In the Gospels, Jesus mentors the disciples through parables (Matt. 13), specific instruction (Mark 6:7–13), and example (John 13:12–16), *walking with them* during his public ministry. Just so do they learn, haltingly, to follow. Occasionally he speaks more sharply to them than he does to the Pharisees and others who overtly oppose him. Slow to learn and more fearful than faithful, the disciples prove incorrigible when confronted with the scandal of the cross and require the mentoring of the risen Lord who surprises them on the road, instructing them again with word and sacrament, *accompanying* them again on the way (Luke 24:13–34). Paul, after encountering the risen Lord on the road to Damascus, confesses to having spent time in Arabia, Syria, and elsewhere, and then only after an additional fourteen years of study and training does he propose his missionary enterprise to the saints in Jerusalem. Following here takes time and requires being mentored in the ordinary, daily, even mundane tasks of ministry, learning not to be contemptuous of the fields in which God has hidden vast treasure.

Eugene Peterson compares the work of ministry "to cleaning out the barn, mucking out stalls, spreading manure, pulling weeds."[6] Just as entering the church's work of theological reflection requires careful listening, apprenticeship in language and study, attentiveness to old arguments and ancient battles, all for the sake of training one's own theological imagination in order to put that in service to the church's witness, so does pastoral ministry involve embracing the messiness of congregational life, undertaking the hard work of listening to text and parishioner, crafting sermons that shed the gospel's healing and bracing light on a particular people in a particular place and time. The

---

5. Cf. Alasdair MacIntyre, *Whose Justice? Which Rationality?* (Notre Dame: University of Notre Dame Press, 1989).

6. Eugene Peterson, *Under the Unpredictable Plant* (Grand Rapids: Eerdmans, 1992), 16.

ordinariness of all of this does not make it easy or amenable to casual effort. The walking is not aimless; the accompanying is not merely congenial. To find a mentor who will show one how to clean up a barn, who will discern in old arguments matters of theological significance, who will exemplify the discipline of making time and having the patience to think and write in the midst of all the messiness is to be given an extraordinary gift. Jesus sent the disciples out, we are told, "two by two" (Mark 6:7), having instructed them in the beginning, and received them upon their return. Paul went on his missionary journey with others, sharing with them in the work. Timothy, he says, has worked with him "like a son with a father" (Phil. 2:22), and his letters instruct him as "my loyal child in the faith" (1 Tim. 1:2). These early disciples, armed with the gospel, were not sent out alone to contrive for themselves their own ministries. They were mentored and companioned.

In his memoir, Stanley Hauerwas tells of growing up as the son of a bricklayer, whose knowledge of the craft carried with it a received wisdom that could not be reduced to mechanical formulas. The wisdom was in the hands and the back, the trowel and the mud. He concludes:

> I think of theology as a craft requiring years of training. Like stonecutters and bricklayers, theologians must come to terms with the material upon which they work. In particular, they must learn to respect the simple complexity of the language of faith, so that they might reflect the radical character of orthodoxy. I think one of the reasons I was never drawn to liberal Protestant theology was that it felt too much like an attempt to avoid the training required of apprentices. In contrast, Karl Barth's work represented for me an uncompromising demand to submit to a master bricklayer, with the hope that in the process one might learn some of the "tricks of the trade."[7]

Learning

How does one learn to become a theologian, a pastor? All begins with a miracle, Father Schmemann insists, a vision that liberates one from the paralysis of many distractions and sets the course of one's life in a particular direction. Even the wisdom of the craft requires such a vision. Without it, all that we are

---

7. Stanley Hauerwas, *Hannah's Child: A Theologian's Memoir* (Grand Rapids: Eerdmans, 2010), 37.

left with is the emptiness of "critical thinking" and endless choices. "Poor are the youth who are offered only 'critical approaches.'"[8] In recounting his own theological journey, Father Schmemann was fond of quoting Julien Green's aphorism: "*Tout est ailleurs.*"[9] All is elsewhere.

But the vision, the mystery, the inexplicable sense of being pulled elsewhere is nourished and shaped, cultivated and confirmed in the equally mysterious gifts of good teachers, who confirm the vision and deepen it. Most pastoral and theological memoirs can recount heartfelt expressions of gratitude for teachers who mentored by helping to clarify, challenge, and expand the vision, revealing in the course of study unexpected delights. Ralph Wood writes movingly of his English professor at a small state university in East Texas, who surprised his young Southern Baptist student not just with the breadth of his learning but with the depth of his decidedly Roman Catholic faith:

> This Christian teacher left his deep mark on me because he was not afraid to face the toughest opponents of the gospel. . . . This teacher wanted to make sure . . . that we naive Christians did not live by what Dietrich Bonhoeffer would call "cheap grace," namely, an easy and convenient faith that costs us nothing in the way of thought or word or deed. . . .
>
> Yet there was a rattle in this splendid teacher's voice that I had been taught not to like. For it turns out that Paul Barrus was not a Baptist nor a Methodist, nor a member of the Church of Christ nor the Assembly of God—the only four churches in my provincial little East Texas town. He wasn't even Presbyterian or a Lutheran or an Episcopalian—whoever they were. He wasn't even a Protestant. God forbid he was a Roman Catholic. Just as I had been taught that blacks are natively inferior, so had I learned that Catholics are not even Christians. . . . Against my will and utterly to my surprise, this Catholic teacher released my little Baptist butterfly from its confining cage. He turned me into an ecumenical Christian.[10]

Or this from Richard Lischer:

> In my final year at seminary I took two courses with theologian Robert Bertram: one entire course on Luther's interpretation of Galatians, "the *magna carta* of Christian freedom," and the other on the philosophy of

---

8. Schmemann, *Journals*, 117.
9. Schmemann, *Journals*, 1.
10. Ralph Wood, *Preaching and Professing* (Grand Rapids: Eerdmans, 2009), 31.

history, in which Marxist notions of the future were brought into dialogue with Christian hope. Bertram was as orthodox as they come, but, unlike my prep school teachers, he had a big picture of the world. He held the tradition up to the light, like a jeweler who patiently turns a stone until it yields its greatest brilliance, and he did it with low-key Socratic patience. By the time one of Bertram's classes ended, we were often passionate about truths we hadn't even suspected at its beginning.[11]

Learning from such a mentor is much more than mastering a text or doing well in a course with a great teacher. Something else is going on, such that one's learning becomes not just the accumulation of information or even of wisdom, but the joyful embrace of one's own vocation, even the happy discovery of the mysterious beauty and power of this particular calling. Fleming Rutledge describes for her fellow students the almost parental nature of such a mentor in her reflections on New Testament scholar J. Louis Martyn:

> Lou Martyn was not only a supreme interpreter of the letters of the apostle Paul—and, earlier of the Fourth Gospel; he was also an authentically nurturing father figure. It is not given to every *doktorvater* to exercise the role of *vater* as well as the *doktor*. In this, Lou Martyn excelled. We will cherish the way he adopted us, supported us, radiated pride in us. To the end of his life his intensely affirming way of greeting us and conversing with us at meetings, gatherings, and other occasions of greater family intimacy was precious to us. He was not without his acerbic side; I'm sure that all of us felt his displeasure from time to time if we disagreed with him. Yet he never ceased to care deeply about each of us and our families in addition to encouraging us in our vocations.[12]

In that same article, Beverly Gaventa reflects on this teacher whose mentoring revealed such a powerfully human commitment to the subject matter, inviting his students to join in this great passion of learning:

> Names, dates, publication title—these all come easily to expression. What is far more challenging to convey to those who did not know him is the character of the man. I have heard the word "Mensch" invoked often for

---

11. Richard Lischer, *Open Secrets* (New York: Broadway, 2002), 38.

12. Fleming Rutledge, "Ruminations: J. Louis Martyn, 1925–2015," *Generous Orthodoxy*; available at ruminations.generousorthodoxy.org/2015/06/j-louis-martyn-1925–2015.html.

him, and that may be the best we have. For all his brilliance, Lou was not concerned with being brilliant. He squirmed at the expression "Martyn School." He cared about the subject matter. What counted was Paul, or as Lou would say, "taking a seat in the early Christian congregation" without succumbing to the temptation "to domesticate the text, to cage the wild tiger." . . . Little in my life can match the pleasure of picking up the telephone and hearing that unique voice, "Is this the Professor Gaventa? Do you have a minute?"[13]

Apprenticeship to a pastor yields similar responses. While he was in seminary in New York, Eugene Peterson interned for a year at Madison Avenue Presbyterian Church under George Arthur Buttrick. He tells of Buttrick's Sunday evening conversations with the seminarians, where Buttrick, sitting on the floor and smoking a pipe, talked with these students about preaching and prayer and worship:

> He kept the conversation local and immediate and personal in a way that I later learned to identify as pastoral. He shied away from "big" truths. On one of these occasions he was asked by one of the students something about preaching. Something on the order of "What is the most important thing you do in preparing to preach each Sunday?" I think we were all surprised by the answer, at least I was. His answer: "For two hours every Tuesday and Thursday afternoon, I walk through the neighborhood and make home visits. There is no way that I can preach the gospel to these people if I don't know how they are living, what they are thinking and talking about. Preaching is proclamation, God's word revealed in Jesus, but only when it gets embedded in conversations in a listening ear and responding tongue, does it become gospel." . . . These Sunday evenings with this prominent preacher sitting on the floor in his slippers and smoking his pipe, were my introduction into the "backroom" of a pastor's life, what went on when the pastor was not in the pulpit, not in the public eye. There was far more to this life of pastor that I had ever had access to.[14]

Learning from a mentor is a gift that does so much more than credential a skill. Such a gift rather shapes the direction of a life and makes of a vocation a joyful service.

13. Beverly Gaventa, quoted in Rutledge, "Ruminations: J. Louis Martyn."
14. Eugene Peterson, *The Pastor: A Memoir* (New York: HarperOne, 2011), 86–87.

Unlearning

Mentors are not always skilled and inspiring teachers who train students to become theologians and pastors. Just as often good mentors can be found in congregations and schools that help apprentices discover the questions that their new context raises, many of which contradict or baffle assumptions picked up in their earlier training. Some things, or better some ways, have to be unlearned. And some mentoring congregations are gifted in helping to train pastors and theologians for work that will only blossom fully elsewhere.

Unlearning seems to have constituted a good deal of Jesus's conversations with his disciples. James and John ask him to grant them positions of prominence in his kingdom of glory. The other disciples, having overheard this request and knowing full well how the world works, are understandably peeved. "So Jesus called them and said to them, 'You know that among the Gentiles those whom they recognize as their rulers lord it over them, and their great ones are tyrants over them. But it is not so among you; but whoever wishes to become great among you must be your servant" (Mark 10:42–43). Indeed, unlearning seems to describe the way Jesus mentors his disciples most of the time: "You have heard it said of old . . . but I say unto you." Or more painfully: "And Peter took him aside and began to rebuke him, saying, 'God forbid it, Lord! This must never happen to you.' But he turned and said to Peter, 'Get behind me, Satan! You are a stumbling block to me'" (Matt. 16:22–23). There is much to unlearn in being mentored as a theologian of this Lord. "'Oh, how foolish you are, and slow of heart to believe all that the prophets have declared! Was it not necessary that the Messiah should suffer these things and then enter into his glory?' Then beginning with Moses and all the prophets, he interpreted to them the things about himself in all the scriptures" (Luke 24:25–27).

Richard Lischer recalls how difficult and even embarrassing this unlearning can be in reflecting on his efforts to preach the gospel to a rural congregation in southern Illinois, having completed his seminary training and graduate studies and with his PhD in hand:

> In my first sermon I explained the meaning of *an* epiphany, not *the* Epiphany of God in the person of Jesus—no, that would have been too obvious—but the *category* of epiphanies in general. . . .
>
> Before I could talk about Jesus, I apparently found it necessary to give my farmers a crash course in the angst-ridden plight of modern man. With the help of clichés from Joyce, Heidegger, Camus, and even Walker Percy, I

first converted them to existential ennui so that later in the sermon I could rescue them with carefully crafted assurances of "meaning" in a meaningless world. . . . It didn't concern me that the problem of meaninglessness had not occurred to my audience or that Marx's critique of religion rarely came up for discussion at the post office. . . .

That year some of the great Epiphany readings came from the letter to the Ephesians, which is Paul's vision of the grandeur of the church. . . .

Why couldn't I see the revelation of God in our little church? In our community everyone pitched in and learned how to "pattern" a little girl with cerebral palsy. We helped one another put up hay before rains came. We grieved when a neighbor lost his farm, and we refused to buy his tools at the auction. As a people, we walked into the fields every April and blessed the seeds before planting them. Weren't these all signs of "church" that were worthy of mention in the Sunday homily? Whatever lay closest to the soul of the congregation I unfailingly omitted from my sermons. I didn't despise these practices. I simply didn't see them.[15]

Unlearning is hard. No small part of it has to do with the growing realization that both mentoring and apprenticeship in the field of theology and pastoral ministry have so little to do with explanations or answers or master concepts. Rather, the gift of mentoring for the apprentice is the training in enduring the questions, in embracing the embarrassment of having no answer save a witness to that one who refuses to be an explanation while graciously drawing us into his life. Pastors sometimes do not learn the chagrin of this embarrassment until they, like Lischer, are called to preach to those whom they have not chosen and might not ever choose as their congregation. Theologians whose work is carried out primarily within the walls of the academy might seem to be better insulated against this embarrassment but often here too their explanations encounter resistance. One theologian who stumbled on the kind of unlearning that can occur here and who was mentored by his congregation as well as by a good friend was Karl Barth. In his essay "The Need and Promise of Christian Preaching," he tells of the theology he had learned at the feet of his teacher and mentor Wilhelm Herrmann. But preaching to the saints in Safenwil, trying to dig into Scripture's story and speak to his own congregation in the depths of their own lives showed him how much he had to unlearn. He writes:

15. Lischer, *Open Secrets*, 73–75.

For twelve years I was a minister. . . . I *had* my theology. It was not really mine, to be sure, but that of my unforgotten teacher, Wilhelm Herrmann, grafted upon the . . . principles of those Reformed Churches which today I represent. . . . Once in the ministry, I found myself growing away from these theological habits of thought and being forced back at every point more and more upon the specific *minister's* problem, the *sermon*. I sought to find my way between the problem of human life on the one hand and the content of the Bible on the other. As a minister I wanted to speak to the *people* in the infinite contradiction of their life, but to speak the no less infinite message of the *Bible*, which was as much of a riddle as life. . . .

It is not as if I had found any way *out* of this critical situation. *Exactly not that.* But this critical situation itself became to me an explanation of the character of all theology. What else can theology be but the truest possible expression of this quest and questioning on the part of the minister, the description of the embarrassment into which a man falls when he ventures upon this task and out of which he cannot find his way—a cry for rescue arising from great need and hope? . . . Embarrassment is certainly the situation most characteristic of the profession of which theology desires to prepare.[16]

Embarrassment, the embarrassment of not knowing an explanation, even unlearning the explanations that otherwise seem so compelling, while, nevertheless bearing witness to the faithfulness of him who sustains us in our stumbling—that is exactly the mentoring gift that congregations often share with their pastors and students their teachers. Discovering such embarrassment and not running away from it or covering it up but rather embracing it as the characteristic situation of both theologian and pastor is the gift that unlearning regularly provides.

Sometimes this gift can be given quite abruptly.

Walter Wangerin tells the story of his attempts to pastor a small urban congregation in the Midwest made up of both poor whites and African Americans unable to escape life in the inner city. The organist of the church was a Black woman named Joselyn Fields. In the second year of his ministry she was diagnosed with cancer, at forty-seven years of age. Wangerin tells how he was determined to be her faithful pastor, visiting her every day, reading the Psalms, praying that God's will be done, and sharing with her in a spirit

---

16. Karl Barth, *The Word of God and the Word of Man*, trans. Douglas Horton (New York: Harper, 1957), 100–102.

of earnest cheerfulness all his activities he had undertaken that day—saying almost anything to keep from dealing with the specter of her dying. At one point, Joselyn looked at him and raised her bony finger to his face and said, "Shut up."

> God help me!—I learned so slowly. But God in Joselyn taught me with an unutterable patience. I, who had thought to give her the world she did not have, was in fact taking away the only world she *did* have.
>
> I shut up, I learned. . . . And the day came when I had nothing, absolutely nothing to say to my Joselyn. . . . I entered her room at noon, saying nothing. I sat beside her through the afternoon, until the sun had slanted into darkness, saying nothing. . . . The evening took us, . . . but with the evening came the Holy Spirit. For the words I finally said were not my own.
>
> I turned to my Joselyn. I opened my mouth and spoke as a Pastor . . . I said, "I love you."
>
> And Joselyn widened her ebony eye. And that lady, she put out her arms. As a parishioner, I suppose. . . . She hugged me. And I hugged those dying bones.
>
> She whispered, "I love you too."
>
> And that was all that was said. But that, dear people, was the power from on high, cloaking both of us in astonished simplicity. . . .
>
> And she died. And I did not grieve.[17]

Friendship

Pastoral ministry and the study of theology can be lonely work. Karl Barth calls this solitude a threat to the theologian and pastor, which must be "endured and borne with dignity and cheerfulness."[18] In a fallen world, this loneliness comes with the territory. Without romanticizing such solitude, those engaged in these tasks soon discover that many find their work odd, even baffling, and perhaps find the pastor and theologian somewhat strange as well. The strangeness of this calling is rooted in the strangeness of the church, whose message is neither self-evidently useful nor always in alignment with

17. Walter Wangerin, *Ragman and Other Cries of Faith* (San Francisco: Harper & Row, 1984), 62–64.
18. Barth, *Evangelical Theology*, 111.

what the world concludes about itself. Yet in that very ecclesial strangeness, the pastor and theologian find the good company of those who help them fulfill the tasks to which they are called. Here, they discover friends.

Theologians and pastors depend upon friends. Not all mentors are friends and certainly not all friends are mentors. But the best mentors in the field of study and teaching and ministry are often those friends and peers who share in the joys and burdens of this work and who are able to suggest, question, and even inspire their colleagues. The list is long of pastors and theologians who recount their friendship with others as the source and strength of their own work. One thinks of the Cappadocian fathers, Basil, his brother Gregory of Nyssa, and their friend Gregory of Nazianzus; or Augustine and his friends Alypius and Simplicianus; or Martin Luther and Philip Melanchthon; or Calvin and Bucer and Farel and Beza; or more recently Karl Barth and his friend Eduard Thurneysen. Stanley Hauerwas even writes that the truth of Christian convictions cannot "be isolated from what is necessary to sustain friendships that are truthful."[19] He cites his friendships with colleagues as varied as Alasdair MacIntyre, John Howard Yoder, and Will Willimon, among many others, as significant for his own theological work.

Nevertheless, the loneliness of this work is often pressing indeed. One temptation is to remedy this loneliness by becoming busy or important. Such remedies can credential one in a world that respects busyness and productivity. In his memoir *The Pastor*, Eugene Peterson tells of the way he and several of his pastor-colleagues sought to combat this loneliness by becoming less busy, discovering in the strangeness of the message to which they were committed a community of friendship that mitigated their isolation. Once a week these pastoral friends gathered to study the text for the next Sunday. They were not all of the same denomination. The group contained both liberals and conservatives, Christians and Jews. But their identity as pastors was under siege, and the loneliness of their work required the gift of friends who could mentor one another and remind one another of the life-giving nature of the work to which they had been called. So they came together to study and there found mentors who were their friends:

> Without quite knowing what we were doing, or even how we were doing it, we were acquiring a vocabulary and a corresponding imagination for seeing ourselves, seeing one another, for what we really were: *pastor*. We were recovering our vocation. And we were doing it in the company of

19. Hauerwas, *Hannah's Child*, 145.

colleagues who were neighbors (not looking for expert advice from non-pastors) and in the actual conditions of our workplace, our congregations (not going to the protected laboratory conditions of a retreat center or campus). . . . We might have been a minority among American pastors, but at least we were not alone.[20]

Becoming a Mentor

In her remarkable essay "The Role of Theological Masters in the Formation of the Pastor-Theologian," Cynthia Jarvis cites Paul's relation to Timothy as a model of mentoring. She notes that Paul had already recognized that God had claimed Timothy for service and, in recognizing this, "wanted Timothy to *accompany* him." She adds: "The word suggests not only the act of traveling together but of living the life given them by God to live together."[21] This *accompanying* is characterized by a life together in which the mentor gives not "*of* himself" but "*himself* to a relationship in which the personhood of both parties [is] central to a relationship in which discipleship to the one Lord was all in all."[22] Mentoring differs from teaching in that teaching (and scholarship and pastoral ministry, for that matter) can be carried on quite independently of the student's vocation. In giving himself or herself, the mentor sacrifices something of his or her individual interests in the recognition of that surpassing vision that animates and draws both the mentor and student toward a common goal. It is in the *shared* passion for the work of ministry, for the goal of theology, for the joyful gratitude that arises from God's gracious act in Jesus Christ that mentoring begins to be possible.

Jarvis's essay suggests that this accompanying is rooted in a vision that invites collaboration and entails a mutual sense of calling to discipleship in Jesus Christ. It is on the basis of life together that mentoring becomes not just a possibility but a necessary gift and task for theologians and pastors. But this vision is not something mystical or redolent of some shared spirituality. Nor does this mentoring take place by cultivating a set of exercises in deeper piety. Rather, to accompany one here is to engage the subject matter itself, sharing a commitment to the subject matter by attending to the craft, the

20. Peterson, *Pastor*, 149, 159.

21. Cynthia Jarvis, "The Role of Theological Masters in the Formation of the Pastor-Theologian," in *The Power to Comprehend with All the Saints*, ed. Wallace M. Alston and Cynthia A. Jarvis (Grand Rapids: Eerdmans, 2009), 88.

22. Jarvis, "Role of Theological Masters," 89.

discipline, and the joy of the work at hand. Teachers and scholars, along with congregations and pastors, become good mentors by falling in love with the subject matter with which they are engaged. Theologians find in the study of theology that "great passion"[23] that perceives the beauty of this undertaking and the joy of sharing in this work with others. Similarly, pastoral mentors become such because they believe the work of pastoral ministry is in some profound sense beautiful, worth doing well, a remarkable gift that resists the tedium of credentialing or professionalization.

One becomes a mentor in theology and pastoral ministry to the extent that one is grasped by the mysteriously humbling and joyfully encouraging word of the gospel. It is that word that saves scholarship from becoming merely an academic career, that redeems ministry from pious self-importance (or, worse, self-hatred), that makes of the sacrifice of one's own interest a passion for the future gifts of one's students. There is something about the gospel—one thinks of Paul and Timothy, Polycarp and Irenaeus, Ambrose and Augustine, Luther and his students, Bonhoeffer and his seminarians—that seeks to share the joy and discipline of the gospel by mentoring others. Here scholarship and the practice of ministry find their true end and goal in the praise and service of him who had time for others, who did not work alone, who entrusted his message to those who followed him.

That is why mentoring and apprenticeship in the field of theology and pastoral ministry can never be boring or tedious chores. Working together toward a common vision of great hope and beauty; learning to follow, to listen, and to read carefully both text and person; learning to unlearn one's own certainties in the course of ministering to those whom God has given us to love; being mentored by peers and friends who accompany us on our way; discovering the fierce passion of God's love for this world and the costly and surprisingly liberating work that marks our participation in that love—these are the ways mentoring and apprenticeship in theology and pastoral ministry are made possible and become occasions for joy.

And perhaps that is what is so often missing and what is most essential here: joy. Theology, Karl Barth, reminds us is a "peculiarly beautiful science,"[24] a joyful enterprise, precisely because of its subject matter. At his memorial service Barth was remembered by one of the students whom he had

23. The phrase is from the lecture fragments of Karl Barth's *Church Dogmatics* IV/4, trans. Geoffrey Bromiley (Grand Rapids: Eerdmans, 1981), 111.

24. Karl Barth, *Church Dogmatics* II/1, ed. G. W. Bromiley and T. F. Torrance (Edinburgh: Clark, 1964), 656.

mentored as a theologian whose thinking and living were the collaborative attempt to indicate that "God" is a delightful word.[25] Mentoring in this field can only be a happy task then, just as being mentored can only be accounted a great gift. To paraphrase Simone Weil, there must be pleasure and joy in this work or it is not mentoring apprentices in the study of theology and ministry of Jesus Christ. For here the joy is as indispensable as breathing is in running. Where it is lacking, there is neither mentor nor apprentice.[26]

25. Eberhard Jüngel, "To Honor Karl Barth," in *Karl Barth, 1886–1968: Gedenkfeier im Basler Münster* (Zurich: EVZ, 1969), 50 (my translation).

26. Simone Weil, *Waiting for God*, trans. Emma Craufurd (New York: Perennial, 2001), 61. Later (p. 78), Weil states: "When an apprentice gets hurt, or complains of being tired, the workmen and peasants have this fine expression: 'It is the trade entering his body.'"

CHAPTER 4

Preacher as Mentor

Thomas G. Long

On my desk stands a small framed photograph of Karl Barth, a picture taken when the great theologian was, I would guess, in his seventies. He is delightfully rumpled in a "Herr Professor Doktor" sort of way. His necktie is a tad askew, one tab of his collar has rebelled and broken free from the captivity of his lapel, and the whitened wisps of his hair are gently wind-blown. He is leaning forward, his large head turned to the right, the eyes behind his owlish glasses dancing with merriment as if someone off camera has just posed a most fascinating question. His mouth is beginning to open, and it is impossible to tell whether he is on the edge of erupting into great billows of laughter or about to explain the significance of the incarnation. Perhaps both.

The reason Barth's picture looks out at me as I work is that I count him as one of my strongest mentors, even though I never met him, even though he was dead by the time I was in my early twenties. But stories about him have guided me along my own path, stories about his intellectual independence, about his dramatic break with the dominant theology of his day, about his courageous opposition to the Third Reich and his penning of the *Barmen Declaration*, about the acrimony and the personal pain he felt in the rupture with fellow theologian Emil Brunner, about the words of hope spoken over the phone on the last night of his life to his friend Eduard Thurneysen: "Keep your chin up. Never mind! He will reign."[1]

---

1. Eberhard Busch, *Karl Barth: His Life from Letters and Autobiographical Texts* (London: SCM, 1975), 499.

Closeness and Distance of Mentors

Barth has been my mentor, and he has guided me along the way in life, but not in ways like the advice of a wise investment counselor pointing out a good opportunity in Brazilian mining shares or a dance instructor trying to guide my leaden feet through the steps of a waltz. No, Barth's mentorship has been more enchanted than mere advice and instruction, and like all good mentorship our relationship has involved a blending of closeness and distance. For me, Barth has been at just the right distance to exert figurative influence. Who knows, if the space between us had been compressed, if, say, I had been a student in Basel and had actually taken a class from old Barth, I might have been disappointed and the force of his mentorship diminished. But Barth stands close enough to me to be known but far enough away to be a symbol of much that I desire to be as a minister, a thinking Christian, and a teacher. Laurent A. Daloz, in his fine book *Mentor*, argues that "mentors are creations of our imaginations, designed to fill a psychic space somewhere between lover and parent. Not surprisingly they are suffused with magic."[2] So Barth has been for me a kind of magical presence. As John Updike's fictional pastor Thomas Marshfield puts it in *A Month of Sundays*: "I did not become a Barthian in blank recoil, but in positive love of Barth's voice, his wholly masculine, wholly informed, wholly unfrightened prose. In his prose thorns become edible, as for the giraffe. In Barth I heard, at the age of eighteen, the voice my father should have had."[3]

There have been, of course, other mentors along the way: among them a high school history teacher who somehow thought I had a brain worth challenging, a pastor in my South Carolina college town who stood tall in his preaching for civil rights in the 1960s at great personal expense, a ruggedly honest supervisor in a Clinical Pastoral Education program who told me truths about myself that cause me to shiver still. Each of these was close enough to exert influence in my life and yet distant enough from me in age, experience, and status to assume symbolic significance. As such, each of them in their own ways shone a light for me on an as-yet-untraveled path, opened up for me experience and wisdom I had not yet acquired, and modeled brave ways I had not yet imagined of navigating life and being human.

2. Laurent A. Daloz, *Mentor: Guiding the Journey of Adult Learners* (San Francisco: Jossey-Bass, 1999), 18.

3. John Updike, *A Month of Sundays* (New York: Knopf, 1974), 24–25.

Heaven knows, we all need mentors, especially in a time when the public markers along the narrow way of wisdom have faded and it seems that our society has a clearer picture of what constitutes *the* good life than what makes for *a* good life. Sometimes we think of mentors as guides we need mostly in our youth, but every phase of life has its unexplored territory and, thus, the need for someone to take us by the hand through the darkness. When a beloved friend of mine, an admired teacher and community leader whose life had been an inspiration for many, was told recently by his physician that he had "about a week" to live, he chose to spend those last hours not in self-pity but in the company of his family and friends. People crowded into his hospice room day and night, laughing at old stories, remembering joyful experiences, desiring to feel one last time the blessing of his presence and to draw strength from the fullness of his life. And yet, that he was so near to death, the reality that he was traveling through the valley of the shadow, constituted a distance from the rest of us that endowed him with mythic powers. He, who had been a wise companion on the pathway of life, was now for us a pioneer on the pathway of death. When he died, I was standing in a long line at the funeral home waiting my turn to speak to his family, and a woman in front of me, a woman I did not know, turned around and said, partly to me and partly to the cosmos, "He taught us how to live, and now he has taught us how to die."

Recently I wrote a commentary on the Pastoral Epistles—1 and 2 Timothy and Titus. These are "mentor letters," epistles that present themselves as the wise counsel of an aging apostle Paul to two younger pastors, Timothy and Titus. While some New Testament scholars see this as historically plausible, the majority do not, finding instead that the Pastorals were written somewhere near the end of the first century. Paul would surely have been dead for years, and Timothy and Titus, even if they were still alive, would certainly no longer have been neophyte pastors. But regardless of one's technical position on the authorship of the Pastorals, the point is that these letters are the expressions not of the Paul who fled Thessalonica and Berea a half step ahead of the mob, or the Paul who cooled his heels in a Roman prison, or the Paul who bitterly takes on his rivals at Corinth. No, this is the Paul for whom all of these experiences have been gathered up into wisdom—in short, the Paul now ready to serve as pastoral mentor. His life in ministry makes him close to young, relatively inexperienced pastors like Timothy and Titus, but he is now an iconic figure, distant enough to be a role model, encouraging them in the face of the kind of strife and hardships many pastors know all too well to be "strong, loving, and wise"[4] in their ministries. Indeed, in one of the loveliest passages in these letters, Paul describes for Timothy the essence of good mentoring: "Now you have observed my teaching, my conduct, my aim in life, my faith, my patience, my love, my steadfastness, my persecutions and suffering the things that happened to me in Antioch, Iconium, and Lystra. What persecutions I endured! . . . But as for you, continue in what you have learned and firmly believed, knowing from whom you learned it, and how from childhood you have known the sacred writings that are able to instruct you for salvation through faith in Christ Jesus" (2 Tim. 3:10–11a, 14–15).

It is all there in these verses, the essence of good mentoring: the mentor's life, in all of its majesty and all of its pain, poured out as a libation and offered as a model; the recognition that the mentee must do her or his own remembering, learning, and dreaming; and the goal of a life worth living.

Pulpit as Mentoring Site

If mentoring can occur in unconventional ways and places—through the biography of a long-dead theologian, via pseudonymous epistles, or in the confines of a hospice room—then there is no reason not to think that mentoring can occur through a preacher in a pulpit. The pulpit is itself a place that blends closeness and distance, and, as such, it can be a place where what Daloz calls "the magic" of mentoring can take place. As for closeness, the era of the "Pulpit Princes"—those royal proclaimers of a previous day who stood above their people in authority, erudition, and moral virtue—has receded into the dim past. In Herman Melville's classic novel *Moby Dick*, a preacher, Father Mapple, delivers a sermon on the book of Jonah from a pulpit fashioned after a ship's prow, a thundering message about sin and the sovereignty of God. As he nears the end of the sermon, Father Mapple imagines moving from the pulpit to the pews, from the role of proclaimer to that of fellow listener: "Shipmates, God has laid but one hand upon you; both his hands press upon me. I have read ye by what murky light may be mine the lesson that Jonah teaches to all sinners; and therefore to ye, and still more to me, for I am a greater sinner than ye. And now how gladly would I come down from this mast-head and sit on the hatches there where you sit, and listen as you listen,

---

4. The phrase "strong, loving, and wise" comes from a translation of 2 Tim. 1:7 by liturgical scholar Robert Hovda.

while some one of you reads *me* that other and more awful lesson which Jonah teaches to *me*, as a pilot of the living God."[5]

Melville wrote during a time when preaching was in fact already in the process of moving from the exalted "masthead" to the lowly "hatches." As historian David S. Reynolds notes, "Between 1800 and 1860, popular sermon style, which had in Puritan times been characterized primarily by theological rigor and restraint of the imagination, came to be dominated by diverting narrative, extensive illustrations, and even colloquial humor."[6] Father Mapple was, in fact, modeled on the wildly popular Boston Methodist preacher at the Seamen's Bethel Church in Boston, Edward Thompson Taylor, whose sermons, which attracted large, diverse, and enthusiastic congregations, were marked by vivid stories and images and "fused the mild theology of Boston liberalism with the daring imagery of colloquial revivalism."[7]

Over the last century and a half, little has stood in the way of the movement of preaching toward the hearers, and the transition from masthead to hatches is now thoroughgoing. In many congregations today, the preacher is more likely to walk around the chancel with a handheld microphone and wearing jeans and a sweatshirt than to stand in a lofty pulpit wearing the robes of ecclesial status. Nearly a century of talk about storytelling and imagery and conversational preaching has brought today's preachers well within the experiential range and communicational space of hearers. Even though he stood in the magnificent pulpit of the even more magnificent Riverside Church in New York, Harry Emerson Fosdick, in the spirit of Edward Taylor, turned his sermons into pastoral conversations and significantly impacted American preaching in the process.

Even though much contemporary American preaching has descended from the masthead to the hatches, from the pulpit heights to the level of the nave, and even though the preacher is now close enough to the hearer to be more a friend than a remote authority figure, some distance—a necessary distance for mentoring—between preacher and hearer remains. Even when preachers try to deny this distinction between themselves and their hearers or to escape it, by, say, wearing khakis and a golf shirt and opening the sermon with a couple of jokes and a self-deprecating anecdote, the distance inevitably remains. I am not speaking here of the kind of distance

5. Herman Melville, *Moby Dick* (New York: Oxford University Press, 1998), 42.

6. David S. Reynolds, *Beneath the American Renaissance: The Subversive Imagination in the Age of Emerson and Melville* (New York: Oxford University Press, 2011), 15.

7. Reynolds, *Beneath the American Renaissance*, 20.

where the preacher refuses to be overbearing and intentionally withdraws from the sermon for the sake of leaving room for the hearer.[8] I am thinking rather of the inescapable difference in roles played by preacher and listener. Theologically we may want to say that preacher and hearer are equals in the sermonic transaction, that they work together to create the event of the sermon, and the difference between them is one of function, not status. True, and yet when the function of one of the partners is to speak for God, then the repeated practice of that function tends to imbue the practitioner with an iconic status, a little like actor Hal Holbrook carrying the aura of Mark Twain with him wherever he went. The preacher is not God, of course, but the preacher speaks *for* God in the sermon, and some of this role inevitably adheres to the person of the preacher, even if the preacher tries to downplay the role as God's spokesperson or is embarrassed by it. Preachers stand in the mentoring space by virtue of their in-between status. They are not God, but for all their attempts to be one of the folks, they are not just like the hearers either.

In some ways the blend of presence and distance in a preacher is akin to the experience of actor Judd Hirsch who played the role of Dr. Tyrone C. Berger, a psychiatrist, in the film *Ordinary People*. Hirsch played the part with such compassion, attractive eccentricity, and warmth that his character leapt off the screen with persuasive and affective force. Letters of appreciation from psychiatrists, grateful for the "image boost" Hirsch's portrayal provided, poured out to Hirsch and also to director Robert Redford.[9] At least one viewer of the film claimed to have received therapeutic benefit from Hirsch's character:

> The film really took on meaning for me here because I had my first real dose of therapeutic treatment at the time I saw the movie. I was very much like Conrad [Dr. Berger's patient]. He didn't want to go to therapy, originally, and neither did I. I had had two prior experiences in therapy when I was a young child and they didn't go over very well. I really didn't want to be there. But this time around I was motivated to get better. Someone had told me that the reason I was a procrastinator was because I subconsciously didn't want to grow up. It made sense to me and now I

8. See an interesting discussion of this dynamic in Michael Brothers, *Distance in Preaching: Room to Speak, Space to Listen* (Grand Rapids: Eerdmans, 2014).

9. Linda B. Martin, "The Psychiatrist in Today's Movies: He's Everywhere and in Deep Trouble," *New York Times* (January 25, 1981); available at nytimes.com/1981/01/25/movies/the-psychiatrist-in-today-s-movies-he-s-everywhere-and-in-deep-trouble.html?pagewanted=all.

was determined to prove this person wrong and act like a man and meet all my responsibilities. I ended up staying with my doctor for eight years and found a needed confidant and friend.[10]

Even though Judd Hirsch obviously moved on to other parts, and even though he has a private life as a nonpsychiatrist, the aura of this role still clings to him. Posters of Hirsch as Dr. Berger have been sold by the thousands, and I would not at all be surprised if strangers approach him in the grocery store seeking wise counsel. Just so, today's preacher may use approachable language and everyday stories and may take on an unassuming "neighbor-next-door" posture, but, for those who hear the sermons, this same preacher is unmistakably God's person in ways that differ from ordinary folk, regardless of all equalizing notions of the priesthood of all believers. It is a distance necessary for the magic of mentoring to take place.

But in what ways can a preacher become a mentor from the pulpit? Daloz, drawing inspiration from the original figure of Mentor in *The Odyssey*, says, "Mentors give us the magic that allows us to enter the darkness, a talisman to protect us from evil spells, a gem of wise advice, and sometimes simply courage. But always the mentor appears near the outset of the journey as a helper, equipping us in some way for what is to come."[11] Although Daloz's language may not seem easily to translate into preaching and pastoral practice (a talisman to protect us from evil spells?), I would nevertheless like to borrow freely from his description of a mentor, to point out several ways in which preachers may serve as mentors.

Helper at the Beginning of the Journey

Daloz notes that "always the mentor appears near the outset of the journey as a helper, equipping us in some way for what is to come." The preacher who serves as a mentor recognizes that the Christian life is a journey that is always beginning. There is the great beginning in baptism when one sets off on the lifelong adventure of being a part of the community of faith and Christ's disciple in the world, but there are countless smaller beginnings—times when people acquire a new sense of call or when they have slipped

---

10. Bud Clayman, "Ordinary People: A Review"; available at oc87recoverydiaries.com /ordinary-people.

11. Daloz, *Mentor*, 18.

off the rails and, like the prodigal, have come to themselves and are heading back home to start anew. As Barbara Brown Taylor observes in *The Preaching Life*, "If my own experience can be trusted, then God does not call us once but many times. There are calls to faith and calls to ordination, but in between there are calls to particular communities and calls to particular tasks within them."[12]

A preacher-mentor, then, will recognize that a significant portion of the listeners are, in ways that are visible and hidden, known to others and not, at crossroads in their lives, personally and vocationally. Many are about to take the first step on some important new journey, and they need a mentor standing along the beckoning path, equipping them out of the gospel for what is to come.

For example, M. Craig Barnes preached "When It Is Time to Leave," a sermon based on the story in Acts 13, about the change of plans that Paul and Barnabas made in their first missionary journey. After a promising beginning to their ministry in Antioch, suddenly resistance arose to Paul and Barnabas and to their preaching. Popular opinion was with them; they could have fought the resistance, but, according to the story, they "shook the dust off their feet" and headed for the next town. Barnes allowed his sermon on this passage to become a mentoring sermon, a guide to Christians who head off with zeal in some new direction, only to find that they need to develop a Plan B. Barnes says:

> Paul and Barnabas knew that sometimes you have to change your plans in order to fulfill your mission. Remember, when Paul said if the Jews wouldn't take salvation to the ends of the earth, God would move to Plan B, which commissioned missionaries to the Gentiles. If God himself has to change plans at times, the chances are great that you will also. The Bible is filled with people who have to go to Plan B. They set off in one direction trying to fulfill their mission. It didn't work out so they went to Plan B. Moses' first plan was to kill the Egyptians. Joshua's first plan was to enter the promised land from the south. Jeremiah's first plan was to prevent the fall of Jerusalem. Peter's first plan was to prevent Jesus from going to the cross and Paul's first plan was to get rid of the church. All of them had to go to Plan B. Some of you, I know, may be up to Plan X, Y, or Z by now, but that's okay. Go to double letters if you have to. Just don't expect to be right all the time. That's called hubris; it's one of the deadlier sins. So they

12. Barbara Brown Taylor, *The Preaching Life* (Lanham: Cowley, 1993), 25.

don't make a statue out of you in Antioch. So what? Move on. Get to the next town because you've got a mission and there's a lot of work to do.[13]

Barnes is preaching here, but he is also mentoring, encouraging his hearers along the way and assuring them that there is no shame in venturing down a new path of mission only to change course in midstride.

Not only do mentor-preachers stand at the trailhead of new journeys with wise advice about the path ahead, they also provide blessings for the pilgrims on their way. The blessing or benediction in worship is not simply an element that marks the end of the liturgy, it is the blessing given as people depart worship to venture out as disciples in the world. Paul W. Pruyser of the Menninger Clinic observes that there is often a moment of awkwardness between therapists and their patients at the close of a therapeutic hour. Both of them, writes Pruyser, often long for more than a businesslike fare-thee-well, for more than "I'll see you next Thursday." What they yearn for, he says, is a blessing.[14]

So the preacher can anticipate that benedictory word in the sermon. The preacher can assure the hearers as they make new beginnings that all may not be free of suffering but that nonetheless "all shall be well and all manner of thing shall be well,"[15] and that the peace of God that passes all understanding will preserve them along the way.

Courageous Presence

In his influential *How to Read the Bible*, Hebrew Bible scholar James L. Kugel presents a vivid and lively description of the prophetic ministry of Jeremiah. Summing up Jeremiah's bold preaching, Kugel tellingly says that "what shines through" in the Jeremiah story is the sheer courage of the man.[16] When preachers display courage, courage in the themes they address, courage in the face of inevitable criticism, the courage of the gospel when 9/11–sized

13. M. Craig Barnes, "When It Is Time to Leave," a sermon preached on the Day1 network, July 16, 2000; available at day1.org/673-when_it_is_time_to_leave.

14. Paul W. Pruyser, "The Master Hand: Psychological Notes on Pastoral Blessing," in *The New Shape of Pastoral Theology: Essays in Honor of Seward Hiltner*, ed. William B. Oglesby Jr. (Nashville: Abingdon, 1969), 352–65, esp. 357.

15. Julian of Norwich, *Revelations of Divine Love*, quoted by T. S. Eliot in *Little Gidding*.

16. James L. Kugel, *How to Read the Bible: A Guide to Scripture, Then and Now* (New York: Free Press, 2008), 581.

events rock society's confidence, they not only display their own character but potentially mentor others in courage. Daloz's comment is again appropriate: "Mentors give us the magic that allows us to enter the darkness, a talisman to protect us from evil spells, a gem of wise advice, and sometimes simply courage," and courage modeled in the pulpit undergirds personal courage in those who hear.

Theologian Al Winn describes the power of this kind of pulpit courage in remembering an extraordinary Sunday in his Alabama town:

> When my children were small, I was writing a dissertation on the Holy Spirit. You can imagine my difficulties when four little people kept asking, "Daddy, what is the Holy Spirit?" We were living in Alabama, in the fifties, and a great riot broke out in our town, protesting the integration of the University of Alabama. Our pastor was a very shy, retiring man. But that Sunday when he entered the pulpit there was something different about him. With a power that none of us had ever seen before, he laid his job on the line—indeed, his life on the line—to tell us clearly and unmistakably that every single human being, regardless of color, is precious in the sight of God. There was a great stillness. New people were being born. Even my children were quiet. In the car on the way home I said quietly, "Now I think you know what the Holy Spirit is." And they nodded.[17]

In another example of mentoring from the pulpit, Nadia Bolz-Weber preached to a gathering of Lutheran pastors, almost all of them buffeted by the howling winds of change in the church. Congregations dwindling, the church embroiled in fierce disputes over sexuality and other hot-button cultural issues, the rise of "nones" among the young—these and many other dispiriting realities were in the minds of the hearers, causing many of them to despair over the future of the church. Bolz-Weber's sermon, titled "Stop Saying the Church Is Dying," began by acknowledging the realities. "It's no news to anyone here," she said, "that there is a lot of hand-wringing these days about the longevity of the Lutheran church. And yeah—to be sure, we used to be bigger, more significant and more impressive."[18] But then her

---

17. Albert C. Winn, *A Christian Primer: The Prayer, the Creed, the Commandments* (Louisville: Westminster John Knox, 1990), 157.

18. Nadia Bolz-Weber, "Stop Saying the Church Is Dying," a sermon preached to the Rocky Mountain ELCA Synod Assembly, May 10, 2014; available at nadiabolzweber.com /uncategorized/stop-saying-the-church-is-dying-a-sermon-for-the-rocky-mountain-synod -assembly.htm.

voice assumed the timbre of courage as she claimed for herself and for her hearers the identity of Easter people who, in the midst of the storm and the earthquake, know the voice that tells them, "Do not be afraid." She closed the sermon by telling the hearers of a trip she and her friend Sara Miles had just taken to Turkey, where they visited caves in which Christians had worshiped centuries before:

> I say this as someone who a week ago was hiking in those desolate valleys of Cappadocia, a land that for 1,000 years was populated with Christians and now is not. That is to say, we are not the first group of Christians to worry about the decline of Christianity.
>
> Sara and I would climb up into caves and look around at ceilings filled with Byzantine Christian iconography. A thousand years of Christianity and now only ruins left. Yes, the big, impressive, successful Byzantine Empire fell, and yet the church of Jesus Christ did not die; if it had, how could two middle-aged women stand in an old cave church 600 years later and sing *Christos Aneste*? Christ is risen. A song that no matter what, will continue to be sung, because worry not, **the tomb is empty, and God will be praised**.

This is preaching, of course, good preaching. But it is also mentoring, speaking with courage and, thereby, giving courage to worried and frightened pastors.

Most of the time, however, preachers are not Jeremiahs or Amoses, charging brashly and boldly into the king's chapel with a revolutionary message. Not even like Jesus, standing in the storm-tossed boat on the churning sea, shouting, "Peace. Be still!" into the winds. Most of the time, preachers mentor listeners by displaying small doses of courage and everyday measures of encouragement (in the literal sense of that word, "en*courage*ment") to their hearers. In an article in *The Christian Century*, Craig Dykstra, then an officer at the Lilly Endowment, described how, as a seminary student, he served as a YMCA swimming instructor for three- and four-year-old children.[19] He remembered how these children, cold and a little frightened, would clutch their bodies and shiver. "Well, it is a law of nature," wrote Dykstra, "that you cannot swim while cramping your body and gnashing your teeth."

So what Dykstra would do was to smile encouragingly at them and, one

---

19. Craig Dykstra, "A Way of Seeing: Imagination and the Christian Life," *Christian Century*, April 8, 2008, 26–31.

by one, take each of them into his arms, hold them gently, and guide them into the water. "Along the way," he said, "I would dip down into the water, allowing them to feel the warmth of it and the flow of it across their skin. After a while—maybe on their third or fourth venture with me into the deep—I would sink them lower and let them feel the water buoying them up." Gradually he would remove his hands. At first, of course, the children would panic a bit, clench up again, and start to sink. But eventually they would learn a key lesson: trust the water. And when they did, they could take courage and swim. Trusting the buoyancy of the water was not, of course, something learned like a principle in a physics book. "One has to come to know it personally," Dykstra said. He continued: "So it is with the life of faith. At the heart of the Christian life there lies a deep, somatic, profoundly personal but very real knowledge. It is the knowledge of the buoyancy of God. It is the knowledge that in struggle and in joy, in conflict and in peace—indeed, in every possible circumstance and condition in life and in death—we are upheld by God's own everlasting arms."[20]

That message is, of course, what wise preachers proclaim in sermon after sermon—on Sunday in the darkness of Good Friday, at graveside—so that "in every possible circumstance and condition in life and in death—we are upheld by God's own everlasting arms." Such proclamation not only deepens people's faith, it also imparts courage and potentially mentors them in their journeys.

Provider of Wise Counsel

Finally, as Daloz says, "Mentors give us . . . a gem of wise advice." In many ways, this advice-giving role goes against much contemporary homiletical wisdom. Preachers are taught not to present themselves as those who have answers to life's dilemmas, not to pretend that they can dispense solutions to problems from the pulpit—a piece of pedagogy that, ironically, is its own form of advice giving. But when it comes to mentoring, the point is not for the preacher to become a bossy parent carping, "Eat your vegetables!" or "Driving is a responsibility, son!" Rather the mentor-preacher speaks caringly and out of shared human experience tempered by the gospel: "Let me tell you, I've been down that road, and the bridge is washed out."

Good resources for preachers in this regard are the New Testament epistles, especially some of the more neglected passages in those documents.

20. Dykstra, "Way of Seeing," 29.

Instead of looking to the letters of the New Testament only for the grand theological themes, such as salvation by grace through faith, preachers can mine them for the wise counsel given to new Christians trying to fashion a distinct way of life in an alien culture.

For example, when the writer of James spends a couple of paragraphs on the power of the tongue both for good and ill ("with it we bless the Lord and Father, and with it we curse those who are made in the likeness of God"; James 3:9), many preachers pass over this text as too small a thing for a sermon. But in a society in which not only families but our whole political discourse is ripped asunder by irresponsible speech, we could all use some mentoring in how to talk with and about each other.

Or take another pertinent issue, the busyness of life and the necessity to make hard choices about how we use our time. Here Ted Wardlaw employs the story of Mary and Martha in Luke not only to preach the gospel in a broad sense but also to provide some wise mentoring advice for his listeners:

> Martha's busyness is ill-timed. It's not the busyness by itself that's the prob-
> lem, but the timing of it. Paul Tillich once put it this way. "There are innu-
> merable concerns in our lives and in human life generally," he says, "which
> demand attention, devotion, passion. But they do not demand infinite
> attention, unconditional devotion, ultimate passion. They are important,
> often very important, for you and me and for the whole of humankind.
> But they are not ultimately important." Figuring out what is ultimately
> important and putting that first—that's the challenge of the Gospel. And
> nothing is more important than receiving the Kingdom of God, wherever
> you are, when it comes near.
>
> Sometimes when we discern that it is near, the faithful thing to do is
> to drop everything and sit still and listen—like Mary. Other times when we
> discern its presence, the faithful thing to do is to get busy and to commit
> to some important task—all of the organizational drive and ability and
> passion we can muster—like Martha.
>
> But if we were to ask Jesus which of these two things we need more
> of—Mary's reflectiveness or Martha's activism—he would probably say yes.
> The truth is that both of these attributes have their time and place; and the
> burden lies in discerning when to do the one and when to do the other.[21]

---

21. Theodore J. Wardlaw, "Only One Thing," a sermon preached on the Day1 network, August 17, 1997; available at day1.org/834-only_one_thing.

A guide at the beginning of a journey, a person of courage in the midst of fear and uncertainty, a wise fellow traveler—the preacher as mentor fills all of these roles and more. To sum up the preacher's mentoring role, we could hardly do better than to recall this beautiful prayer from Matins: "O God, you have called your servants to ventures of which we cannot see the ending, by paths as yet untrodden, through perils unknown. Give us faith to go out with good courage, not knowing where we go, but only that your hand is leading us and your love supporting us; through Jesus Christ our Lord. Amen."[22]

---

22. Eric Milner-White and George Wallace Briggs, *Daily Prayer* (London: Oxford University Press, 1941), 14.

CHAPTER 5

Ethical Perspectives on Mentoring

Rebekah Miles

We cannot do good mentoring without ethics. Ethics is necessary as we reflect on mentoring, set up and implement mentoring programs, and engage in mentoring relationships.[1] Mentoring without ethics is unethical.

The Need for Mentors and Protégés to Reflect on Ethics

The evidence is convincing that mentoring is ethically potent; it can make people more ethical *or less*. In a large-scale study of early to midcareer scientists with grants from the National Institutes of Health, researchers found that mentoring was linked, both positively and negatively, with ethical behavior in research. The good news is that protégés whose mentoring had focused on ethical research engaged in fewer ethically questionable behaviors in their research. The bad news is that protégés whose mentoring centered on winning grants and professional success actually had *more* ethical lapses than average. In other words, when mentoring focused primarily on utility, it fostered vice over virtue. The protégés got the message; getting ahead matters.[2] Mentoring without an ethics component is morally hazardous.

---

1. For other reflections on ethics and mentoring, see Peter Wilson and Brad Johnson, "Core Virtues for the Practice of Mentoring," *Journal of Psychology and Theology* 29.2 (2001): 121–30; Dennis Moberg and Manuel Velasquez, "The Ethics of Mentoring," *Business Ethics Quarterly* 14.1 (January 2004): 95–122; Chong Siow-Ann, "An Asian Perspective on the Ethics of Mentoring," *Asian Bioethics Review* 1.4 (2009): 445–48; Brad Johnson and Nancy Nelson, "Mentor-Protégé Relationships in Graduate Training: Some Ethical Concerns," *Ethics and Behavior* 9.3 (1999): 189–210.

2. Melissa Anderson et al., "What Do Mentoring and Training in the Responsible Con-

The NIH study also found that workshops on ethical research were not as successful as ethical reflection with a mentor. A group of Johns Hopkins scientists made a similar claim: "No type of research ethics training will be more effective ultimately than mentoring. There is no substitute for watching senior faculty grapple with a question of research ethics as it emerges, in real time, in the lab, the field, or the clinic."[3] For mentoring to be ethical and to promote ethical behavior within a field, then, it must focus in part on ethics.

Ethical reflection in mentoring not only helps people engage in more ethical behavior, it also helps them become more ethically discerning. In a study of mentoring and ethics in nursing, researchers found that most new nurses were unable, without assistance, to identify the ethical issues in their nursing practice, even when they had covered those issues in their nursing courses. Regular ethical reflection with a mentor, however, helped the nurses learn to identify and respond appropriately to the key ethical problems in their practice.[4] Likewise a physician and researcher at MD Anderson Cancer Center calls for the inclusion of ethical reflection in the mentoring relationship, especially in the areas of care for patients with advanced cancer who are considering high-risk, experimental treatments. It is not enough to go over the issues in medical school and other ethics training; the new physician needs interaction with an elder to discuss how to weigh the risks and benefits for the patient, how to deal with the realities of informed consent, and how to rightly balance the needs of the patient with possible benefits for the field and the research physician's career.[5]

In recent years, many professional organizations—including those of physicians, nurses, attorneys, clergy, and counselors—have mandated more ethics training both in school courses and in continuing education workshops, and they are to be commended. The research reviewed above suggests, however, that the more effective strategy is ethical reflection with senior colleagues in mentoring relationships. Classes and continuing education about ethics are not enough.

---

duct of Research Have to Do with Scientists' Misbehavior? Findings from a National Survey of NIH-Funded Scientists," *Academic Medicine* 82.9 (September 2007): 853–60. See also Brian Martinson et al., "Scientists Behaving Badly," *Nature* 435 (2005): 737–38.

3. Ruth Faden et al., "On the Importance of Research Ethics and Mentoring," *American Journal of Bioethics* 2.4 (Fall 2002): 51.

4. Gert Hunink et al., "Moral issues in Mentoring Sessions," *Nursing Ethics* 16.4 (July 2009): 487–98.

5. Maurie Markman, "Mentoring in the Ethics of Clinical Research: An Ongoing Need," *Current Oncology Reports* 9.4 (July 2007): 235–36.

Ethical Challenges

Systemic Challenges within Mentoring Programs

Discussion of the ethics of mentoring should include not only ethical reflection within the mentoring relationships itself but also ethical reflection on the broader practices and understanding of mentoring. Those who are not only mentors but are responsible for setting up or overseeing mentoring programs need to think clearly about the larger ethical issues of mentoring.

Any ethical analysis of mentoring should be shaped by the context of current conversation and practice. Sustained interest in mentoring arose in the 1970s when several research studies found that those who were most successful in their fields often shared in common the early guidance of a senior trusted and wise sponsor or mentor. Daniel Levinson saw these mentors as important catalysts in adult psychological development, especially as the protégé moved successfully from one stage of adult development to the next.[6]

The 1980s saw a continuing rise of interest followed by a sharp increase in the late 1980s and 1990s. The new focus on mentoring came from several areas—an attempt by social and governmental agencies to offer aid and improve the lives of people, especially young people, who were socially disadvantaged—and a corporate effort to train and get the most out of employees in an efficient and inexpensive way. This became especially important after the economic downturn in the late 1990s when there was a greater demand for efficiency and cost cutting; mentoring is, among other things, efficient and cheap.[7]

Although the literature in other professions such as academia and medicine has increased significantly, the corporate understanding of mentoring has become dominant. Much of this mentoring discussion was centered on corporate life in the United States, though the conversations spread globally by the late 1990s. The US corporate dominance of the recent resurgence of interest in mentoring is a significant factor. Mentoring has even been called an "American management innovation."[8] That may be overstated, but certainly US corporate life has left its mark on mentoring.

---

6. Daniel Levinson et al., *Seasons of a Man's Life* (New York: Random House, 1978).

7. Jeremiah Barondess, "A Brief History of Mentoring," *Transactions of the Clinical and Climatological Association* 106 (1995): 1–24; and Helen Colley, "Righting Rewritings of the Myth of Mentor," *British Journal of Guidance and Counselling* 29.2 (2001): 177–97.

8. George Odiorne, "Mentoring—An American Management Innovation," *Personnel Administrator* 30 (1985): 63–65.

What is this corporate mark on mentoring? Corporate mentoring generally focuses on career advancement, professional skills, and utility and material success—both the success of the company and of the protégé. At the same time, there is often little focus on character formation, the reduction of vice, and the growth of virtue, with little reflection on the larger goals of a good life that go beyond material success, such as improving the common good. There is also little place for critical reflection on the weaknesses of one's self, one's institution, and one's larger culture.

Part of the problem may be that much of the mentoring literature is secular and lacks the obvious overarching worldview of a religious system with fully developed ideas about human nature and temptations, the common good, and the ends toward which individuals and groups should be striving. Instead professional mentoring in the United States is often supported by an unarticulated materialist/corporate worldview that values material success, profit, and efficiency. It lacks a full picture of the common good, settles for a focus on short-term material gain, and offers few models of the good moral life or particular figures who live it out as saints and moral exemplars. Mentoring today offers socialization to a particular profession, but it rarely gives a structure of value to support that socialization. Consequently, it may or may not be socialization for the good.

One response to the dominance of a corporate mindset in mentoring would be to look at past models that are similar to mentoring yet offer richer traditions and worldviews such as the older tradition of Christian spiritual friendship and spiritual direction.[9] This is a richer tradition that offers grounding and a more substantive ethical worldview with a sense of vocation, purpose, and meaning. Another response would be for the mentoring relationships to include critical reflection on dominant culture and to explore larger worldviews that might offer grounding. This could include discussions of what constitutes success from different perspectives, what is the good toward which the mentoring relationship should move, and what is a virtuous person.

---

9. For discussion of mentoring in relation to the tradition of spiritual direction, see Wilson and Johnson, "Core Virtues for the Practice of Mentoring," 121–30.

Formal or Informal Mentoring

Even the question of whether to set up a formal system of mentoring or to let the mentoring relationships arise informally and naturally has ethical implications. We know that informal mentoring relationships tend to have better professional outcomes, more success.[10] That would be a great testimony for informal mentoring programs except for one problem. Informal mentoring is notoriously exclusive. One of the reasons for formal mentoring is to give everyone an opportunity. If left to informal connections, mentors tend to choose people like them. In other words, senior men of means from the dominant culture will tend to choose younger men of means from the dominant culture. This makes it very difficult for potential protégés who are female, persons of color, or in some other way not of the dominant culture. One response to this problem would be to assign several mentors in the hope that one would be a more natural fit and would offer something closer to the similar interests found in informal relationships. Another option would be to wait to assign mentors until junior colleagues have already begun to establish informal relationships and can identify who they would like to have as mentors.

Dual Roles

One of the most common ethical problems is the conflict among the various roles of the person who is a mentor. In many cases, especially in business, healthcare, or education, the mentor has several overlapping roles that can cause tension in the interactions. The mentor offering the advice and modeling is often also a part of the structure that evaluates, compensates, and sometimes even terminates. Consequently, when the mentor and protégé interact, they are not thinking simply about the obvious tasks before them. The protégé will likely wonder how their conversation will impact his or her future career and will hesitate to be too honest about weaknesses and problems. The mentor may wonder if the protégé is going to make it at their institution and if he or she is ready for promotion. One response to this problem would be to set up mentoring programs in ways that ensure that the mentor is not and will not become involved in any way in the supervision of the protégé.

10. Christina Underhill, "The Effectiveness of Mentoring Programs in Corporate Settings: A Meta-Analytical Review of the Literature," *Journal of Vocational Behavior* 68 (2006): 292–307.

The tension in overlapping roles brings us to another potential ethical landmine in mentoring relationships—romantic and sexual intimacy. In the mentoring relationship, as in any other dependent professional relationship, sexual and romantic intimacy are inappropriate, and it is the responsibility of the person with greater power, in this case the mentor, to keep the boundaries. In the most obvious case, it is the responsibility of the mentor not to have any sexual contact with the protégé. In addition, to avoid sexual contact or even the appearance of sexual contact, protocols need to be developed and followed. Sexual, teasing banter is out of place in a mentoring relationship. If there is sexual or romantic attraction on one or both sides, the mentor is responsible for keeping the boundaries. This should include not only avoiding sexual contact or even the appearance of impropriety, but also keeping faithful to sensible processes and protocols. This could include meeting in public places or a conference room with a window and avoiding certain intimate topics.

It is not just sex we need to worry about. Mentoring can founder on other grounds. Protégés can become too dependent on the mentor. Mentors can show inappropriate preference to the protégé in a way that disadvantages other junior colleagues.

Vices

When mentors are asked about difficulties in the mentoring relationships, a common complaint is deceit.[11] The protégé is not always telling the truth but instead projecting an image. The protégé may not acknowledge work problems or may put too positive a spin on a work disaster. Withholding the truth undercuts the mentor/protégé relationship and effectiveness. Even so, as noted earlier, if the mentor has a dual role and is also involved in any way with the protégé's advancement, one can see why the protégé is not totally forthcoming. It may not be in his or her interest. For their part, the mentors may not be fully open or even self-aware about the dual nature of the relationship and the tension between their roles in mentoring and the ongoing evaluation and review of the protégé. Again, an appropriate response would be to assign mentors without supervisory roles over the protégé and at least

---

11. Moberg and Velasquez, "Ethics of Mentoring," 97. See also Lillian Eby and Angie Lockwood, "Proteges' and Mentors' Reactions to Participating in Formal Mentoring Programs," *Journal of Vocational Behavior* 67 (2005): 442–58.

to talk openly about these questions and fears and come to an agreement about confidentiality.

When asked about the difficulties with mentors, protégés complained primarily about mentors failing to fulfill their mentoring responsibilities or being manipulative, heavy handed, and tyrannical.[12] These are ethical problems involving the shirking of duty and the abuse of power. For mentoring to be successful, mentors must continue to commit to the fulfillment of their duties in relation to the protégé. In addition, supervisors need to pick and train mentors who are responsible to their duties and who are not manipulative. Unfortunately, this may mean that the mentoring workload is not spread evenly among senior colleagues.

Ethical Principles

In addition to looking at ethical challenges faced in mentoring, it is also critical to explore ethical resources, especially principles. Given the mentoring challenges, what ethical principles are especially helpful? The four principles often used in biomedical ethics and many other professional fields are relevant here as well: autonomy, nonmaleficence, beneficence, and justice.[13]

Autonomy

One of the most important principles for our purposes is autonomy, because mentoring presents particular challenges in this area. The principle of autonomy emphasizes independence, freedom from coercion, and the right of self-control. This principle works to counter the loss of agency that can arise in mentoring.

Why are mentoring programs a challenge for autonomy? First, there is a paternalistic aspect built into mentoring that is in tension with autonomy. A senior person with greater power is advising a junior person with less

12. Moberg and Velasquez, "Ethics of Mentoring," 97.

13. The classic treatment of these four principles in biomedical ethics is Tom Beauchamp and James Childress, *Principles of Biomedical Ethics* (New York: Oxford University Press, 1977). These principles have been taken up in discussion about many ethical topics and within many professions. See, for example, Sondra Wheeler's *Stewards of Life: Bioethics and Pastoral Care* (Nashville: Abingdon, 1996); and Sarah Banks, *Ethics and Values in Social Work* (New York: Palgrave Macmillan, 2012).

power. Moreover, mentoring programs are set up by employers or judicatory organizations that often require or strongly recommend participation. In addition, particular mentors are often provided to the protégé with little or no choice offered; it is an arranged relationship. Moreover, the mentors, though perhaps not directly in a supervisory role, often have a part in the protégés' futures and in their evaluations. This sets up a difficult dynamic. Because the protégé may not feel free to decline the mentoring relationship, free consent is nearly impossible. Because the protégé often has not chosen the person or the format and process for the mentoring and because the person who has made these choices often has control over his or her future career, the protégé may enter the process with a sense of weakened autonomy and heightened resentment. This is a common problem among protégés. It is important, then, to give greater autonomy to protégés, offering them choice about whether to participate, about whom to have as mentors, and about how to set up a process by which the protégé and the mentor can work together to formulate structures and goals.

Autonomy can be a challenge not only in setting up a mentoring program but also within a mentoring relationship itself. Mentors complain not only of dishonesty among some protégés but also overdependence. It is ironic that mentoring is a dependent relationship that seeks to foster autonomous, independent action on the part of the protégé. In addition, protégés commonly complain about mentors being tyrannical or manipulative, characteristics that are, at base, threats to autonomy. Mentors and mentoring programs need to be set up and then enacted in ways that encourage greater autonomy and independence.

In ethics, autonomy often includes not only freedom to self-determination but also informed consent, that is, consent in light of the full knowledge of the issues and choices in question. If the protégé does not know from the beginning what the mentoring relationship will involve and has little choice in the matter, then it is near impossible to have true consent. It is crucial, then, to be clear from the beginning about what is entailed in the mentoring relationship and to give the protégé as much choice as is feasible in the situation.

Confidentiality is often considered under the principle of autonomy. People are to have some control not only over their own selves but also their private information. This can create tensions in a mentoring relationship, if a protégé mentions something that could impact the organization. For example, what if a protégé reveals that she is considering taking another position? Does the mentor reveal that information to others in the organization? Some essays on mentoring in the business context suggest that a mentor would need to weigh not only the good of the protégé but also the potential harm or benefit to the individuals and the organization.[14] As someone who has written in the area of pastoral care, I am taken aback by this interpretation of confidentiality. If confidentiality in the mentor relationship is taken so lightly, then, of course, the protégé should not disclose everything and would be justified in putting a positive spin on any information given to a mentor. In other words, if one wants honesty and full disclosure in mentoring relationships and thinks that is necessary for the mentoring to be successful, then confidentiality has to be honored, except, of course, in extreme circumstances when there is a threat of serious bodily injury.

Nonmaleficence

In medical ethics and other contexts, the principle of nonmaleficence, doing no harm, takes priority over the principle of beneficence or doing good. This is true in mentoring as well. A mentor seeks to benefit the mentee but at minimum wants to avoid harm. How might mentors harm protégés? A mentor could give bad advice that the protégé takes more seriously, precisely because it is from the mentor. This advice could hurt the protégé and his or her career. The mentoring relationship could create too great a dependence of the protégé on the mentor. The mentor could be heavy handed with the protégé or use confidential information in work evaluations. The mentor could neglect and fail to engage the protégé. Moreover, both parties could fail to address larger social questions about public responsibility, such as how does this employment or activity affect the larger social good? Mentors need to be aware that it is a complex relationship and that it takes intentional reflection and work to avoid these problems. Nonmaleficence is not easy or automatic.

Beneficence

If nonmaleficence is the negative obligation to do no harm, beneficence is the positive obligation to do good. This is sometimes framed in grander terms as the obligation to love and care for others. In the field of medicine, the focus is primarily on what is good for the patient or research subject. In many mentoring discussions, the focus is chiefly on the good of the protégé

14. Moberg and Velasquez, "Ethics of Mentoring," 108–9.

as well as the institution, with an occasional reference to the good for the mentor. (These reflections often note some benefits, but more sacrifice on the part of the mentor.)[15]

There are several obvious gaps here. First, most mentoring programs have a very circumscribed notion of whose good is important and focus primarily on the good of the protégé and the institution. What is missing is the consideration of what is good for the people who are served by the protégé and institution as well as the common good of the larger human society and even the nonhuman parts of the global environment. This shift of focus could change the mentoring relationship dramatically.

Second, there is little talk about what constitutes the good. Many studies on the benefits of mentoring assume a focus on the utilitarian, material goods for the protégé and the institution. They measure success of mentoring for the protégé by the rates of career accomplishment, promotion, salary increase, and employee job satisfaction. Business mentoring often focuses also on the good of the institution, which is framed as increase in sales and profits as well as employee retention and productivity. What is missing here is a broader understanding of the good that includes growth in virtue, character, and justice as well as an increase in awareness of and responsibility to the common good.

In my reading, there is also no critical moment built into most mentoring processes. If the mentoring process focuses on success within an institution without fostering ethical reflection on the institution and its goals, mentoring is suspect. How do persons and communities find regular ways within mentoring to think about and critically reflect on their own complicity and blindness and that of their institutions?

Those who set up mentoring programs, then, would do well to think more broadly about the good, both about whose good is being sought and about what constitutes the good. And likewise, mentors should include in their discussions not only material goods like career success or increased productivity but also the larger goals of a moral life and the improvement of the society and world.[16] This inclusion would foster beneficent, ethical mentoring.

15. Tammy Allen, Elizabeth Lentz, and Rachel Day, "Career Success Outcomes Associated with Mentoring Others: A Comparison of Mentors and Nonmentors," *Journal of Career Development* 34.3 (March 2006): 272–85.

16. Aquinas and Aristotle could be helpful here in thinking about what constitutes the highest level of friendship. In friendship at its best, the two friends share goals that go beyond their own interests and extend to a shared common good.

Justice

The final principle is justice, which at its most basic is fairness or giving each what is due to each. Ethicists often look at several different types of justice. Distributive justice is fairness in distributing benefits and burdens. Procedural justice calls for fairness in setting up processes and procedures. Commutative justice is fairness in relationships and in agreements within relationships. Corrective justice is fairness in correcting, providing restitution, and even instituting punishment for past wrongs. Each of these relates to the mentoring process.

In distributive justice the benefits to be distributed could include any goods, services, or privileges. The burdens could include costs in money, goods, time, and energy. In relation to mentoring, this model of justice could suggest that the opportunity of having a mentor should be distributed fairly to protégés and that the burden of mentoring should be distributed fairly among senior persons. Of course, one still has to ask what fairness is in any particular case. The distribution could be based on equality, in which case everyone gets the same benefits and burdens; or on equity, where everyone gets what is appropriate given their contribution; or on need, where all get a share commensurate with their needs. If, for example, one had a mentoring program based on need, then one could give preferential treatment to some employees who had particular deficits or a specific task that necessitated greater assistance. The problem here, of course, is that this is a subjective judgment that could, if mistaken, lead to unfair, unjust treatment. Moreover, it is not helpful to a mentoring program to give people the impression that it is remedial! If an institution is operating out of fairness as equality, then all junior employees should have the opportunity to be mentored and all senior employees should share the burden of mentoring. The difficulty with this option is that it does not take into account that some employees may not want to participate (autonomy) and that some potential mentors may not have the gifts or inclination for the task and might become the neglectful or tyrannical mentors about which protégés often complain.

Procedural justice, or fairness in setting up processes and procedures, demands that institutional leaders think carefully about how they set up mentoring programs. Are the procedures fair throughout? Are the expectations clear? Is there enough structure and flexibility? Are there ethics components? This reflection on procedure and process is especially important given that many mentoring programs are thrown together without much thought about ethical principles, including justice.

Commutative justice, fairness in relationships and in agreements within relationships, is also especially important early in the mentoring process. When a mentor and protégé begin, their relationship can be more just if the institution is clear about the nature of the relationship and if the mentor and protégé work out clear expectations at the beginning and follow through with their commitments. (See the preceding paragraph on procedural justice.)

Corrective justice is fairness in correcting, providing restitution, and even instituting punishment for past wrongs. Mentoring programs could themselves be expressions of corrective justice if they are focused on giving aid to people who are disadvantaged in an activity or profession. For example, if women have been largely absent in a field, a mentoring program could be established specifically to help women succeed in that male-dominated field. Corrective justice may be needed within the mentoring relationship itself. Ideally mentoring programs would be set up and implemented in a just and fair way so that corrective justice within the mentoring relationships is not necessary. It would come into play only when there has been a failure in some other part of the mentoring program. But in the face of mentoring failures, this is an important part of justice. For example, if a mentor were to give bad advice to the protégé that led to poor performance, the institution's leaders might take into account that the protégé was not entirely to blame.

In addition to reflecting on these four principles (including the different models of justice), institutional leaders and mentors also need to consider tensions among them. For example, what if the duty of beneficence to a protégé calls for partiality of treatment that disadvantages another employee with whom the mentor is not in a special relationship. Might not this be a violation of distributive justice? Also, beneficence and autonomy often conflict. For example, what if the good that could be done for a protégé is something that the protégé does not want? Moreover, what if the mentor and protégé face a choice that would be good for the protégé but not good for others? In addition to these tensions among the four principles, one also can draw on other principles such as truthfulness, fairness, fidelity, love, and concern for the larger common good.

Larger Frameworks for Ethics

As we have seen, one of the major ethical challenges facing mentoring is that these relationships often exist in a context with no shared worldview or with only a partially articulated corporate worldview that is morally shallow at best. Mentoring, and any moral reflection on or within mentoring, can be done more deftly and successfully in a community with a shared worldview that has substantive moral depth. Religious traditions, for example, offer this framework, as might American liberal democratic tradition or the classical traditions of the West growing out of Aristotle and Plato. These traditions would offer a framework from which to understand and practice mentoring.

These frameworks can often be found in or near institutions that offer mentoring. Religious institutions, including seminaries, colleges, and hospitals, can draw on the framework of their religious traditions. While no framework is rejected out of hand, some may not be as well suited. Again, the US corporate framework has its own values and virtues but not ones that work very well for forming and maintaining a moral life and character.

Of course, many institutions may have these larger frameworks and find that their members still live out of and offer mentoring not from that tradition but from the more secular mentoring process that comes from business and other professional contexts. Consequently, institutions and leaders that have a shared tradition need to be explicit about drawing on those traditions within mentoring. As an example of the way a larger framework would help the mentoring process, I turn to the tradition I know best—Christianity.

Mentoring programs are most often set up in workplaces in relation to employment and other forms of work. Consequently, Christian theological and ethical reflections on work and vocation are especially important to this discussion of mentoring. For centuries among many Christians, human work has been seen as vocation—a part of our service to and an expression of our love for God and neighbor. This would be true not only of ordinary tasks of our employment but also of the mentoring process; mentoring itself is an expression of the vocation of both mentor and protégé. To talk about employment or mentoring primarily as a means to material success and prestige is morally bankrupt from a Christian point of view. Our work (including mentoring) is service to God and neighbor.

Many Christian theologians and leaders emphasize that employment offers a way for us to provide for ourselves and our families and even for our future security, to avoid debt, and to give to the poor. The excess beyond our necessities is to be given away, because it belongs not to us but to God and to those who have too little. The material aspects of our employment are important, then, but only to a point. The goal should not be to get promotions and raises to amass wealth and privilege for ourselves. That perspective is antithetical to the heart of Christianity. In a highly materialistic culture with an unprecedented gap between the rich and the poor, these topics must be at the heart of Christian mentoring.

Our employment is only one part of our vocation and is to be balanced with our vocations as Christians, citizens, and family members. In a culture that places an extremely high value on workplace success, any responsible Christian mentoring process has to place discussions of paid work in the context of our prior vocation as Christians and as family members. Work–life balance is not just about stress reduction; it is primarily about moral faithfulness to our calling as Christians.

Our work in the world, in whatever part of our vocation, is governed by ethical rules, principles, and duties set forth in Scripture and in our traditions. These include injunctions not to cheat, deceive, or charge usurious interest; to care for and never harm the poor, the orphan, and the immigrant; to provide and care for our families; to be responsible stewards of the created world; and to be cautious of the temptations offered in material goods and worldly success. One can easily imagine conflicts between these injunctions and one's employment, if, for example, one's work harms the vulnerable or requires deception. Christian mentoring needs to include moral reflection not only on the internal codes specific to that profession but also these broader rules for faithful living.

As moral people, our work in the world, in whatever part of our vocation, also depends upon us becoming certain kinds of moral people. The Christian tradition offers models of what it means to be a good and virtuous person. The mentoring process should reflect on these models. In addition, the mentor should strive to exemplify these virtues for the protégé, and both should be growing together in grace and virtue. Both mentor and protégé should be seeking forgiveness for inevitable failure and relying always on God's grace. These considerations could be a part of the mentoring contract and process set up at the beginning of the relationship.

In the early chapters of Genesis, humans were created for work, to till the ground and keep it. Our created capacity and God's injunction to work and to care for all of creation are good parts of our human nature. As we see in those same chapters, work can also be part of the pain of living in separation from God and all that we are intended to be. These realities, too, need to be in the background of mentoring discussions.

We also remember that as creatures we are finite and sinful. We are subject to death. This means that our work and its fruits will not last. As we hear in Ecclesiastes it is vanity—literally, vapor or breath. We will also make mistakes—some because of chance or error and others because of outright sin. Our work is an expression not only of our lives as good creatures created by God but also as fallen creatures whose actions are always clouded by and subject to temptation and self-deceit. Christian mentoring is always done in the context of the sin and frailty of the mentor, the protégé, and the institutions in which they work as well as the fleeting nature of all human projects.

We also do our work in the face of the realities of this finite world where many do not have enough to live and therefore suffer tragedies and abuse. Throughout Scripture we see that the faithful have special responsibilities to the vulnerable. The mentoring process can be a part of our Christian *examen* or self-reflection where we ask, "Are we, in our work, harming anyone, especially the vulnerable? Are we, in our employment, doing good for others, especially the poor and suffering?"

Given our sin and frailty, and that of the world, it is easy to despair and come to believe that our work (including mentoring) makes no difference. That despair would be warranted if it were all up to us. But the good news, from a Christian framework, is that it is never all up to us. Our work—including the care for others expressed in mentoring—is in God's hands. In our work we participate in God's work in the world. Through the transformation offered in Christ and the ongoing power of the Holy Spirit, we are empowered for that work, including the work of mentoring.

Christ also serves as a model for mentoring. As a mentor to his disciples he chided them for seeking prestige and power, and he reinterpreted the meaning of power and lifted up the value of suffering for others. He encouraged his followers to put the needs of others before their own and to be willing to suffer for the sake of others.

Our work in the world, in whatever part of our vocation, is also a part of a larger vision of the Christian moral life. We operate out of a vision of the good life, of the destiny toward which we are moving. Christian mentoring should include discussion of the ways that our professional goals contribute to these larger goals of the Christian life; that could include justification, repentance, personal sanctification, and social transformation. Of course even our ultimate goals in this life are always seen in relation to the final redemption for which Christians wait. Our work, including mentoring, is a part of this ultimate goal but is also relativized by it.

Summary

Mentoring without ethics is unethical. Ethical reflection is required to set up just mentoring programs. Moral action and character are required of mentors to fulfill commitments to protégés, value their autonomy, honor confidentiality, and keep appropriate boundaries. Ethical reflection is also a necessary topic of conversation between mentors and protégés. Both mentor and protégé, if they are to respond effectively to the challenges of their field, need practiced capacities for moral discernment. They need hard conversations about moral conflicts within their profession, where the senior person reflects honestly on failures and successes and provides a moral model. Mentoring needs to include conversations not only about the ethics of the shared profession but also of a good human life. How does the work in which they engage in their profession (including the work of mentoring) contribute to a better, more ethical life not only for the mentor and protégé but also for others in their families, local communities, and wider society? If the mentor and protégé share a religious worldview, what resources from that worldview inform their ethical reflection? Are there laws and principles that are especially relevant? Does this tradition offer models of the good life and the good society toward which all people are to be working? In brief, ethics is a necessary component of responsible mentoring; we cannot do good mentoring without ethics.

CHAPTER 6

Expanding the Perimeters of Feminist Mentoring

Cynthia L. Rigby

Every now and then, at our faculty meetings at Austin Seminary, President Ted Wardlaw turns to a member of the faculty and asks: "Dr. So-and-So, what is recruitment?" And the person responds: "Recruitment is everyone's business."

Every time this little ritual occurs, everyone present is reminded that the day is over when academic institutions can rely on a person or small team of persons to go out and spread the word about a school to prospective students who have a range of ministerial callings and very different educational backgrounds and who represent a variety of ages, ethnicities, races, genders, and economic classes. All of us are needed if the message is to get out that our doors are open wide.

There may have been a day when "feminist mentoring" was the work of one or two wise women privately advising up-and-coming women about how to sustain themselves and their work in largely patriarchal church and academic cultures. Such mentoring will always be invaluable, of course. But if we pigeonhole our understanding of feminist mentoring in such a way that we leave the work of feminist mentoring to others, humbly opting out by describing ourselves as "not yet wise enough women," or "not really feminist women," or "men who are *not* women and are therefore not qualified"—if we take on these labels in the name of humility and deference to those who are more obviously qualified to do the work, if we do these things while insisting that we actually *support* this work, we are not qualified to engage ourselves, make no mistake: we have actually undercut it. The truth is, as I argue in this chapter: feminist mentoring is *everyone's* business.

Overview

In this chapter I develop a broad understanding of what constitutes feminist mentoring in the context of the United States. I do it, first, by suggesting there are ways that those not identified as feminists may still take on the work of feminist mentoring, using Jesus as an example of a feminist mentor. I then compare feminist mentoring to mentoring more generally in an attempt to establish a working definition. Next I offer examples from my own life of a range of interactions that might be understood as feminist mentoring in order to show that potential feminist mentoring has to be used as a vehicle of transformation. Finally, I offer three common theological handles that can be used as potential starting points for coaching women (and many men) in being who God created them to be.

It is important, before I proceed, to note that I am imagining all of this in my own life and context in the United States. The stories I tell take place in Rhode Island, Atlanta, and Austin. Their possibility is contingent on there being some modicum of commitment both to gender equality and to the importance of individuals flourishing, values that are not present everywhere. These are values that, due to the privileges of my own upbringing and context, I am able to access for myself and for others even when they are not adequately in play. Thus, as much as this chapter is about broadening our understanding of what constitutes feminist mentoring so it can have greater influence, the examples here are narrow in the broad scheme of things. I hope for a day when all women and girls—all people—have access to the values and freedoms that make feminist mentoring possible.[1] Remembering that it is not equally possible everywhere, I am more determined not to squander its possibilities. The way I look at it, to advocate for feminist mentoring is not only and perhaps not even primarily to name what women do not have, but to celebrate and insist on giving women the opportunities to develop and utilize the abilities and gifts they do have.

Jesus as Feminist Mentor

I surprised myself as I typed the header over this section, since I generally refrain from applying the label "feminist" to Jesus (given that it was not in-

---

1. A book that incisively outlines what must happen even before women can benefit from feminist mentoring is Jimmy Carter's *A Call to Action: Women, Religion, Violence, and Power* (New York: Simon & Schuster, 1994).

vented for close to two thousand years after his time!). But saying someone is a feminist mentor is a bit different from calling that person a feminist. Grammatically, the use of the term *feminist* here is an adjective, not a noun. One can *act* feminist without necessarily being understood to *be* a feminist.

Let me try to explain this with an analogy. It might well be problematic to tell someone who is not a literal mother that we think she *is* a mother, when we see her caring for children. But to describe her as "motherly," whether or not she is in fact a mother, is to offer a powerful description of the character of her caretaking. Along these same lines, Alice Walker explains that Black communities often tell young girls, as a compliment to their taking responsibility and gaining in maturity, that they are acting "womanish."[2] This is said even when it is clear that the person being described is not old enough, yet, to be called a woman.

In identifying Jesus as a feminist mentor, I am aiming to say something about the character of Jesus's mentoring. I still need to explain what I mean by calling Jesus's mentoring feminist, of course! In order to do this, I reflect on a biblical story—Jesus's visit with Martha and Mary in Luke 10—in which I describe Jesus's mentoring as feminist:

Martha: "Tell her to help me!"

Jesus: "Mary has chosen what is better, and it will not be taken from her." (Luke 10:40, 42 New International Version)

Jesus is often understood to be mentoring Mary in this story. Mary is sitting at his feet, soaking in his words and wisdom. She is not helping in the kitchen, which upsets Martha. So Jesus also extends guidance to Martha, correcting her for being overly worried and for questioning the "better" position Mary has chosen.

I argue that Jesus is not only a mentor to Mary and Martha in this story, but a feminist mentor. His emphasis is not on all the important things *he* has to teach, but on *Mary's* having chosen what is important and Martha should not interfere. The purpose of his mentoring is not to recapitulate himself or to reinforce the system that others might then step into. It is, rather, to affirm what Mary has chosen *despite* the expectations of those around her and the regular patterns of the system. Jesus does not care about these at all; he cares about Mary and is determined to support her growth and decisions.

2. Alice Walker, *In Search of Our Mothers' Gardens* (San Diego: Harcourt, 1983), xi.

Mentoring versus Feminist Mentoring

Feminist mentoring is often distinguished from mentoring in the literature as placing less emphasis on disseminating wisdom and more on drawing out of the mentee her or his best self, gifts, and strengths. Mentoring is traditionally framed by the important acknowledgment that some have more knowledge and power than others.[3] Recognizing their relative expertise and privilege, mentors commit both to disseminating what they know and to creating opportunities for mentees to network in ways that gain them more power and status in the system.[4] Feminist mentoring also acknowledges power differentials, but is less focused on helping individuals gain more power and influence in already established systems than in helping individuals negotiate, defy, and transform systems that depend on their being less than who they really are. Some feminist mentors, in fact, reject the language of feminist mentoring altogether because they view it as oxymoronic: mentoring, as such, reinforces the very hierarchies and power differentials that feminists want to equalize, they say, emphasizing instead mutuality. Suggestions for better terms include "co-mentoring,"[5] which immediately complicates hierarchical presuppositions about mentoring, and "midwife teaching" or "coaching," both of which center more on bringing to fruition the person and capacities of the mentee than on mimicking the gifts and contributions of the mentor.[6] If traditional mentoring can be depicted, metaphorically, by the image of a master forming an apprentice in something of his own image, a good and very different metaphor for feminist mentoring might be midwifery. The feminist mentor coaches the mentee in birthing what she (or he) has to offer to the world.[7]

3. Aine M. Humble et al., "Feminism and Mentoring of Graduate Students," *Family Relations* 55.1 (January 2006): 2–15.

4. A classic book on mentoring that is well described in this way is *The Elements of Mentoring* by W. Brad Johnson and Charles R. Ridley (New York: Macmillan, 2004). This guide contains discussion of how gender and race factor into mentoring relationships, but only insofar as they come into play in relation to women and persons of color being successfully "networked in" to the patterns of the dominant system. The focus, in other words, is not on the flourishing of individuals except insofar as they participate in, and rise in the ranks of, the existing system.

5. Gail M. McGuire and Jo Reger, "Feminist Co-Mentoring: A Model for Academic Professional Development," *NWSA Journal* 15.1 (Spring 2003): 54–72.

6. Tina Huyck Carter, "Feminist Mentoring" (unpublished paper). I am indebted to my friend Tina, a scientist, pastor, and "coach," for helping me think through the difference between "mentoring" and "feminist mentoring" as well as for identifying some specific ways I have served as a feminist mentor, in her observation.

7. Humble et al., "Feminism and Mentoring of Graduate Students."

It might be objected that this differentiation between mentoring and feminist mentoring does a disservice to mentoring insofar as it leans on certain stereotypes of mentoring, overlooking approaches that do not aim to perpetuate hierarchical systems and that do want to focus on drawing out the best of what the mentee has to offer.[8] This volume no doubt demonstrates that there are a range of ways mentoring can be understood, with some approaches being more mutual and/or more attuned to coaching than others. The question is: if mentoring moves away from more hierarchal-oriented models (i.e., master to apprentice) to more mutual paradigms (midwifery), in what way can it then be differentiated from feminist mentoring? In other words, is what distinguishes mentoring as feminist its being mutual and focused on the mentee, or is there something more to its uniqueness?

I would say that what makes mentoring feminist is not only what has thus far been mentioned, but one more crucial element: feminist mentoring insists on keeping at front and center those experiences of women that are not taken into adequate account in systems of power that perpetuate themselves by way of traditional patterns of mentoring. This does *not* mean feminist mentoring can be accomplished only when women are in the roles of mentors and/or mentees. It does mean, however, that the content and progression of feminist mentoring is oriented around an awareness of and concern with the being, value, and flourishing of those women whom the system generally excludes, whether actively or passively. This awareness of women and their experiences can also challenge and/or benefit men who are mentors and mentees, particularly when the men in the mentoring relationships want to have more egalitarian relationships with women or when they themselves are experiencing exclusion due to race, economic class, sexual preference, or physical disability.

There is at least one potential problem with setting the perimeters of feminist mentoring as I have done, namely, mentors and mentees who are actively considering how women can maneuver and/or engage structural dynamics in ways that enable them to flourish are engaged in the work of feminist mentoring, whether they would accept this identification or not. I understand the problems that come with assigning labels, especially when the labels contain politicized terms such as "feminist." For the purposes of this chapter, however, I will use the terminology and definition not in order to coopt the efforts of others, but for the purpose of acknowledging the participation of as many as possible. To be frank, I would rather err by

8. Humble et al., "Feminism and Mentoring of Graduate Students."

understanding the perimeter of feminist mentoring too broadly than by too narrowly delineating what feminist mentoring is all about.

Along these lines, feminist mentoring, as I see it, is not a delicate art that should be dared by only a select few. It is a responsibility of any and all who believe half the population should be equal to the other half, which should be all of us. As long as men leave feminist mentoring only to women, the structures will never change enough for women to flourish. What might have been really interesting, along these lines, would have been to have a man write this chapter of this book. How might a male senior pastor act as a feminist mentor to a female associate? It seems to me that, if he were to do this effectively, he could do it only in a co-mentoring relationship with her. Otherwise, the very structure that has impeded her flourishing would only be recapitulated. We will break free of this recapitulation not by women sharing power with other women, since this will only leave the men at liberty to maintain more traditional patterns of mentoring that exclude women. New patterns of engagement will be seen in the land only when the men who have the power to sustain the system choose to mentor in ways that change the patterns that leave women (and less privileged men) behind. For men to be involved in feminist mentoring is to shake up the structures that have excluded, to reverse the "kingdoms" that have hitherto been recapitulated.

In the reflections that follow, I aim to keep my focus on my assignment, which is to reflect on *feminist* mentoring. To do this responsibly, I believe, requires that I say something about what might constitute *womanist* mentoring. If feminist mentoring always has in mind the flourishing of women, and therefore the experiences of women,[9] it must not neglect the flourishing of women of all ethnicities, races, and socioeconomic levels. The experiences of women kept at the front and center of consideration in feminist mentoring cannot be only the experiences of white, middle-class and upper-class women, but also must be the experiences of women who are economically disadvantaged, and women of color whether they are economically disadvantaged or middle/upper class. *Womanist* mentoring is feminist mentoring that pays special attention to the ways in which women of color are generally excluded from the systems they are a part of, not only because they are female but also because they are not white.[10]

9. Rosemary Radford Ruether, *Sexism and God-talk* (Boston: Beacon, 1993).

10. For more on womanist mentoring, which is not given adequate consideration in this chapter, see Anne Wimberly and Maisha Handy, "Conversations on Word and Deed: Forming Wisdom through Female Mentoring," in *In Search of Wisdom: Faith Formation in the Black Church* (Nashville: Abingdon, 2002); and Kathleen E. Gillon and Lissa D. Stapleton, "'My Story Ain't

Feminist Mentoring Is Everyone's Business

With these definitions and limitations in mind, I offer four examples of what might constitute feminist mentoring drawn from my own life, including two times I have been mentored and two times I have mentored others. The point of offering these is to demonstrate what feminist mentoring might look like for those who want to take seriously that it is their business to participate.

Story #1: Feminist Mentoring of a Not-Feminist Mentee by a Not-Feminist Mentor

I graduated from Brown University in 1986, having received a bachelor of arts degree in religious studies. I had many teachers there who were superb. But one, in particular, stands out in my memory as making all the difference in the path I took in life. Professor D. was an Anglo, male, full professor who had a great deal of status in the department. While my other teachers told me I should move directly into a PhD program and were somewhat baffled by my conviction that I should, in one form or another, enter into Christian ministry, this professor made it a point to try to understand where I had come from so he could help me make a next step consistent with my abilities and calling.

In asking me questions about my perceived vocation, Professor D. was disturbed to discover that I was unclear (at the time) about whether it was permissible, biblically, for women to be ordained. Instead of telling me this was incorrect, or even inconsistent with my changing hermeneutics, and despite my having told him I was *not* a feminist, he presented me with copies of two new publications: Rosemary Radford Ruether's *Sexism and God-talk* and Elisabeth Schüssler Fiorenza's *In Memory of Her.*[11] While I may have written a lot of snide remarks in the margins of these books, I read them multiple times and used them extensively in my final college paper.

In my senior year, Professor D. called me in for a meeting. (I do not think I realized, at the time, how unusual it was to be called in for a meeting one has not requested.) "I have been praying for you," he told me. (Again, this was not something my professors at Brown habitually said to me!) "And I am led

---

Got Nothin to Do with You,' or Does It? Black Female Faculty's Critical Considerations of Mentoring White Female Students," *Journal of Critical Scholarship on Higher Education and Student Affairs* 1 (2015): article 3.

11. Elisabeth Schüssler Fiorenza, *In Memory of Her: Feminist Theological Reconstruction of Christian Origins*, tenth anniv. ed. (New York: Crossroad, 1994).

to believe that God wants you to do an MDiv at Princeton Theological Seminary." Years later, after I had earned both an MDiv and a PhD at Princeton Seminary, this professor—now a colleague in the field—told me that he had been very strategic in the way he phrased this suggestion to me. He knew that, at that time in my life, I would take very seriously his having committed the matter of my future to prayer. "I knew you would not go straight to the PhD," he told me, "but I guessed right that we could keep you in academia if we got you to Princeton, working on your MDiv."

Looking back, I realize that this professor was one of the most influential feminist mentors I ever had. He did not lecture me on what I should and should not believe; he did not tell me I should be more confident or hurry up to get my plans caught up with my brain; he did not spend hours telling me stories about himself and how he got to where he had gotten. He figured out how to coach me by meeting me where I was, by coaching me to the next workable step he knew I could take, and by giving me dialogue partners (feminist thinkers) who would help me continue to become who I was already becoming.

Story #2: Feminist Mentoring of a Feminist Mentee by a Feminist Mentor

Directly following the very first academic paper I delivered at the American Academy of Religion, I was asked to take a few questions. Looking out at the audience of a couple of hundred people, I felt happy and competent. The paper had been well received. I answered one question well, and then another. Then a third questioner began. He rose up from the first row, turned, faced the audience, and made an announcement about a group that he led; a group that, he assured us, would welcome papers in the genre of the one I had presented; papers, he explained, that worked with both Karl Barth's theology and feminist insights. "If anyone is interested," he said, with his back toward me (I was still standing at the podium), "just let me know."

"I am interested," I said into the mic. Everyone laughed. I got the room back for a few seconds until it was time to turn to the next session presenter.

I walked out of the meeting room feeling depressed, but at the time not able to identify why. After all, the paper had gone well, as had the Q&A, and even the announcement was in significant ways an affirmation of my work. Why did I feel so down?

"I will tell you why," said the feminist mentor who helped me process what happened. "It is because you were coopted. The Q&A should have been focused on you and your work. What he did was take the energy in the room and turn it toward himself and his agenda."

While that analysis hurt, I knew my mentor was right. She had not been at the presentation, but had seen the pain in my eyes as I was moving through the crowds at the AAR meeting. As busy as she was, she had stopped, and stopped me, and asked me what was up. The story spilled out of me, and so she took me by the arm, sat me down with a cup of coffee, and told me what had happened. And then she told me what I had done that helped disarm the coopting (I had made that joke from the microphone) and what I could have done better (cut him off sooner, possibly also with a joke that named the problem).

This feminist mentor, again, did not talk a lot about her own experiences or focus on giving me tips for the ways she has found to avoid or manage such situations. Instead, she focused on what had happened to me in that session, analyzing it and coaching me through it, pointing out how I could do more of what I did right to circumvent the coopting, next time around.

Story #3: Feminist Mentoring of Female Students
by a Feminist Mentor Teacher

Once I became a professor myself, I noticed something disturbing. The men in my seminary classes were speaking up far more than the women were. I tried to figure out why. The ratio of men to women was about equal. There was a woman (me!) standing up front and teaching, which one might presume would pave the way for other women to speak. I checked myself, lest I was somehow encouraging the men more than the women, making sure I was equally affirming and gave equal time to those women who did speak up. I even tried creating spaces for the women to speak, by naming the phenomenon out loud. "I have noticed that those who have spoken are all men," I would say; "are there any women who would like a chance to speak?"

Occasionally, there would be a knock on my office door, and I would open it to find a receding female student, apologizing to me for having said too much in class. On almost every one of these occasions, I had to work really hard to remember that the apologizing student had said anything at all. "I actually wish you would speak up a little *more* often," I would tell them, at first. Over time I risked pushing this point a little harder. "You need to speak up more," I would say. Eventually, I became known not only for encouraging and challenging reticent students to speak, but for *requiring* them to do so.

"No matter what," I now tell them, "you *have* to speak at least one time, and preferably two times, in every single class period."

Most of those on whom I impose this contrived command get a little smile on their faces and look very, very relieved. They are almost entirely women. In order to be good girls, now, they need to *speak* rather than to be *quiet.* Finally, a rule they can keep that gives them permission to put forward who they are rather than keeping who they are under wraps.[12]

Inevitably, that smile of the students grows fuller and fuller as they heed this subversive rule I give them for how to participate in class. I have only anecdotal evidence for this, but former students who were given this rule in the past, now pastors, tell me it made all the difference to their capacity to use their voices confidently on day one of their ministries, whether chairing meetings or leading in worship.

Story #4: Feminist Mentoring of a Latino Male Student by an Anglo Female Teacher

A fourth story is one I would never have thought to tell, were it not for the encouragement of a friend, Tina, who is a better feminist mentor than I am and who insists I would be remiss if I left it out. It is the story of an Anglo middle-class feminist professor (me) who mentored a Latino male who came from generational poverty. This man (I will call him Juan) was a student in my feminist theologies class. Juan resonated with many of the struggles the women in the class articulated, as well as with the strategies we discussed for engaging them. He connected with the feminist theological idea, for example, that the doctrine of sin has to be understood from a different vantage point when ministering to people who come from the margins. It made sense to him that the sin he needed to be healed from was more often self-deprecation than the more traditional sin of pride. While the other two men in the feminist class had difficulty even imagining any other way of conceiving of sin, Juan in some ways felt that he understood sin as self-deprecation better than some of the women in the class who were economically and racially privileged.

But there was a day that the discussion turned into a kind of pep talk for those who thought in self-deprecating ways about themselves. The theme of

12. For more on how women are socialized to use their voices, see Susan Brownmiller's "Voice" in *Femininity* (New York: Simon & Schuster, 1984).

the discussion became something like "we need to remember that we have more options than we often think we do, as women." Juan did not speak up because, in the course of the discussion, he felt that those who were economically disadvantaged were diminished, as though someone who was poor was inevitably someone who had not been able to realize all the options they actually had. He did not, in the course of this particular discussion, figure out quickly enough what he wanted to say or how he could say it. I think he was trying to discern whether there even *was* a place left for him in the class, and where it was.

When Juan approached me after class, I had a difficult time at first understanding what his concern was. I myself am quite practiced at overriding any feeling that I am stuck by remembering that I probably have more options than I think I do, so it took a few minutes for me to hear what Juan was telling me. What he was explaining is that some people do not actually have many, or even any, other options than those they are already living. If they are to succeed in moving into a different life space where they can thrive, they need to think in an entirely different way than in the way I (and many privileged feminists) think, by realizing and stepping into options we actually have, but have had trouble seeing.

In the context of this conversation, I did not let Juan off the hook when he lamented that "he should have spoken up" in class. I remember telling him it was not too late to reflect with his colleagues, asking him to prepare five to ten minutes worth of comments for the beginning of the following class. Juan turned out to be a natural teacher. In the next class session, he explained what it was like *not* to have options, or many options, for moving out of the dynamics of generational poverty. He went on to share the kinds of strategies that are helpful when people really are stuck. That presentation helped shape our class discussion for the remainder of the course. In short, what Juan taught me is that, though self-deprecation is a real problem even when there are unrealized options before us, self-deprecation also emerges in relation to life circumstances in which options cannot be recognized because they do not, as yet, exist. What we need to do before we can *recognize* them is to *create* them, Juan taught me.

How did I serve as a feminist mentor to Juan, in that situation? By agreeing, as he noted, that he should have spoken up in class, but even more by engaging with him after class for the time it took to understand what he was saying. I was then able to tell him, "We need your voice!" We needed it not in some abstracted, principled, politically correct way, but because it was the voice of a person who had glimpsed the specifics of his real and unique contribution and who genuinely believed I and the members of my class would be lesser people without it. Professor D. had created space for me to grow, in relation to who I am, when he gave me books by Ruether and Schüssler Fiorenza, and when he went out of his way to recommend a graduate school where being a theologian, as a woman, was a nonissue. Similarly, I created space for Juan to be who he is simply by giving him a handful of minutes at the start of the next class. Together, in that space, we all came to a deeper understanding of what hope we have, as women and as other marginalized persons, for making bricks out of straw when there really are not a plentitude of unrealized options before us.

These four example stories suggest what our interactions might look like once we consider feminist mentoring to be everyone's business rather than as work done primarily by more experienced women in service to less experienced women and their related institutions. I am present in all of these stories, but I have different roles in each of them. In the first I am extended feminist mentoring by a male professor who is not a feminist, and in the second by a wise, more experienced feminist mentor. In the third and fourth I am the mentor, but I take very different actions. In story three I contrive a rule that effectively subverts the stymying societal expectation that women suppress their voices; in story four, the most I am capable of doing as a mentor is creating space for another to speak. In this space I, *as a feminist mentor who values reciprocity*, am also gifted with the opportunity to learn.

Theological Handles for Feminist Mentoring

What remains is to invite you, the reader, to accept the thesis that feminist mentoring is everyone's business and to join in the work. In that spirit I offer three theological handles that might be helpful for participating in the work and calling of feminist mentoring.

First, the reason for taking women's experiences into account is not simply to even the score because men's experiences historically have been the dominant reference point for the development of theologies and cultures. The reason for honoring, exploring, and learning from women's experiences is that we believe the Holy Spirit is just as likely to move, communicate, and act in and through women's experiences as in and through the experiences of men. In order to hear what the Holy Spirit is saying we have to listen to these experiences and discern what is true about them. And in order to be able to give these experiences a hearing, we have to create spaces in which they can be shared with the church at large, and we need to empower women to tell them. This is where feminist mentoring comes into play: it is committed to helping women and other marginalized persons use their voices and other means of communication; it is committed to seeking spaces in which others can hear their voices and engage their ideas. The purpose of keeping women's experiences in play is that the Spirit might teach all of us something through them, and through them change us, our churches, our institutions, and the world.

Second, the sin of women and others located at the margins is not—or at least is not generally speaking—pride. It is self-deprecation.[13] If pride leads persons to think *more* of themselves than they should, self-deprecation leads us to think of ourselves as *less* than God made us. To repent of self-deprecation is not to put on sackcloth and ashes and sit on the ground. It is, with Mary, to claim one's exaltation as a bearer of God: to stand, and sing, and prophesy, and celebrate. Further, sin as self-deprecation is not helped by the idea of Jesus dying on the cross to pay penalties we have accrued. Such an understanding of the cross only furthers self-deprecatory sinfulness. Feminist mentoring, if it includes sharing with the mentee the message of salvation, should focus its reflection on the cross instead on the truth that God in Christ entered all the way into the very worst kind of diminishment. But it was not the end of the story for him, and it is not the end for us. We, with him, can rise to new and abundant life.

Third and finally, the hope of resurrection includes the bodies of women, men, and all people in the "now" as well as in the "not yet." So often, the disparities between men's and women's experiences, between the more privileged and the less privileged, between those who appear whole and those who appear broken, are glossed over by appeal to the life to come. And yet the Christian tradition insists, again and again, that it is *this* world that God so loves, *this* world for which Christ died, and *these* bodies that Jesus Christ took along with his when he rose, embodied, from that grave. We make the radical confessional claim that Jesus "sits at the right hand of the Father," as though that resurrected body that ate fish and bread with the disciples still *is* in some way. What are the implications of this for how we mentor women and others who have been socialized to feel ambivalent about their bodies—bodies that have been objectified or even abused?[14]

13. For more on the "feminine sin" of self-deprecation, see Valerie Saiving, "The Human Situation: A Feminine View," *Journal of Religion* 40.2 (April 1960): 100–112.

14. For more on how the doctrine of the resurrection of the body is a balm to feelings

Feminist mentoring must attend to these issues if women are, indeed, going to have the opportunity with Mary to choose what is better. Even more to the point, anyone who truly believes the Holy Spirit is working in the lives and experiences of women, anyone who understands that self-deprecation is just as problematic and even more incapacitating than the sin of pride, anyone who insists that resurrection is not only something we are waiting for, but something that should be manifest in the here and now—anyone who believes, understands, or insists on these theological handles is ready for this work. Even if we do not understand or agree with all things feminist, we can undertake the work of trusting the lives and callings of women enough to create spaces for their voices and their gifts.

---

of shame and self-deprecation, see my "Chains Fall Off: The Resurrection of the Body and Our Healing from Shame," in *Reimagining with Christian Doctrines: Responding to Global Gender Injustices*, ed. Grace Kim and Jenny Daggers (New York: Palgrave, 2014), 49–70.

PART 3

Diverse National and International Communities of Mentoring

CHAPTER 7

Mentoring Magnificent Men—
African American Perspectives

Alton B. Pollard III

"Don't worry. I know his parents." It was one of the most jarring and defining moments of my young life. The year was 1968. I was just learning to enjoy the freedom that comes with leaving childhood behind, more or less, coming of age as an adolescent male and embarking on that educational rite of passage once commonly known as junior high school. It was the first day of seventh grade and I was starting to "feel my oats." Blaring from a transistor radio that belonged to one of my new classmates was Marvin Gaye's transcendent blues-inflected Motown hit "I Heard It through the Grapevine." In the rich cultural parlance of African America, "the grapevine" is a reference to the informal and often confidential networks of communication that have linked Black communities dating back to the antebellum period.

I was the sole student dancing enthusiastically on top of their desk when our new teacher walked into the room on that fateful morning. Her name was Mrs. Lois Dobbins. I grew up in the Upper Midwest. The junior high school I attended was located in an all-white middle-class neighborhood, with the unwanted exception of my family. The community and its children, angered by the encroachments of racial integration, grew more resentful and hostile with every passing year. Mrs. Dobbins was my first and only Black teacher. Not coincidentally, she also belonged to our church.

Manhood Signs

The 1950s and 1960s represented the height of the Black-led freedom movement in the United States. The pivotal events of the Civil Rights and Black Consciousness (or Black Power) period were part of an ongoing legacy of Black freedom struggles challenging and redefining the life of the nation. By the middle of the twentieth century, the children of Africa in America numbered well over twenty million. There were harsh truths to contend with as African Americans increasingly dispensed with their former miseducation and turned instead to the critical task of unmasking the American metanarrative of democracy, equality, and freedom.[1] The egalitarian myth promulgated by white America was empirically contradicted by Black America's carceral reality: the great injuries of white racial supremacy, structural inequality, the status quo ante, and a cautious federal government in matters of just civil and human rights policy.

In Birmingham, Alabama, school-aged children—girls and boys—faced police dogs, rubber batons, and high-power hoses and withstood the political indifference emanating from the corridors of power in Washington, DC. In hundreds of cities, towns, and rural communities young women and men conducted sit-ins, kneel-ins, teach-ins, wade-ins, freedom rides, and more in the face of what appeared to be inalterable, intractable, and impenetrable realities. Black women who labored by day as secretaries, cooks, seamstresses, laundrywomen, caregivers, nurses, teachers, and more (only to be excised from the historical record) organized local communities, conducted meetings, and led boycotts as pivotal communal agents of change. Black America was learning, growing, and pressing for a world that was not so exclusively governed by the principles of white supremacy.

Nineteen sixty-eight was a watershed year in the Black-led freedom struggle and in the history of the United States. A major Tet Offensive was launched by the North Vietnamese against South Vietnam and its allies, including the United States; feminist struggles and theories were emergent; quadrennial campaigning for the presidency of the United States was in full force; the Black Panther Party for Self-Defense had become a leading force for liberation in urban settings; and the Poor People's Campaign was preparing to launch a movement that would fundamentally challenge the federal government and society to work to eliminate systemic and structural poverty. Individuals who ascended to national public leadership during this period embraced with great reluctance, even to their own peril, the fierce and unrelenting demands of the time.

Among the most vivid memories for me as a young Black male coming of age at that time were the photos that appeared in print and broadcast

---

1. Kelly Brown Douglas offers a theological summation of America's myth of racial superiority and grand narrative of exceptionalism in *Stand Your Ground: Black Bodies and the Justice of God* (Maryknoll, NY: Orbis, 2015), 3–47.

media, the daily barrage of signs and placards carried by hundreds of Black sanitation workers in Memphis, Tennessee, emphatically declaring in bold, black print: "I AM A MAN." I took careful note of the fearless dedication of those men and not a few sympathetic women. I committed to memory their fierce and unflagging determination.

Noteworthy among the insurgents were angry young Black men with their fists raised defiantly in the Black power salute and with whom I readily identified. But it was the tremendous resolve and majestic dignity etched in the faces of old Black men, the elders who had seized the initiative to organize for just wages and humane working conditions, and the near endless phalanx of manhood signs that moved me above all else. For at least one very impressionable young man, the courageous struggle of garbage collectors in the face of relentless and oppressive forces was the best possible witness to the insurgent power of truth and to the incredible magnificence of conscious Black manhood.

Mrs. Lois Dobbins was my seventh grade English teacher. Much to my chagrin, she was also a member in good standing at the Black Baptist church that both our families attended. Ours was a rather large church, a prominent and well-respected church, whose membership primarily consisted of blue-collar workers like my parents and a good number of people in the professions. We worshiped together under a common refrain: "There are no big I's or little U's in the church." My father served as superintendent of the Sunday school, and my mother was a teacher. As with most Black churches, educational and vocational expectations for its young men and women ran high, and communal integrity, social identity, and personal dignity were regularly invoked as articles of faith. Their bestowal of knowledge and experiences transmitted to the next generation helped me to navigate my path.[2]

Mrs. Dobbins was widely respected in both church and community as a leading educator and student advocate. She brooked no nonsense, gave no quarter, and took no prisoners no matter the context. She saw resident in me, one of her rare young Black male charges, future prospects for magnificence that I had yet to even begin to contemplate. Through demanding assignments, repeated reprimand, before- and after-school detention, and regular and often devastating reports to my mother and father, she mentored me against my will with the requirement that I embrace my full capabilities.

2. The pioneering educator Laurent A. Daloz writes, "By their very existence, mentors provide proof that the journey can be made"; *Mentor: Guiding the Journey of Adult Learners* (San Francisco: Jossey-Bass, 1999), 207.

Much to my surprise and astonishment, I was awarded our school's highest honor for academic achievement at the end of the year, my grade point average and behavior notwithstanding. The awards ceremony was a pivotal moment in my life. In the midst of racist, unjust, and oppressive social realities raging on the national level and in the microcosm of my own locale and school, Mrs. Dobbins challenged me with the radical imperative to rise and learn to confront my circumstance. In addition to my mother and my father, who were constantly teaching, admonishing, and requiring much, she taught me by word and deed to believe in myself. The mentoring challenge was not hers alone.

Mentoring Networks: Howard Thurman

As I have already illustrated, the most important institution for mentoring and mobilization in the African American community has been the extended family network inclusive of church and community. This is not to deny the prominent influence in the workplace of tailored mentor-to-protégé approaches.[3] But the daily care of children and youth entrusted to the extended family—parents, grandparents, aunts, uncles, cousins, and more—is a longstanding tradition based on a more holistic model with roots deeply interwoven in African antecedents. In contrast to mixed messages coming from the social order or worse, cultural provisions were made available, including the empowering declaration of individual dignity and significance grounded in the embrace of community.

An outstanding case in point of the mentoring impact of the extended family network is the life and biography of the twentieth-century mystic and ancestral griot Howard Thurman. Thurman was born in 1900 in Daytona, Florida, deep in the segregated South. He was the middle of three children, the only son from the union of Alice Ambrose and Saul Solomon Thurman. His father, a railroad crewman who held little regard for churches and preachers, died when Thurman was young.

With his mother working long hours as a domestic cook and laundress for white families, the daily care of young Howard and his sisters was largely entrusted to "Grandma Nancy." Nancy Ambrose did not have access to formal education but set high academic standards for Thurman. She modeled for

3. David DuBois and Michael Karcher, *Handbook of Youth Mentoring* (Los Angeles: Sage, 2005).

him the transformative power of religion, challenging the hegemony of white racism and the religious parochialism of their local Black church, and creating her own hermeneutics of resistance and recovery. Grandma Nancy insisted that religion, whatever else it does, must begin with the utter affirmation of an individual's dignity and worth. Her reasoning was derived from slavery's harsh lessons. When she was a child, a white preacher in league with the slave master consistently preached: "Slaves, be obedient to your masters." In contrast, the furtive message of the Black preacher was positive and enabling: "You are not niggers! You are not slaves! You are God's children!"[4]

Saul Thurman died when young Howard was seven. With the death of his biological father, several men served as elder role models for Thurman, including his two stepfathers, the public school principal, and the "stranger in the railroad station in Daytona Beach" who purchased the train ticket for him to travel to high school.[5] The most important of his male mentoring influences, however, were a cousin, Thornton Smith, and the family physician, Dr. Stocking. Thurman held these men in high esteem as "my masculine idols."[6]

Young men frequently seek out mentors according to an admired quality or skill they possess and often the person's visibility in the larger community. It was well known that in the segregationist South, an African American male who had the audacity to display healthy self-esteem in the public square risked losing his life. Thurman described his cousin Thornton Smith as "a wise man, unacquainted with fear," who helped African Americans in Daytona gain the vote, a new school, and Black police officers.[7] In similar fashion, Dr. Stocking's clear disdain for organized religion upset traditionalists, but his piercing intellect attracted the young Thurman. Although Thurman's decision to enter the Christian ministry dismayed Dr. Stocking (Thurman declined his offer of financial assistance to attend medical school), they remained lifelong friends.

Much like the elders in African traditional society, this coterie of men provided a strong mentoring presence as role models and served as impor-

4. Howard Thurman, *With Head and Heart* (New York: Harcourt Brace Jovanovich, 1979), 60.

5. In Daytona, Florida, the public school system was carefully structured to end the education of African American youth at the seventh grade. At the time there were only three public high schools for African Americans in the state. Thurman would go to the closest church-supported school one hundred miles away in Jacksonville. Only the intercession of his principal, who taught him the eighth grade on his own time, enabled him to secure the diploma necessary to attend high school. See Thurman, *With Head and Heart*, 24–25.

6. Thurman, *With Head and Heart*, 21.

7. Thurman, *With Head and Heart*, 21.

tant transmitters of African American male magnificence for Thurman. Surrounded by a dynamic, interdependent, and coalescent network consisting of family, church and community, and children, women, and men, Thurman's talents and sensitivities were at once valued and cultivated. Always at the center of Thurman's moral, cognitive, and affective development were his mother and grandmother, who invested in and supported his success by nurturing, providing, and holding him to high educational, vocational, and communal standards. Instilled with high aspirations from a wealth of sources, Thurman drew on insights that enabled him to establish a liberating emphasis within the world he knew and ultimately prepared him for a life of profound engagement with the religious and social world.

The benefits of mentorship are evidenced throughout Thurman's spiritual journey and his redemptive movement through the impediments of racism. Despite Thurman's personal experiences of deep suffering exacted by white supremacy, they would not be the final arbiters or determinative influences on his self-concept. He had been well inoculated against the affronts of enmity and its bitter fruits—self-doubt, despair, disappointment, social and existential death—by oppositional values deeply embedded in African American culture. Writes Thurman, "My roots are deep in the throbbing reality of the Negro idiom and from it I draw a measure of inspiration and vitality. I know that a person must be at home somewhere before they can be at home anywhere." His intense dedication to the African American freedom struggle led him to this protestation: "I believe, with my foreparents, that this is God's world. This faith has had to fight against disillusionment, despair, and the vicissitudes of American history."[8]

Thurman went on to graduate from Morehouse College. While in graduate school, as the only African American student attending then Rochester Theological Seminary in New York, he was urged by a prominent professor to lay aside racial matters and, instead, apply himself to facing the "timeless issues of the human spirit." Thurman well understood the complimentary intent behind his theological mentor's statement. But his own reflections on the nature of the struggle against racism were far more critical, nuanced, and discerning: "A man and his black skin must face the 'timeless issues of the human spirit' together."[9] Says Thurman: "Always the sense of separateness that is an essential part of individual consciousness must be overcome as it sustains

8. Howard Thurman, *Deep River and the Negro Spiritual Speaks of Life and Death* (Richmond, IN: Friends United, 1975), 13, 111.

9. Thurman, *With Head and Heart*, 60.

and supports. This is the crucial paradox in the achievement of an integrated personality as well as of an integrated society. To work as if the walls did not exist, to be nourished by the strength of one's ethnic idiom, and at the same time to be victimized by the walls is as exhilarating as it is hazardous."[10]

Historically the Black church, school, and related institutions have been indispensable contributors to the extended family network.[11] Churches were the spiritual face of the African American community, and social identity and personal dignity were deeply intertwined with their existence. Schools, whether established under state, philanthropic, or religious auspices, for elementary, secondary, and tertiary education also melded with the life of the larger community, validating individual talents and skill-sets, and encouraging collective agency. Religious and educational leaders were generally held in high esteem and functioned as crucial transmitters of African American sacred and cultural wisdom to empower current and future generations. The repressive external environment was thus constantly being contested through a Black interdependent network of relationships or holistic model consisting of family, school, and church. However, to date not even the most resilient of Black counternarratives and resourceful challenges to the nation's racial calculus and animus have succeeded in making oppression a relic of the past.

A Constant Struggle

For communities of African descent there is no historical closure to our freedom movement but rather ongoing continuities. Over the last fifty years the struggle in the United States has dialectically waxed and waned and deepened and expanded. Challenges facing this resurgent freedom movement include Africa, the Diaspora and global communities, apartheid, gender justice, lesbian, gay, bisexual, queer, intersectional and transgender people's rights, the HIV/AIDS epidemic, mass incarceration, human trafficking, social stigma, bullying, misogyny, healthcare equity, reproductive freedoms, diverse religiosity, immigration, globalization, gun control, living wages, sustainable

10. Howard Thurman, *The Luminous Darkness: A Personal Interpretation of the Anatomy of Segregation and the Ground of Hope* (New York: Harper & Row, 1965), x.

11. The Black church is analytical shorthand for the vast network of racial-ethnic communities of Christian faith, worship, and life born out of, and informed by, the historic and present-day experiences of people of African descent, whatever the tradition and wherever they are found. See Alton B. Pollard III and Carol B. Duncan, "Introduction," *The Black Church Studies Reader* (New York: Palgrave Macmillan, 2016), 6.

community, ecology, and so much more. One of the core elements of mentoring Black boys and men for magnificence in the present generation, now more than ever, must be the care and respect for all persons and advocacy for all creation, human and nonhuman alike. Holistic, intergenerational, and multifaceted, our mentoring work has only just begun. In the prescient words of Black feminist and activist Angela Davis: "Freedom is a constant struggle."[12]

There is a pervasive myth that the United States is comprised of a common citizenry living in a postracial, color-blind, and inclusive society. It is a persistent myth, one that has especially gained traction since the administration of the first African American president, whose very election was heralded as proof positive that we live in a just and democratic society. In point of fact, the oppressive legacies of the past are far from ended, and they are never so easily dismissed. Disparity and death, violence and abuse, stigma and structural unemployment, food deserts and unhealthy dietary options, educational malfeasance and urban disinvestment, the War on Drugs and the economics of mass incarceration, racial profiling and anti-immigration xenophobia, voter identification and vigilante justice—all function as contemporary forms of hegemonic social control grounded in but certainly not limited to the machinations of race.

Twenty-first-century life in the United States also seems favorable to those whose principal interpretation of the world is seen through a postmodern lens. Postmodernity is a term loosely associated with progressive social and political views arguably without a hegemonic worldview or empirical agenda. A litany of prominent themes includes the shift from industrial to information-technology and service-sector economies; the ascendancy of market capitalist forces in India, Brazil, South Africa, and particularly China, and other so-called developing or developed countries; the reshaping of Western Europe and the United States by the children of the once colonized; old and new forms of domestic and global extremism; the decline of mainline Protestant Christian churches and the concomitant rise of "spiritual but not religious" (frequently interpreted as cultural beliefs rooted in religion); and the political reemergence of the "Solid South," a euphemism for former Dixiecrats/white Democrats turned Republicans seeking a return to ideological if not racial advantage.

Other postmodern priorities include the national elevation of STEM education at the expense of the arts and humanities with their representations

---

12. Angela Y. Davis, *Freedom Is a Constant Struggle: Ferguson, Palestine, and the Foundations of a Movement* (Chicago: Haymarket, 2016).

of what is real and good and true; the elimination of clear social-class markers and identity formations; the emergence of such contested epithets as "special interest groups," "political correctness," and "multiculturalism"; the absence of a foundation for objectivity and the reliance on one's "personal truth"; the internationalization of monopolies and the decline of the nation-state; the ascendancy of social media platforms with their respective publics; the chief preferment of consumption over production, sampling instead of creating, fantasy rather than the actual, and the virtual over the real.[13]

Conspicuously absent from most postmodern depictions are the life experiences and narratives of peoples and communities who continue their existence on the underside and margins of history. It is not by coincidence that a nation skilled in the ways of conquest, violence, domination, concealment, and greed continues to translate unjust and repressive beliefs and practices into new and unrecognizable forms. Bipartisan obstructionism and market forces dictate the new racial reality. Race-relations management forged in civic and corporate spaces masquerades as principled public policy. Intersections between race and other socially contested realities—gender, generation, sexuality, ethnicity, ability, and class among others—are denied critical nuance, coalescent recognition, and emancipating capacity under a variety of derisive guises. The nation's crisis of confidence in living out the full meaning of its creed remains unabated. Racism, America's original sin, lives on.

In 2015 I was asked to contribute an article for a powerful online series called "28 Black Lives That Matter." The designation pays bleak homage to a Black person being reported killed in the United States every twenty-eight hours by state-sanctioned means. My own essay was a tribute to the life of a magnificent family man and mentoring presence, Mr. Bernard Bailey. To the people of Eutawville, South Carolina, Bernard Bailey's life will always have meaning beyond the death he endured. I began my commentary with these words:

> The most defining moments in our lives often come like a thief in the night, quietly and unsuspectingly, preceded perhaps by premonition or foreshadowed by force of circumstance, but usually with little or no advanced warning. Such is the nature of the valley of the shadow of death experienced by people of African descent in the Americas for five hundred years. Today, much has changed; little has changed. Harsh and oppressive

---

13. For an in-depth theological treatment of postmodernity, see Dwight N. Hopkins, *Head and Heart: Black Theology—Past, Present, and Future* (New York: Palgrave, 2002), 53–74.

conditions, under the cover of new names, continue to short-circuit the life expectancy of many Black people in America. For African Americans, the specter of death is everywhere. Death and the conditions of death are the lived reality we contend with still.[14]

On August 24, 1955, fourteen-year-old Emmett Till of Chicago was visiting family in Money, Mississippi, where he ventured into a grocery store to buy gum and reportedly whistled at a young white woman. Four days later, two white men roused Till from his bed in the middle of the night, brutally beat him, shot him in the head, and dumped his body in the river. The men were tried for murder and acquitted by a jury of their peers—all white, all male, and, in all probability, all Christian.

The date is February 26, 2012. It is a Sunday evening. Seventeen-year-old Trayvon Martin walked into a 7-Eleven near a gated community in Sanford, Florida, to buy a bag of Skittles and an iced tea. He was later shot to death at close range by a neighborhood "watch captain" who claimed Trayvon had acted suspiciously and looked "out of place." Trayvon's killer was tried for murder and manslaughter and acquitted on all counts. Out of the mayhem and madness, the mantra and social media hashtag #BlackLivesMatter was born.[15]

Separated by nearly six decades, several states, and hundreds of miles, two young African American men experienced violent deaths that pierced the delusion of America as "the land of the free." The reality of violence and death perpetrated against Black boys and men, women and girls, has been a consistent theme in the history of people of African descent in the United States. Untold numbers of Black people have been killed by official and extralegal means since before the founding of the republic. The killings of Emmett Till and Trayvon Martin represent an ominous and unbroken stream of violence from the slave patrols and the Ku Klux Klan to the bombing of Birmingham's Sixteenth Street Baptist Church and the murder of four young girls and the ubiquitous profiling practices of the present day.

There is a disease ravaging our land, a deadly form of racial detritus born of moral and social pathology. During the civil rights years, Dr. Martin Luther King Jr. repeatedly described America as an extremely sick nation. Today the

14. Alton B. Pollard III, "Bernard Bailey: A Consequential Life," *Huffington Post*, April 19, 2015; available at huffingtonpost.com/alton-b-pollard-iii/bernard-bailey-a-conseque_b _6699320.html.

15. Alicia Garza, "A Herstory of the #BlackLivesMatter Movement," *Feminist Wire*, October 7, 2014; available at thefeministwire.com/2014/10/blacklivesmatter-2.

face of racism has changed but the deadly force of its impact has not. Poverty, homelessness, and people with mental illness are de facto criminalized. Patriarchy and misogyny destroy Black girls and women.[16] Incarceration is the principal instrument of social policy directed toward Black boys and men. Black lives, irrespective of gender, sexuality, or class, are deemed to matter less and can be terminated with extreme prejudice.

The sheer persistence of the killing of Black children, women, and men contradicts representations of these events as limited to isolated individuals or extraordinary incidents. Officially condoned racist violence advances to a long and steady beat. Twelve-year-old Tamir Rice of Cleveland was carrying a toy gun when he was fired upon by a police officer. His fourteen-year-old sister Tajai, running to come to his aid, was thrown to the ground, helpless as she watched her brother die. It was Tamir's fault that he died, the city would claim and was later forced to retract. Young Aiyana Stanley-Jones (age seven) of Detroit was sleeping on her living room sofa when an officer, conducting a "no knock" raid of her home, discharged his gun.

Freddie Gray (age twenty-five) of Baltimore was killed by excessive force while in the midst of transport. On the one-year anniversary of protests marking his death, police chased, shot, and wounded a thirteen-year-old boy who was carrying a toy BB gun. Sandra Bland, a college student, died in the Waller County, Texas, jail three days after an improper traffic stop. There are twenty-two-year-old Amadou Diallo of New York and Guinea, West Africa; twenty-year-old Rekia Boyd of Chicago; twenty-six-year-old Tarika Wilson of Lima, Ohio; nineteen-year-old Renisha McBride of Detroit; twenty-four-year-old Jamar Clark of Minneapolis; and the nine members of Charleston's Mother Emanuel African Methodist Episcopal Church, ranging from twenty-six to eighty-seven years of age, who were gunned down during Bible study.

Then, of course, there is Michael Brown Jr. It happened just after noon on August 9, 2014, in the Canfield Green apartment community of Ferguson, Missouri.[17] Eighteen-year-old Mike Brown was walking down the middle of the street with a friend. A police officer approached them both and ordered them onto the sidewalk. What happened next remains a matter of public

---

16. Eboni Marshall Turman, "Fighting for Amy: On Bullies, Bathrooms, and Violence against Black Girls"; available at huffingtonpost.com/eboni-marshall-turman/fighting-for-amy -on-bulli_b_9769158.html.

17. Leah Gunning Francis offers a theological memoir of the movement for justice in Ferguson in *Ferguson and Faith: Sparking Leadership and Awakening Community* (St. Louis: Chalice, 2015).

dispute. What is clear is that Brown was unarmed when the officer shot him multiple times. The authorities left his lifeless body lying uncovered in the street for the next several hours.

It is hard to identify the precise spark that ignites the fires of urban rebellion. It is even more difficult to isolate what incites inclusive and uncharted struggle. But for reasons that will never be fully known, Brown's slaying was a breaking point for the people of Ferguson and for countless numbers of Black, Brown, and all people of conscience acting in solidarity across the United States. There is seemingly no end to racist violence in America. Black life expectancies are being cut short. To be young, Black, and poor almost always means that your death will go unprosecuted and unpunished. Another day, another week, another community, another news cycle, another death, another mother and father pour out their souls in anguish to God.

For African Americans and particularly young boys and men, the focus of this chapter, the conditions of death are everywhere. In American communities, towns, and municipalities everywhere, from sea to shining sea, racialized culture and its lethal accomplice, violence, are deeply and distressingly entrenched. The carnage, meant to be confined by the larger forces of racism to Black contexts, is not in the slightest contained. James Baldwin called it, with his usual prophetic candor, "The Fire Next Time." Like a fiery inferno the anarchy of our inhumanity spreads one person, one family, and one community at a time—into our personal relationships, within the privacy of our homes, in darkened movie theaters, on secured military bases, on enlightened college campuses, in public spaces, behind bars, on death row, to our houses of worship, and more—without respect of person or of race. There is an old African American saying, "A dog gone mad knows no master—only the taste of blood."[18]

This is a season of searing and searching pain for Black America. It is also a time for serious self-examination by American citizens from every walk of life. Angela Davis persuasively states that it is our inability as a society to understand the complex interplay between cultural and structural forms of racism that deflects attention away from systemic factors and reinforces assumptions "that there is an independent phenomenon that we can call 'Black-on-Black crime' that has nothing to do with racism."[19] Stand your ground, stop and frisk, conceal and carry, law and order, and public vigilan-

18. C. Eric Lincoln, *Race, Religion, and the Continuing American Dilemma* (New York: Macmillan, 2011), 6.

19. Davis, *Freedom Is a Constant Struggle*, 89.

tism require an incisive and compelling analysis of racism and a companion vocabulary and advocacy in support of new recognitions that the struggle for our common humanity is not over nor is the battle won. The character assassination of Black people, the militarization and immunity of law enforcement, the mass incarceration of our young, and so much more require a new movement and a new set of practices in "the new Jim Crow" era.[20] Of particular moment is the task of mentoring our Black boys to embrace their magnificent potential as men.

Black Lives Matter

As I emphasize throughout this chapter, one of the major consequences of the violence of racism is that it leads to other forms of violence in families and communities—violence against children, violence against partners, violence against friends, violence against ourselves—like a contagion the force of violence spreads in the social order without respect of persons or institution. Often we too unconsciously contribute to the stigmatizing work of racism, assuming that the violence is individual and sui generis.[21]

It is not always useful to compare eras. Yet for Black America, remembering painful continuities between past and present is a crucial element when it comes to the question of mentoring. In matters of race, the past is not always past. Ta-Nehisi Coates, in his book *Between the World and Me*, brilliantly captures the sensibilities of young Black people and particularly boys and men whose lives are being destroyed and diminished in our day and time in legal and extrajudicial terms by the ravages of poverty, police violence, misogyny, and mass incarceration.[22] The book is a letter to his fifteen-year-old son styled in the manner of Baldwin's *The Fire Next Time*, but far more reminiscent in my estimation of the writings of Baldwin's crucial predecessor, Richard Wright, from whom the title and starkness of tone derive.[23] The absence in the text of any religious rhetoric of hope is distressing for some

20. Michelle Alexander, *The New Jim Crow: Mass Incarceration in the Age of Colorblindness* (New York: New Press, 2010).

21. A powerful critique of the canard of color-blindness and the denial of institutional racism as a central explanation for racial inequality is found in Keeanga-Yamahtta Taylor, *From #Blacklivesmatter to Black Liberation* (Chicago: Haymarket, 2016), 51–74.

22. Ta-Nehisi Coates, *Between the World and Me* (New York: Spiegel & Grau, 2015).

23. Richard Wright, "Between the World and Me," in *Black Voices: An Anthology of African American Literature*, ed. Abraham Chapman (New York: Signet, 2001), 431.

and noteworthy for others. In articulating Black life, the liberation struggle does not always turn to prayer, although there is substantial precedent. Is there another witness?

Coates fiercely and lovingly wants for his son to grapple with the hard facts of what it means to live within a Black male body, to reside in a world that will for reasons of "hue and hair" refuse to guarantee for him the freedoms that so many others take for granted.[24] The pain and horror of American racial injustice throughout history are well known to African Americans but discredited by our refusal to capitulate to oppression. The Black interdependent mentoring model from the not so distant past—comprised of family, church, and school—repeatedly emphasized the agency of young Black men and women against all odds, claiming the magnificence of our lives, even in the midst of those who would destroy and demean us.

Many young Black people today find themselves on the opposite end of anything remotely resembling holistic communal support. They live in a season where growing up is not necessarily counted in years, but "in the thickness of the trauma they have endured."[25] They live in a world that is made even more opaque by the heterogeneities of geography and social class. Often, they do not have access to emancipating resources sufficient to help them awaken to their own magnificent power. They have no aspirational capital to envision the future in the face of clear and present danger. A growing number of younger African Americans under age thirty (19 percent) express no religious affiliation.[26] Deeply enmeshed in a world of social death, they have little margin for error and, perhaps, even less margin for hope.

Tragically, many Black churches and schools, enmeshed in their own quest to become upwardly mobile and comfortably middle class, have become distant and removed from neighborhoods in need. Oblivious to the translucent testimonies of the past, they betray their communal responsibility to contest deathbed contexts as instruments of hope. Black-led institutions are called to be the extended family of concern, an authentic mentoring presence, sharing in the struggles of young Black men and women, embodying other alternatives for their lives. The path to personal freedom and the long work of social change requires internal as well as external organizing values

24. Coates, *Between the World and Me*, 7.

25. Goldie Taylor, "Does 'Black Lives Matter' Really Matter?"; available at thedailybeast .com/articles/2016/04/22/does-black-lives-matter-really-matter.html.

26. Pew Research Center, "A Religious Portrait of African Americans"; available at pew forum.org/2009/01/30/a-religious-portrait-of-african-americans.

and skills. Often for young people, irrespective of background, such humanizing awareness comes as an unexpected gift. At times, the opening to their own inner universe occurs outside the customary pathways of organized faith. For religious and academic leaders and institutions to serve as deep spiritual and educational touchstones, to work in solidarity with our young and invite us all to our own best possibilities, especially in dire circumstances, is a magnificent privilege and the least we can do.[27]

Toward a New Black Future

Now well into the second decade of the twenty-first century, a new social network of extended family mentoring and partnering has emerged. It is bringing people together in communities across the nation and world, people of profound dedication and commitment, who recognize that racism is alive and well and that structural racism in particular will not be eliminated without a sustained mass challenge. Many in the leadership of #BlackLivesMatter—perhaps the most well known of the new generation of activists—are young, female, transgender, and queer. Happening before our very eyes, the current moment is transforming into a leader-full movement. They seek to focus our attention on structural and systemic racism in society, even when de jure segregation has been declared historically obsolete, racist symbols do disappear, and individual expressions are not at all easily condoned.[28]

Vast numbers of African Americans are still deprived of the right to vote. Many more do not achieve living wages, quality education, housing, and healthcare. Black millennials regularly report being victimized by violence or harassed by law enforcement. Police officers just as often avoid indictment and criminal charges. The intransigence of patriarchy and misogyny in American society continues to threaten and harm Black girls and women.

Along with such organizations as Dream Defenders, Black Youth Proj-

---

27. For example, Vincent Harding, *Hope and History: Why We Must Share the History of the Movement* (Maryknoll, NY: Orbis, 1990); Tamelyn N. Tucker-Worgs, *The Black Mega-Church: Theology, Gender, and the Politics of Public Engagement* (Waco: Baylor University Press, 2011); and Raphael G. Warnock, *The Divided Mind of the Black Church* (New York: New York University Press, 2014).

28. Patrisse Marie Cullors-Brignac, "We Didn't Start a Movement. We started a Network"; available at medium.com/@patrissemariecullorsbrignac/we-didn-t-start-a-movement-we -started-a-network-90f9b5717668#.a8ktn1pda.

ect 100, Ferguson 100, Hands Up United, We Charge Genocide, Color of Change, and others, new models of leadership and insight are surfacing. These groups are affirming the ancestral struggle even while envisioning and moving toward a new Black future. Theirs is a marvelously intersectional movement that refuses to be discredited and is developing solidarity with Latin@s (immigration rights), Arabs and Muslims (Islamophobia/Palestine), Native Americans (self-determination), and other communities of the marginalized and oppressed. Kairos is happening again.

Magnificent Manhood

What does all this mean for the mentoring of African American boys and men in the twenty-first century? The historic Black extended family network, now in the crucial role of learner, has much to gain from the lessons of #BlackLivesMatter and other new organizations and still has much to offer in terms of liberating support. Contrary to popular opinion, the current movement welcomes its foreparents to partner, resource, mentor, and pray. They have a special sense of appreciation for those legions of freedom fighters who were once their young forerunners. The mentoring function of elders is to help the younger generation continue to plumb the deepest power of their humanity. The movement is still in formation. Together, transformative and comprehensive solutions will be found. And that to my mind is a very good thing.

If a revolution in American society is to take place, then a progressive kind of consciousness must be encouraged, cultivated, and claimed by Black males. Young Black boys and men—sons, siblings, husbands, fathers, lovers, partners, guardians, exes, and friends—must learn from and model womanism and commit to uncommon forms of mass activism that demonstrate a new meme.[29] This means that men will have to embrace women's struggles as their own. It also means that men will have to learn to struggle for the full humanity of men in such a way that more men are encouraged to participate in their own liberation.

Finally, as Black men we will have to recognize ourselves as integral to the lives of entire communities—as lovers, partners, and nurturers to children, family members, and friends—and the world as a whole. Mentoring magnificent men and boys requires that we model for one another the emphatic

---

29. For more on the term *womanism*, see the chapter by Katie G. Cannon in this book.

belief that the just society is possible. Dedication to the struggle to make this our reality is a sacred endeavor. Being the change we seek is a laudable goal. Perhaps Coretta Scott King said it best: "Struggle is a never ending process. Freedom is never really won, you earn it and win it in every generation."[30] Dismantling a racist system and ushering in beloved community will require all of this and more.

---

30. Alton B. Pollard III, "Assassinations, Anniversaries, and the New America Now"; available at huffingtonpost.com/alton-b-pollard-iii-phd/assassinations-anniversar_b_4283257.html.

CHAPTER 8

Womanist Mentoring—
African American Perspectives

Katie G. Cannon

My aim in this chapter is to answer the following set of questions: What parts of womanist mentoring demystify the deadly onslaught of lies underpinning systemic mechanisms that facilitate and maintain white supremacy? What is the impact of the continuous play of racism and androcentric patriarchy in the everyday lives of Black women?[1] As professors nurturing graduate students, specifically in the discipline of theological ethics, how can women intellectuals embrace the richness of traditional scholarship and the established academic canons and not fall into pedagogical patterns we abhor? How should African American women scholars deal with our presence as professors in the classroom creating all kinds of cognitive dissonance in customary communities of thought?[2] How frequently do we need to give considerable attention to cultural mythologies perpetuating microaggression in the body politic? Within this soul-wrestling inquiry is the crucial question: Why even teach the next generation of African American students how to survive and thrive in a system of academic fascism? The foundations of womanist mentoring directly address these questions and other challenges confronting Black women intellectuals who do not fit neatly in learned societies and traditional disciplines.

For instance, womanist mentors engage in continuous defiance against demeaning racist, sexist stereotypes like the fictional characters enshrined in

---

1. Melanie L. Harris, Carolyn M. Jones Medine, and Helen Rhee, "Racial-Ethnic Women in Religious Studies Classroom: Silent Scripts and Contested Spaces," *Journal of Feminist Studies* (Spring 2016); and Gabriella Gutierrez y Muhs et al., eds., *Presumed Incompetence: The Intersections of Race and Class for Women in Academia* (Logan: Utah State University Press, 2012).

2. Carmen Kynard, "Teaching While Black: Witnessing and Countering Disciplinary Whiteness, Racial Violence, and University Race-Management," *Literacy in Composition Studies* 3.1 (March 2015); available at licsjournal.org/OJS/index.php/LiCS/article/viewFile/62/84.

Harriet Beecher Stowe's epic melodrama *Uncle Tom's Cabin; or, Life among the Lowly*.[3] When asked where she was from, Topsy, a young, faceless, depraved, Black female outcast, the symbol of ascension from death-dealing chaos to life-affirming possibilities, responds, "I spect I grow'd." In essence she says she just "popped up." Such zero-sum people do not exist, nor do ahistorical realities.[4]

Thus, it is important to note that Afrocentric mentoring did not just pop up. For fifteen or more centuries African mentoring resources and wisdom literature have been inseparable. The oldest examples of mentoring intertwined with wisdom are the teachings of African monarchs that extended over a period of about three thousand years.[5] These ancient African teachings, consisting largely of succinct proverbs and extended treatises, were a sort of encyclopedia of utilitarian knowledge. The original purpose of mentoring was to train worthy males to be rulers and attendants of the royal household.[6]

The association between mentoring and royalty meant that pharaohs and kings educated their sons as their successors, while officers of the court trained their sons to act in ways befitting those who would serve nobility. These young men were expected to memorize and observe certain rules so that they would know how to behave with prudence in given situations. The main focus of this type of didactic instruction was to enable men by clever strategy to achieve status and power.[7]

In view of these historical facts, women of African ancestry who live in the African Diaspora in the United States understand that mentoring operates differently across generational, religious, racial/ethnic, socio-gendered, geopolitical, and economic terrains. Womanist mentoring not only challenges the basic assumptions and prevailing paradigms embedded in Afrocentric wisdom traditions, but we shift our view-from-above to an epistemological

3. Harriet Beecher Stowe, *Uncle Tom's Cabin*, ed. Amanda Claybaugh (New York: Barnes & Noble, 2003), 279.

4. I am indebted to Emilie M. Townes for her excellent analysis of structural and cultural evil. Townes's writings focus on delineating negative, pathological stereotypes about Black women that originate in the hegemonic imagination of White men and women. See, in particular, *Womanist Ethics and the Cultural Production of Evil* (New York: Palgrave Macmillan, 2006).

5. For detailed historical commentary, see Gerald Massey, *Ancient Egypt: The Light of the World* (Baltimore: Black Classic, 1992); and William Kelly Simpson, ed., *The Literature of Ancient Egypt: An Anthology of Stories, Instructions, and Poetry* (New Haven: Yale University Press, 1972).

6. Maimba Ani, *Yurugu: An African-Centered Critique of European Cultural Thought and Behavior* (Trenton, NJ: Africa World Press, 1994).

7. E. A. Wallis Budge, *The Life, History, and Literature of the Ancient Egyptians* (New York: Dover, 1977).

view-from-below. Womanists use creative ethical concepts and cutting-edge methodologies to move the analyses of inherited forms of mentoring into a wider sociocultural context, placing Black women's experiences, perspectives, and realities at the center of the discourse, rather than at its margins. In order to understand how our foremothers and foresisters withheld obedience from official powerbrokers who defrauded and exploited the masses, womanists direct our attention to injustices, for by doing so we grasp the underlying causes of and factors involved in institutionalizing domination and marginalization. Besides being provided with inherited wisdom, we are able to sketch womanist mentoring in terms of the knowledge we deliver, transmit, and pass on as being consistent with our African American identity, cultural heritage, and the cohesively layered consciousness instructing our survivalist intentions in the here and now.[8]

Furthermore, in order to elaborate and exemplify the epistemological framework I use as a womanist mentor, I include throughout this chapter a variety of quotations from students who have participated in my womanist theological ethics seminars since 1983. I am indebted to graduate students for sharpening womanist discourse with reports from their *discussion triads* and *conscientization working groups*. In each of my womanist seminars, students learn how to interface texts with their real-life contexts. In judicious ways, these graduate students exemplify the momentum and substance of womanism with clarity and dynamism.

A Point of Departure: Embodied Mediated Knowledge

My point of departure in advising seminarians, ministers, doctoral candidates, and undergraduate students is *embodied mediated knowledge*. Since the beginning of womanist discourse in the early 1980s, embodied mediated knowledge simultaneously engages in the dialectic of town and gown. Our communities of origin and the learned academy are not separate and inimical, but each is a fundamental and ethically charged repository of data. One of the conscientization working groups summed up their understanding of this idea in these words:

8. For further, in-depth discussions of theology and ethics in relation to African American identity, cultural heritage, and consciousness instructing our survivalist intentions, see Katie G. Cannon and Anthony B. Pinn, eds., *The Oxford Handbook of African American Theology* (New York: Oxford University Press, 2014).

Our personal identities are guided through the world with sources from home that convey our sense of identity. The majority of these sources come from our hometown community, and more particularly, are within our extended family. When we have strong women to refer to and lean on, our personal sense of self is being shaped from the inside out. There are also numerous men who educate us in ways that only men can, i.e., about loving a woman and about losing a dream. Perhaps it is the stability amidst the dynamic weaving of life-lessons that enables us to fulfill our ambitions, to achieve a voice for ourselves in the world.

Womanist mentoring continues to be done by connecting our social-self in existential contexts to the destabilization of status quo norms. Due to pronounced emphasis on embodied knowledge, another conscientization working group wrote about embodiment in this way:

> When we recount events of the past and present shared with family members, especially our thoughts, dreams, sadness, struggles, tragedies and joys, we peek into our family's most intimate moments with genuine tenderness and sensitivity. The remembering and retelling stories about our communities-of-origin are ways to keep alive our kith and kin. We are particularly mindful of conditions in which family members were forced to make a living in situations that sapped the life out of them.
>
> Our commitment to keep our ancestors alive through the telling of their stories serves as a cleansing and healing process for us to rediscover our thoughts, actions, and feelings, and come face to face with the reality of what our homes of origin represent.

The focal point of all this is employing memory as embodiment strategy so that there is no disjunction between multiplicative dynamics in our personal lives and our socially engaged public scholarship.

One of the discussion triads summarized the delicate balancing act of embodied mediated knowledge and the specificity of our race/sex/class social location in this way: "When we trade our extended family communities for urban isolation, we disconnect ourselves from our traditional 'mothers,' our ancestral carriers of culture, and we become the walking dead, destroyed by ignorance of our woman power." In other words, embodied mediated knowledge calls attention to Black women's moral agency as self-determining human beings. That is, womanists resist becoming talking heads and armchair academicians represented by colleagues who embrace the notion of abstract, objective, detached, dispassionate, contemplative, mathematically calculated, spectator knowledge. Another discussion triad wrote about embodied mediated knowledge in this way:

> In contrast to much of Western theological traditions and normative ethics, women liberationists value the body and sexuality as essential sources of knowledge about the Divine. Bodily experiences are regarded as opportunities for theo-ethical learning and growth. Embracing embodiment, we focus our attention on immanent theology, instead of transcendent theology. In transcendent theology, a deity stands above and over us, and sometimes even, over and against us, to whom we must appeal from our position as subordinates in a cosmic hierarchy. However, with immanent theology, the Divine lives with and indwells among us, interconnecting us to one another.

When womanists engage in the work of embodiment our point of entry acknowledges what W. E. B. Du Bois coined "double consciousness"—Black people looking at ourselves through the eyes of others.[9] It is worth mentioning at this point that womanists take an additional step, to increase our depth and breadth by moving from double consciousness to multiple consciousness. Sociologist Deborah H. King contends that multiple consciousness includes "interactive oppressions" experienced by Black women.[10] What womanists have in mind when incorporating multiple consciousness is immediately apparent. African American women combine seeing ourselves as others see us with simultaneously speaking in our own voices, addressing our own issues, and seeing ourselves through our own eyes.

This understanding of embodied knowledge is the testimony a discussion triad had in mind when they wrote:

> Womanist's embodied mediated knowledge enables us to juxtapose freedom with the existence of chattel slavery, to define humanity without hegemony, and to celebrate blackness in terms beyond negative "otherness," so that "otherness" and differences will no longer support the so-called unique nature of what it means to be a real American (white propertied male).

9. W. E. B. Du Bois, *The Souls of Black Folk* (Chicago: McClurg, 1903), 3.

10. Deborah H. King, "Multiple Jeopardy, Multiple Consciousness: The Context of a Black Feminist Ideology," *Signs: Journal of Women and Culture and Society* 14.1 (1988): 42–72.

With a focus on evidence-based configurations of our families and communities of origin, instead of emulating the ruling elite in learned societies, womanist discourse exposes students to acts of resistance over and against the ordinariness of racialized gender roles that serve as microstructures of oppression.[11] This idea is reported from a conscientization working group in these words: "It is important to note that Western culture has traditionally viewed 'difference' as problematic, and has established a dualistic hierarchy of hegemonic norms by which persons who are different are often viewed as inferior and demonic."

Throughout these pages I contend that the kinetic mining of women's subjective experiences situated in particular time and specific place is central to justice-making transformation. Based on the cultural milieu and sociopolitical settings, the stories of Black women serve as counternarratives that critique the received interpretations of mentoring lying beneath traditional educational institutions.

Mentoring and the Work Your Soul Must Have

In essence, mentoring is my ministry. My vocational call is to share the parameter of inquiry in relation to my specific process of womanist discourse, by discussing the innovative, theological framework that supports the soul-wrestling invitation I extend to all—*to do the work your soul must have.* My line of reasoning is for women and men I mentor to recognize the synergy between being and doing, personal and political, ethical autonomy and justice-making community.

In order for me to mentor persons in relation to their soul-work, I begin the initial mentoring conversation by asking each person three specific questions:

- If you had time, money, and energy to research any topic in the whole wide world, what subject matter sparks your creativity?
- Since doctoral studies is a process of refiner's fire, wherein any person, place, or thing in our bio-text that might cause us to self-sabotage will surface, what real-life trauma, torture, tragedy, or terror do you need to face, front and center?

---

11. For an excellent critique of macroaggressions in today's struggle against outrageous injustice, read Angela Y. Davis, *Freedom Is a Constant Struggle: Ferguson, Palestine, and the Foundations of a Movement* (Chicago: Haymarket, 2016).

- When you open yourself morning by morning to God's revelation, what is God calling you to do?

I listen carefully and give much attention to each answer in order to identify the raw materials and the definitive forces shaping the student's research sensibilities. As the conversation continues I am able to discern if a person's vocational call as a scholarly researcher will be accepted or rejected by various academic disciplines and intellectual circles. If there are clear evidence and realistic possibilities for the inquirer to proceed as a graduate student, together we begin our work as colearners.

In other words, the theological question I pose to each person I mentor—*what is the work your soul must have?*—provides an answer to the crucial question I raised at the beginning of this chapter: "Why even teach the next generation of African American students how to survive and thrive in a system of academic fascism?" My presupposition is that every human is born with a purpose. God wrote it on our hearts in the process of creation. Even if powers and principalities, institutionalized into societal systems of racism, sexism, and class elitism, attempt to isolate, alienate, and exterminate our divine purpose as African Americans in the United States, the teaching I learned as a member of the Black church community is that faithful living and authentic Christian discipleship require us to press against entrenched social evils. The sermons I heard, both at home and at church, taught Black girls and boys how to possess an intolerability to civil arrangements that result in injustice. Our ultimate Christian allegiance is to do the specific work God is calling for each of us to do.

Each person must work toward fulfilling her or his sacred task. If we want to be whole, it is essential for us to realize we are morally bound to resist oppression, to oppose authorities, to disobey immoral laws, to challenge lies that rob us of our divine birthright and God-given dignity. African American intellectuals blessed with the ability to cogitate, speculate, read, write, and think must refuse to acquiesce to any person or thing that interferes with actualizing our vocational call.

At this juncture, I divide my womanist-mentoring work into three separate but intertwined movements: (1) *debunking* the matrix of power, (2) *unmasking* the pedagogy of the opposable thumb, and (3) *disentangling* deliberate distortions in biblical hermeneutics, wherein we make visible intentional falsification of biblical interpretations, enabling us to know who we are and how we work and, most importantly, how to proceed in *doing the work our souls must have.*

Debunking—Analyzing the Matrix of Power

First and foremost, debunking is the "what" in the womanist-mentoring process. When we debunk, we connect women-centered resources to engines of
knowledge in texts, and real-life existential contexts, so that students develop
critical tools that enable users to analyze the deadly onslaught of lies underpinning prescriptive authorities and systemic mechanisms that facilitate white
supremacy and male superiority. At the core of our African Americanness,
women know that in the pursuit of knowledge we will face "a complex of
discouraging realities—sexual discrimination, racism, few role models and
mentors, isolation, competing personal and career demands, shifting social
norms and expectations."[12] Using the Black women's wisdom tradition as
our foundational underpinning, I teach advisees how to analyze the matrix
of androcentric patriarchal power in order to avoid tragic, devastating consequences. The intersectionality of discriminatory legacies of race, sex, and
class oppression creates enormous problems. Womanist professors and students
who want to eradicate the multiplicative dynamics of discrimination present
a paradigmatic seriousness:

> Our lives embody numerous "isms." We cannot pretend we are able se-
> lectively to address just one or the other "ism." Some can do this, and
> some might even find creating a hit-parade list of oppressions desirable.
> We can't and we don't. Women, men and children living on life's margins
> deal with the intersection of "isms" every day. Debunking is a difficult
> task, but it equips the oppressed with a broader range of plural visions and
> consciousness.

One of the discussion triads talked about the fundamental necessity of
debunking hegemonic logic that holds everyday racism and sexism in place:

> There are numerous reasons white benefactors strive to maintain white
> supremacy. There is a reluctance to acknowledge race at all. They consider
> it "more polite," more liberal to exclude any recognition of the social
> construct of racism and its consequences in the lives of African Americans.
> To deconstruct the all-American characteristics of individualism, sports-
> manlike masculinity, the heroic frontiersman's boundless opportunities

12. Patricia A. Farrant, "From the Editor's Desk," in "Black Women in Higher Education,"
special issue of *Initiatives* 53.1 (Spring 1990): iii.

mixed with innocence, would catapult the responsibly conscientious to deconstruct layers of sadistic configurations of masters as enslavers and to interrogate transgressed racial boundaries.

The general theme of debunking requires womanists, and all who cast their lot with us, to expose the impact of the continuous play of sexualized racism, to shine light on the pretentious and exaggerated lies about the Black woman's unnatural capacity to handle conflicts, complexities, and contradictions as superwomen. Thus, a womanist-mentoring mandate is to create strategic action plans to eradicate ruthless, volatile, calibrated violence, both verbal and physical assaults. African Americans must be able to take conscious and constructive steps to ensure that our lives and overall well-being will no longer be exaggerated, distorted, silenced, erased, or absent from the master narratives. A conscientization working group wrote about this nuanced understanding of debunking by exegeting the abuse and misuse of Black people's contributions in the American story:

> We need to explore the contributions of African American people in the structuring and development of this country, especially the essential role race played in the evolution of the principles upon which this country is founded. We think it is important to uncover the truth that the USA is premised on a notion that all men are created equal, yet what the statement really means is that white men of wealth, property, and privilege are the only ones counted as equal.
>
> We teach our children that if they work hard they will succeed; that America believes in life, liberty, and the pursuit of happiness, that democracy is vested in equality of the people, by the people, and for the people. And yet this country refutes these notions and concepts in relation to people of color. We must expose the fact that the American dream intentionally excludes African Americans, and yet the existence of this nation is inexplicably connected to the blood, sweat, and toil of African Americans. In several preaching venues, Dr. Prathia Hall Winn summed it up this way—all factors indicate, Black people are the capital upon which capitalism was built.

In a very real sense, generating new knowledge pertinent to debunking the continuous play of androcentric patriarchal oppression, womanists broaden our perspectival resources. Understood as both form and substance, womanist mentoring as a structural procedure passes on essential teachings to subsequent generations, wherein African Americans connect authoritative bodies of knowledge from the past with the intellectual uncertainties, mysteries, and doubts we wrestle with in the present.

Unmasking—Grasping the Pedagogy of the Opposable Thumb

Unmasking is the "how" in my womanist-mentoring process. The general objective of unmasking is to teach students how to mine the mother lode of diasporic women, by capturing moments in time that show the multistranded and thickly textured experiences in the dailiness of Black women's lives. My pedagogy of the opposable thumb enables us to delineate the various ways women of color are demonized, infantilized, pedestalized, idealized, or presented as free and independent persons created in the image of God. A discussion triad articulated the "why crisis" that emerges when women are demonized, infantilized, pedestalized, and idealized; we become "thingafied":

> By succumbing to the toxic ploy wherein women are placed either on top of the pedestal or forced to crouch beneath the pedestal, we lose our strength and lose sight of our God given dignity, which is our divine birthright. When we become duped by forces in society and succumb to being manipulated, our moral agency as doers-of-justice decreases and we lose sight of our vision, becoming so impotent we cannot rise from the complex, messy inhabitance where others have named and placed us.

Black women who are members of the American Academy of Religion and the Society of Biblical Literature displace the notion of objective, value-free, neutral, dispassionate, abstract principles with radically relativized values and contextualized truths. Womanist mentoring is not either/or. It is both/and. Black women professors resist oppositional binaries that place our minds, reasoning, and facts into dueling polarity over and against our bodies, emotions, and intuition. Before adjourning from a womanist plenary session, a conscientization working group summed it up this way:

> A critical engagement between wholeness, harmony, and self-authenticity is an active effort in the face of unhealthy social constructs. It is our responsibility to interrogate status quo norms which conflict with our *embodied mediated knowledge.* Where there is a conflict between texts and our real-life contexts, we use reliable, liberationist resources to determine

which understanding of the nature of reality is privileged. In other words, to create a dialectical tension between texts and contexts trifurcates body, mind and soul, no one of which can exist in wholeness without the other.

As a womanist mentor, I research, write, and teach about African American women in the past and present, who refuse to separate, to dichotomize, to detach with remoteness from God's presence. As doers-of-justice, womanist work requires us to work collaboratively in wrestling moral legitimacy from theological teachings in which religious superiors dominate so-called inferiors.

Womanists will do well if we stay acutely aware that it is possible to focus even more specifically on unmasking by teaching students my two-step opposable-thumb methodology: how to use the anatomy-of-the-idea and how to create theoethical templates. Here I accept my responsibility to teach the people I mentor constructive ways to analyze required canonized texts. We begin critically evaluating facts about each author relevant to her or his qualifications to write about their subject. The next important thing is to state the author's central thesis and the methodology or methodologies used.

Within the matrix of shifting power, we use research tools and intellectual strategies to probe both the purpose of texts and the profiles of specific audiences within the established canons of the academy. A nonnegotiable component in womanist work is to question the portrayal of Blackness and femaleness. Feeling both fascinated and challenged by the work of creating theoethical templates in relation to the established academic canon, a conscientization working group wrote:

> To plunge into in-depths critiques of our required, standardized texts, to examine books labeled as authoritative and must-reads, bring up all that is fearful in our relentless pursuit of truth and justice. Tapping into deep primordial resources of our wisdom will sharpen our analytical skills and frame our questions so that we are able to explore patterns in normative discourses that sustain certain politics, interactions, and practices.

Now that we are sharpening exegetical skills by synthesizing our findings from the anatomy-of-the-idea, we are in a position to evaluate if our inherited scholarly traditions help or hinder our struggle to overcome institutionalized oppression. By studying the origin of the idea in the genesis of each book, we are able to note what is crucial and central to women's liberation in texts designated by the theological academy as essential readings. From what

I have said up to now it may be clear that the anatomy-of-the-idea enables self-identified womanists, and others who cast their lot with us, to name destructive social forces and embedded patterns of habitual indoctrination that must be eradicated. And on the basis of keen analyses we create theoethical templates with little difficulty. The significance of each template is clear. They convey concrete, microstructural injustices impacting people's lives in this postindustrialist, hyper-connected, digitized, technocratic, robotized world.

To be more specific, when we identify social trends as structurally constructed instruments situated within patriarchal traditions, we are better equipped to challenge inscribed principles that demean females and ask women to sacrifice our dignity and well-being. These straightforward procedures of unmasking illuminate hidden controls that have become habitual responses. Unmasking has its home in the sphere of opposable-thumb pedagogy that indicates how important it is to know what we are seeing when powerbrokers situated at the top of hierarchal pyramids continually assume forces of power maintenance. The hierarchies of White supremacy, male superiority, and social-class elitism are not natural, not normative, and certainly not ordained by God. The purpose of womanist mentoring at this juncture is to prepare students to unmask unequal power relations in the dailiness of life.

In order to move beyond impasses by which contemporary Black women are constrained, the women and men I mentor need to understand how Black women's life lessons serve as counternarratives. Womanist mentoring gives confidence to people who are marginalized to become a seismic force, filled with holy boldness, so much so that we are willing and able to address the lingering injustices in the fight to actualize our vocational call as first-rate scholars no matter the cost.

Disentangling—Making Visible Deliberate Distortions in Biblical Hermeneutics

And finally, disentangling is the "why" in my womanist-mentoring process. This third and final movement parallels the two previous movements in terms of function, meaning, and significance. In general, disentangling is the movement in my womanist mentoring where I teach students how to complete the anatomy-of-the-idea, by exploring the intellectual breadth, conceptual depth, and structural linkage in established academic canons, with particular focus on the multiplicative vectors of racism, sexism, and class elitism. Next, my task as mentor is to equip students with tools for interpreting data revealed in theoethical templates so that they can carve out space where "silenced" voices of Black women can be heard. A discussion triad points out the power of "womanist-in-voicing"[13] this way: "Womanist work is about listening to the silences, naming the silences, deconstructing the silences, and then acting to eradicate the silences. According to Audre Lorde,[14] the fact we are here and speaking and writing these words, we are breaking the silences. We must use our voice to speak out against the perpetuation of oppression in all forms."

During this final stage in my womanist-mentoring process, I direct students' attention to the various ways womanist hermeneutics[15] enables discernment of the rhetorical powers of individuals responsible for dispersing funds, making decisions, receiving foundational monies, and determining standards of excellence in a one-way unaccommodating monopoly of power.

Elisabeth Schüssler Fiorenza's feminist liberation hermeneutics is given much attention in my womanist process of disentangling.[16] When Schüssler Fiorenza discusses principles for interpreting texts, her hermeneutical method provides tools for keen, critical analysis of domination, violence, and injustice linguistically inscribed in Scripture and formative church traditions.[17] The reason this hermeneutical method is of utmost importance in my work as a womanist mentor is that Schüssler Fiorenza's four areas of pyramidal relations in analyzing hegemonic intellectual work dominated by men—sociopolitical, ethical-cultural, biological-natural, and linguistic-symbolic—place the spotlight on primary strengths and major weaknesses in antebellum biblical exegesis and interpretations of sacred texts.

Womanist hermeneutics, in tandem with feminist liberation hermeneutics, peels back the complex layers of cultural mythologies perpetuating microaggression in the body politic. Womanist and feminist exegetes reveal multiple ways to embody humanity, the intersection of race, sex, class, age,

---

13. Dr. Jaqueline Grant coined the concept "womanist in-voicing." She discussed the meaning of "in-voicing" during the filming of Anika Gibbon's documentary "Journey to Liberation," December 2013, at Union Theological Seminary in New York City.

14. Audre Lorde, *Sister Outsider: Essays and Speeches* (Berkeley: Crossing, 2007).

15. Nyasha Junior, *Introduction to Womanist Biblical Interpretation* (Louisville: Westminster John Knox, 2015); Wilda C. Gafney, *Womanist Midrash: A Reintroduction to the Women of the Torah and the Throne* (Louisville: Westminster John Knox, 2016); and Mitzi J. Smith, ed., *I Found God in Me: A Womanist Biblical Hermeneutics Reader* (Eugene, OR: Cascade, 2015).

16. Elisabeth Schüssler Fiorenza, *But She Said: Feminist Practices of Biblical Interpretation* (Boston: Beacon, 1992).

17. Elisabeth Schüssler Fiorenza, *Empowering Memory and Movement: Thinking across Borders* (Minneapolis: Fortress, 2014).

ethnicity, sexuality, gender, and so on.[18] Womanist mentors must enable others to stay mindful that there is no unitary essence of human being-ness. For those of us who live day in and day out surrounded by "the pervasiveness of whiteness, the viciousness of racism, racialized constructions of safety and space, distorted notions of justice, and the process of 'writing the wrongs,'"[19] we understand the written words of Scripture as more than literal. The social location and historical circumstances of biblical interpreters and writers of commentaries are crucial for determining the relevance of exegesis. Therefore, in womanist mentoring I teach the analytical tools for assessing how biased interpreters lead to faulty interpretations.

Tracing back more than three centuries, scholars in the white church community, who pledged their allegiance to slavocracy, used the Bible to justify calibrated violence and forced brutality against enslaved Africans.[20] Within the common world of discourse and antebellum experiences, white religious powerbrokers and ecclesiastical leaders translated Genesis 4:16 ("then Cain went away from the presence of the LORD, and settled in the land of Nod, east of Eden") in ways that fueled relentless negative and hate-filled stereotypes about African Americans.[21] Pervasive, pernicious, and persistently dishonest and inaccurate interpretations of Genesis 4:16 assigned enslaved Black Americans to the lowest rung and in last place in the great chain of humanity. To make this point another way: all forms of biased, hate-filled communication processes were used to rationalize situating African Americans permanently on the outside of salvation history.[22]

What womanists observe in this work of disentangling is how the US slave economy and biblical hermeneutics grew up together, each supporting the other.[23] There was a moment of revelation about warped biblical exegesis supporting chattel slavery when a discussion triad wrote:

18. Elisabeth Schüssler Fiorenza, *Wisdom Ways: Introducing Feminist Biblical Interpretation* (Maryknoll, NY: Orbis, 2001).

19. Kenneth J. Fasching-Varner et al., eds., *Trayvon Martin, Race, and American Justice: Writing Wrong* (Rotterdam: Sense, 2014), xiii.

20. John Boles, *Masters and Slaves in the House of the Lord: Race and Religion in the American South, 1740–1870* (Lexington: University Press of Kentucky, 1988).

21. H. Shelton Smith, *In His Image . . . : Racism in Southern Religion, 1780–1910* (Durham: Duke University Press, 1972).

22. George D. Kelsey, *Racism and the Christian Understanding of Man: An Analysis and Criticism of Racism as an Idolatrous Religion* (New York: Scribner, 1965).

23. Albert Barnes, *An Inquiry into the Scriptural Views of Slavery* (Detroit: Negro History Press, 1969).

During the centuries of chattel slavery in the USA, it became necessary for enslavers and others whose livelihood depended on slavocracy to create theological justifications for the enslavement of persons of African ancestry. This was achieved by creating nefarious connections between chattel slavery and the Bible, connections supposedly ordained by God. Christian Scriptures were misinterpreted and preached as prescriptive mandates relegating enslaved Africans to the status of subhuman. Whiteness was held up as the norm and Blackness was classified as deviant. When the merger of racist myths comingled with the creation of biblical hermeneutics, the outcome was a thickly textured, multistranded web of lies.

It ought to be noted that anti-Black racist thinking was used both in preaching and teaching[24] to convince white parishioners that African Americans are deemed disposable because they were the so-called descendants of the ape that Cain supposedly married in the land of Nod.[25] Other exegetes provided intellectual cover in their translation of Genesis 9:18–27. Their argument was that people of African ancestry are the descendants of Ham, Noah's son who was cursed for laughing at his drunk father.[26] Fraudulent biblical exegetes in various mainline Christian denominations identified African Americans as the so-called descendants of Ham (via Canaan).[27] As such, Black people were classified as being deficient in reasoning and innately criminal, and must be subjected to special scrutiny and around-the-clock surveillance.[28] With straightforward words, a conscientization working group wrote:

> Those in power benefit from distorted interpretations of Scriptures. Such distortions serve as rationale for the hegemonic enslavement of African people. Moreover, white supremacy is presented as a natural phenomenon, the normal and accepted prior knowledge necessary for biblical exegesis.

24. Joseph R. Washington Jr., *Anti-Blackness in English Religion, 1500–1800* (New York: Edwin Mellen, 1984).

25. Josiah Priest, *Bible Defence of Slavery* (Glasgow, KY: Brown, 1852).

26. Stephen Haynes, *Noah's Curse: The Biblical Justification of American Slavery* (New York: Oxford University Press, 2002).

27. David M. Goldenberg, *The Curse of Ham: Race and Slavery in Early Judaism, Christianity, and Islam* (Princeton: Princeton University Press, 2003); and Thomas Virgil Peterson, *Ham and Japheth: The Mythic World of Whites in the Antebellum South* (Metuchen, NJ: Scarecrow, 1978).

28. Kelly Brown Douglas, *Stand Your Ground: Black Bodies and the Justice of God* (Maryknoll, NY: Orbis, 2015).

Societal institutions, including the church, communicated racist rhetoric. When ruthless and sadistic acts against Black people were thought to be based on the Bible, exegetes and interpreters communicated to their audiences that calibrated violence against enslaved Africans was acceptable cultural custom and practice.

Cleverly crafted fraudulent exegesis of selected scriptural passages argued that enslaved Black people were inferior to the enslaving white people, and in turn, subjecting enslaved ancestors to overt hostility and violent abuse was not a sin.[29] Multiple forces railing against the humanity of African Americans used the Bible to support the horrors of systemic racial and sexual wrongdoing.[30] Antebellum Christians were taught that Black people were destined by God to fulfill subservient, menial roles in society, in accordance with the biblical verse found in Joshua 9:23: "Now therefore you are cursed, and some of you shall always be slaves, hewers of wood and drawers of water for the house of my God."

To further exemplify how Bible-toting Christians used everything within their power to deny African Americans access to equality at all levels, Philemon 10–18 was often used as a sermonic text to rationalize why enslaved African Americans could be baptized spiritually as Christians and remain physically bound in chains as slaves.[31] Another more clarifying way to address this point of view is to acknowledge how white missionaries assigned to evangelize women, men, and children living in slave quarters often preached about Paul, in the book of Philemon, sending the enslaved Onesimus back to the enslaver, Philemon.[32] Thus, this interpretation of the book of Philemon was used by "Christian enslavers"[33] to revoke, to make void the English law wherein a person was freed by the act of baptism.[34]

29. David B. Davis, *Inhuman Bondage: The Rise and Fall of Slavery in the New World* (New York: Oxford University Press, 2006).

30. Frederick A. Ross, *Slavery Ordained by God* (Philadelphia: Lippincott, 1857); and David Brion Davis, *In the Image of God: Religion, Moral Values, and Our Heritage of Slavery* (New Haven: Yale University Press, 2001).

31. John Daly, *When Slavery Was Called Freedom: Evangelism, Proslavery, and the Causes of the Civil War* (Lexington: University Press of Kentucky, 2002).

32. Lester B. Scherer, *Slavery and the Churches in Early America, 1619–1819* (Grand Rapids: Eerdmans, 1975).

33. Samuel Blanchard How, *Slaveholding Not Sinful, Slavery, the Punishment of Man's Sin, Its Remedy, the Gospel of Jesus Christ* (New Brunswick: Terhune, 1856).

34. Katie G. Cannon, "The Sign of Hope in Three Centuries of Despair: Women in the Black Church Community," *Human Rights and the Global Mission of the Church*, Boston Theo-

The result of this type of wrongheaded thinking was adopted by interpreters of Scripture who wrenched the following pericopes out of their contexts and used them to communicate justification of harsh systemic racial segregation from 1865 to 1965. The focal point of these three scriptural passages, Colossians 3:22–4:1; 1 Timothy 6:20–21; and Acts 17:22–31, connected together, operated as a formula in the creation of rigid, institutionalized Jim Crow policies and practices. Recurring behavior among the majority of Christians was using these texts to bolster a false self-esteem of white superiority and to create laws supporting racial segregation as part of God's overall divine plan.

Womanist mentoring facilitates the understanding, in spite of hermeneutical distortions and exegetical misinterpretations by white supremacists, that the majority of people active in the Black church community continue to fulfill our mission, offering incisive and vivid examinations of biblical messages of liberation and wholeness. Heroically, we must right, as well as write, the wrongs of the past, by resisting the reduction of the Bible as another tool in the hands of oppressors.[35]

Conclusion

To conclude, it is widely recognized that there is no single, predominant, monolithic, pedagogical unity regarding the work of womanist mentoring. Each self-identified womanist professor makes her own choices in pursuit of the goal. However, it is my hope that in the course of this chapter I have contributed to mentoring from my specific womanist perspective.

My emphasis is on providing intellectual tools for members of oppressed communities who are willing and able to do the work our souls must have. Our threefold task of debunking the matrix of power, unmasking the pedagogy of the opposable thumb, and disentangling deliberate distortions in biblical hermeneutics equip us for academic battles. My work as a womanist mentor, in the discipline of theological ethics, does not waver in my

---

logical Institute Annual Series 1 (1985): 44–50. See also Albert J. Raboteau, *Slave Religion: The "Invisible Institution" in the Antebellum South*, updated ed. (New York: Oxford University Press, 2004 [orig. 1978]).

35. Cain Hope Felder, ed., *Stony the Road We Trod: African American Biblical Interpretation* (Minneapolis: Fortress, 1991); Brian K. Blount et al., eds., *True to Our Native Land: An African American New Testament Commentary* (Minneapolis: Fortress, 2007); and Allen D. Callahan, *The Talking Book: African Americans and the Bible* (New Haven: Yale University Press, 2006).

insistence that each person's vocational call is essential in discerning one's responsibilities as an activist scholar. My "what," "how," and "why" are re-sources that can become incarnate within us, affirming our authentic selves, while simultaneously extending us far beyond our physical, spiritual, and intellectual development.

CHAPTER 9

Mentoring in the Roman Catholic Tradition

Luke Timothy Johnson

In the centuries-long tradition of Catholicism, mentoring has played a prominent role and has had several distinctive features. It has had little or no connection with the sort of mentoring for worldly success in a career or profession that current use of the term suggests. Rather, its main goal has always been the transformation of personal character in the search for sanctity. This sort of mentoring has deep roots in Greco-Roman moral philosophy and Hellenistic Judaism, in which the "guidance of souls" (*psychagoge*) had a significant place. The expressions of such mentoring have been various across the centuries, but every form includes a teacher/disciple relationship, the transmission of wisdom through oral instruction, and (perhaps most critical) imitation of the teacher by the disciple. Over time, a considerable body of devotional literature was generated, which enabled even those excluded from such a personal mentoring relationship to follow the same path.

In this chapter, I first sketch the historical antecedents and the successive expressions of mentoring within the Catholic tradition. And since being "Catholic" means embracing the entire tradition rather than the short period since the Counter-Reformation when the modifier "Roman" became necessary, my survey goes back to the beginning. Along the way, I note significant literary expressions of this mentoring tradition. Then, I spend some time on the actual shape of such mentoring: how was the path to sanctity understood, why was it thought to be perilous, and why was careful guidance required for those who undertook it? I close with some comments about the effects within Catholicism of the loss, or at least the substantial weakening, of this mentoring tradition.

Background and First Stages

Christianity inherited an already well-developed tradition of mentoring in the philosophical life. In the time of the early empire, philosophy had become a matter more of therapy than of theory. Moral philosophy paid close attention to the formation of virtue (health) as opposed to vice (sickness). Although philosophical schools differed on many points of doctrine, they agreed on the need for the transformation of character and that such transformation required a special form of *paideia* (education/discipline). Wisdom was a matter of practical living and was best learned through imitation of a living example.

Thus, in the patriarchal structure of the ancient household, a father was expected to provide both wise sayings (maxims) for the guidance of his son and to serve as a living exemplar of proper behavior. For those seeking more than merely conventional morality, however, training in the philosophical life required the instruction, but even more, the example of the philosophical mentor. The Stoic Epictetus, for example, praised the way his own teacher, Musonius Rufus, had insight into even the secret vices of his students; and Epictetus offered himself to his own students not only through his lively sermons (discourses) but as well through the manner of his life. The condemnation of false philosophers, in turn, tended to focus on the disparity between their words and their practice; it was important to learn authentic virtue from an authentic exemplification of virtue.

Attention to the formation of would-be philosophers was given more formal structural expression among the Pythagoreans, whose communal life featured the sharing of possessions and the ordered transmission of the *apophthegmata* (wise maxims) of Pythagoras. Entrants to the Pythagorean community had to undergo a period of probation before they were admitted among the mature members. Such structural elements are found as well among the Essenes at Qumran, who resemble the Pythagoreans not least in their exceptional practice of communal possessions. Philo of Alexandria's description of the *therapeutai* suggests as well the goal of spiritual transformation among such Jewish practitioners of the philosophical life through the study of Scripture, teaching, and prayer.

The canonical Gospels contain elements that situate the activity of Jesus and the apostles within this mentoring tradition: Jesus is portrayed as a teacher who instructs his disciples, and his command to "follow me" points to his role as a model to be imitated. In his letters, Paul presents himself as a model to his readers and instructs them in the moral life. But mentoring in any real sense is not found in the New Testament writings, which are directed primarily to the formation of communities, rather than the transformation of individuals. The same is true of the extant Christian literature of the pre-Constantinian period. With the very partial exception of such Gnostic writings as Ptolemy's *Letter to Flora*, little attention is given to the spiritual progress of individuals. As the figures of Ignatius and Polycarp and Justin and Origen remind us, the centuries when the church lived under the threat of persecution and martyrdom demanded a posture of public witness in the face of death more than the patient cultivation of the virtues under the guidance of a mentor.

A clearer expression of mentoring emerges after Constantine, when Christianity was established as the imperial religion. The relatively comfortable circumstances of Christian life in urban centers led some to become discontented with what they regarded as a compromised form of discipleship and to seek a more strenuous form of witness—a "white martyrdom"—in the wilderness of Egypt, Palestine, and Syria. The conflict these fathers and mothers of the desert engaged was not with the demonic forces of the empire threatening death through martyrdom, but with the demons of their own passions (desire, lust, envy, avarice, sloth) that threatened to turn disciples from the way of Christ. The publicity gained by some of these early saints (see Athanasius's *Life of Antony*) led thousands to seek their presence and their guidance, so that virtual "cities in the desert" grew up around the men and women who could provide direction to others in the quest for holiness.

Many of their maxims on the spiritual combat, as well as anecdotes about their practice of prayer and fasting, were collected and published (see the *apophthegmata patrum*), enabling those who could not physically be in their presence to share in their wisdom. The fourth-century *Lausiac History* by Palladius describes the way in which wealthy men and women from cities would travel from one holy person to another seeking such guidance; the literary expression of their quest similarly enabled readers to participate in the same mentoring at a distance. And the early-fifth-century monastic founder John Cassian, who had studied with monks in Palestine and Egypt, compiled the wisdom of the desert monks concerning the path to God in his *Conferences*, which enabled readers to virtually hear from the lips of those ancient saints themselves in a form of secondhand mentoring.

In the cenobitic monasticism established in Egypt by Pachomius (292–348), the communal expression of *paideia* pioneered by Pythagoreans and Essenes found renewal within Christianity. Responsibility for the shaping of monastic character—which meant simply a life in search of perfection—was shifted from the one-to-one relationship of sage and student to the structure of life governed by the rule. The classic form of Western monasticism in Benedict of Nursia's *Rule for Monks* (early sixth century) followed this essentially communal focus without losing a concern for individual formation. Thus, in the prologue to the *Rule*, the individual monk is called to "return by the labor of obedience to him from whom you had departed by the sloth of disobedience." The applicant to the monastery is to undergo a period of "testing of spirits" before being admitted to the novitiate, where "a senior is assigned to them who is skilled in winning souls to watch over them with the utmost care" (*Rule* 58).

The novice master provides the sort of hands-on mentoring in the monastic ethos and practice that reinforces the positive elements of what young monks could observe also (it was hoped) in the behavior of the entire community. Benedict was also aware of the need for personal attention when the framework of obedience to rule and abbot failed. Thus, the *Rule* exhorts the abbot to be solicitous toward the excommunicated (for faults), sending them sympathetic "brothers of mature years and wisdom" who might offer them counsel and support (*Rule* 27). In the final chapter, Benedict acknowledges that he has provided only the "rudiments of the religious life," and for those "who would hasten to the perfection of that life," he offers the study of the Old and New Testaments, the writings of the "holy Fathers" (patristic authors), the *Conferences* of John Cassian, the *Lives of the Fathers*, and the *Rule of Saint Basil* (*Rule* 73). And in fact, the course of *lectio divina* within the long monastic tradition included the close and sustained reading of such spiritual authorities and the imitation of the examples they provided.

The Long Tradition

Catholic mentoring in the spiritual life—before and after the Protestant Reformation—continued to take place almost entirely within the frame of religious vows, among men and women who, like ancient philosophers, chose to commit themselves to (what they regarded as) a higher and more difficult expression of Christian identity. Whether in Benedictine monasteries (male and female) and in the families of monks in the West that derived from the Benedictines (Cistercians, Trappists), or in male and female religious orders that sprang up in the Middle Ages and beyond—Dominicans, Franciscans, Carmelites, and many others—the basic pattern set by the monastic life continued.

From one perspective, such religious life was remarkably stable and predictable, with monks and mendicants passing through stages of postulancy, novitiate, simple vows, and solemn vows while living out their obedience to the order's rules and authority structure. From another perspective, those driven by the desire for unity with God entered upon an arduous journey of the soul that required careful guidance. The role of the individual "spiritual director" was therefore a key element in the mentoring process. Patriarchal arrangements obtained: male monks and mendicants often served as spiritual directors as well as confessors for women religious (as, in the sixteenth century, John of the Cross was for Teresa of Avila, even though he was a follower of her reform movement). Among the many classics of mysticism written over this long span of time, several of them are noteworthy for adopting a mentoring stance toward the reader, leading him or her along on the path of mystical ascent: the anonymous *Cloud of Unknowing* (late fourteenth century), Teresa of Avila's *Way of Perfection* (late sixteenth century), and John of the Cross's *Ascent of Mount Carmel* (late sixteenth century).

When the Council of Trent, seeking to reform the clergy who did not belong to religious orders, mandated the establishment of seminaries for the training of priests (session 23 in 1563), the model of spiritual formation in monasteries and religious orders was transposed to the preparation of diocesan clergy. Seminary life in many ways imitated the routine of monasteries. A formal position within Roman Catholic seminaries was therefore that of spiritual director, whose responsibilities included conferences on the spiritual life. In addition to the official spiritual director, seminarians were encouraged to choose a personal director, who would serve both as confessor and as spiritual guide. Depending on the individual gifts of such directors, personal advice could range from the obtuse and purely formal to the personally engaging and psychologically discerning. Just as the monastery's novice master was to "test spirits," so in the Roman Catholic seminary, the spiritual director played a key role in helping the seminarian (and institution) to discern the authenticity of his vocation.

An unspoken premise of this system was that the seminarian's experience of spiritual direction would also serve to make a young priest a better confessor for lay Christians and capable of offering spiritual direction to those who sought it. The mentoring found within seminaries, moreover, was assumed to be carried on after ordination in pastoral placements, where senior clergy—the priest or monsignor who served as pastor—was to provide both personal example and verbal instruction to the younger associates assigned to the parish. Sometimes this happened, sometimes it did not. But this on-the-job mentoring came as close as anything in the Roman Catholic tradition to what is currently understood as professional mentoring, that is, dealing not only with personal spiritual progress but also with competence in ministerial practice.

The practices of spiritual mentoring within this long Catholic tradition were found almost exclusively within monasteries, religious houses, seminaries, and rectories. Laypeople had little access to such guidance, unless they made personal contact with such religious professionals or joined one of the Third Order sodalities that offered participation in the life of a religious organization. Otherwise, laypeople depended on whatever counsel and advice could be delivered by their parish priests in the context of confession. Seldom did this become more than a hit-or-miss proposition. The content of spiritual instruction, moreover, remained largely monastic in form. Thus, although *The Imitation of Christ* by Thomas à Kempis (early fifteenth century) enjoyed an astonishingly wide readership—and in book 3 had the reader directly addressed as "my son" by Jesus—its message remained shaped by a "flee the world" disposition that ill fitted the lives of lay readers. What made Francis de Sales's masterpiece, *Introduction to the Devout Life* (1609), so remarkable was its wholehearted appreciation for the worldly circumstances of lay readers and its effort to build a spiritual life in completely lay terms.

Why Mentoring Is Needed

The commitment to "seek the face of God," to pursue a life of sanctity beyond that expected of ordinary discipleship, is inherently exceptional and perilous. It is exceptional: by no means did all Christians make such a commitment; thus the decision to become a monk or join a religious order was a choice for "the way of perfection," understood as bearing greater blessing and greater risk for those who chose it. For those who made the commitment, then and now (now less and less within the frame of a religious institution), it is the ultimate decision that measures all other choices. It is not like taking up a hobby or cultivating a certain craft. It is rather a religious commitment that utterly defines one's life. Since it is a matter of living one's life in a certain way, it is imperative that guidance come from someone who has made the same commitment earlier and has made significant progress along the same path.

The commitment is also perilous: seeking intimate communion with God is a dangerous pursuit. It is not like finding a friend or enjoying the company of other persons. God is not a person among other persons or an object among other objects. The living God is Spirit, the source and goal of all that exists. The journey is dangerous, first, then, because it deals with the Lord of all creation, and the letter to the Hebrews reminds us that "it is a fearful thing to fall into the hands of the living God" (Heb. 10:31); this is not a trivial enterprise but one dealing with ultimate reality. And since the journey is not one along material paths but through the very soul of the seeker, it is subject to all the perils that can befall a psyche that is reaching beyond its own capacity.

Mentoring in the Catholic tradition has therefore taken the form of a spiritual companionship and support during a long and lonely journey of the soul. The journey is long. It is not accomplished by reaching external marks of advancement. It is, indeed, never accomplished before death and is incapable of being measured by any external marks. It is a lifelong commitment to transformation of one's self according to the mind of Christ, to a renewal of one's mind and heart through the power of the Holy Spirit. The temptation to give up the quest out of fatigue and frustration is real; equally real is the temptation to cease questing out of the delusion that one *is* finished before death.

The journey is also inherently lonely. Not only do few undertake such a commitment, the process of transformation itself involves alienation from the comforts of the flesh, including the precious comfort of human companionship. The interior struggle is not easily shared with those not also engaged in the struggle—even within a monastery or religious order. Even in such contexts, there are not many who understand or are even appreciative of the secret journey that the one who seeks God's presence has undertaken. The sense of being alone on such a perilous journey heightens the psychic dangers and increases the need for a spiritual guide.

The notion of progress is built into the image of a journey, so an obvious aspect of spiritual direction is identifying the stages of such progress as they were lived by the pioneers and trail-markers of old and helping adjust the perceptions and expectations of the one who is seeking to make a way through such spiritual stages. The classic stages of growth in the spiritual life are called the purgative way, the illuminative way, and the unitive way. The first represents the turning from vice and the cultivation of virtue; it involves what is usually thought of as asceticism: the disciplined cultivation of "a life worthy of God, who calls you into his own kingdom and glory" (1 Thess. 2:12). Here, there is an emphasis on prayer, fasting, and almsgiving at a level more radical and absolute than the same practices as found among ordinary believers. The second signifies sporadic moments and states of spiritual insight or illumination, a more palpable experience of God. In this stage, more attention is given to the effects of "pray[ing] without ceasing" (1 Thess. 5:17).

The third stage points to the end of the journey available in the present life, an enduring condition of unity with God that is not to be identified with either purgation or illumination but that builds upon and subsumes those earlier stages.

Although the distinction between such stages seems clear enough, the actual movement through them is filled with uncertainty and ambiguity, making the discernment of a spiritual mentor critical. By no means, for example, does the purgative way ever end; the struggle to control the passions remains real throughout life. And that struggle raises all kinds of questions: When are fasting and other forms of fleshly mortification appropriate, and when are they excessive? How does genuine humility manifest itself? How is religious obedience to be distinguished from will-lessness or masochism? The advanced stages of the spiritual quest raise even more questions: How can one distinguish between genuine divine visitations and self-generated visions? How can one follow the lead of such experiences and also be guided by religious obedience?

Spiritual mentoring is necessary above all because of the constant threat of delusion and self-deception in those engaged in such an exalted yet isolating quest. How easy it is to mistake states of dissociation arising from acute fasting with spiritual advancement, or periods of depression with the dark night of the soul, or erotic attraction with spiritual intimacy. Self-examination is not sufficient, for it can equally be compromised by fantasy and desire. The sane voice of another is required to cut through the tangle of self-delusion. The voice of sanity is especially valuable for those whose exercises have brought them to the brink of psychic exhaustion and confusion. The companion who has undertaken the same journey is best able to identify its dangers and wrong turnings, is best capable of reminding the one seeking sanctity that it is not a matter of spectacular works but of simple and ever-deepening faith, expressed most authentically not in flights of mystical exaltation but in loving-kindness toward the neighbor.

The best of the mentoring tradition within the long Catholic tradition combined a spirit of companionship arising from commitment to the same quest with a tough-minded detachment that enables a true testing of the spirits. At its best, as exemplified by the experience of many we call saints, spiritual direction is one of the true (if seldom acknowledged) glories of a tradition that is too often identified with externals rather than with internal transformation.

But spiritual mentoring has by no means always been at its best, and it is important to remember the ways in which the practice of spiritual direction has itself been corrupted. There is no lack of stories recounting the ways in which spiritual directors manipulated those they advised, sometimes through authoritarian demands for obedience, sometimes through forms of persuasion that became sexually seductive, sometimes both. The breaking of boundaries that properly appalls us in the case of doctors and teachers and therapists is even more shocking—though seldom surprising—in the case of those whose help is sought in the most psychically demanding exercise of all: the quest of perfection. The abuse of power displayed by confessors seducing those seeking repentance or by spiritual directors coopting the freedom of choice properly belonging to those they direct are all the more heinous because they are done in secret and under the cloak of the highest and best of human endeavors.

Breakdown of a Tradition

Much of this chapter has been cast in the past tense, because the tradition of spiritual mentoring within Catholicism has changed in fundamental ways, and its future is uncertain. To some extent, the alteration is one of the unintended consequences of the Second Vatican Council. The council's documents effected important shifts in focus. In contrast to the "flee the world" piety and intellectual stance that characterized the church in previous centuries, the council called for an engagement with the modern world. Rather than focus exclusively on clergy and religious, the council sought to empower laity within the church. In its earliest proclamation, the council called for the reform of the liturgy, making it the center of Catholic identity and calling in particular for full participation by all in the Eucharist. The council advocated a more Scripture-based spirituality, at the same time approving of contemporary historical-critical approaches to the Bible. Empowerment of the laity, participation in public worship, the critical reading of Scripture, engagement with modernity—all these make an activist and communal form of Christian discipleship more attractive than an individual's quest for interior perfection. Asceticism, prayer, and contemplation were not proscribed, but neither were they highlighted.

The decades following the council saw the virtual collapse of the vast interlocking network of institutions that for centuries had been the natural setting for mentoring in the spiritual life. Monks and nuns left their houses, and many fewer young people joined contemplative communities; religious orders as well found their numbers decimated; vocations to the priesthood almost disappeared; seminaries were forced to shut down. Those who remained in traditional forms of religious life were far fewer than before and were aging as a group, without a younger cohort of eager men and women surging through the door seeking to be mentored in the spiritual life. The crisis of diminished numbers exacerbated a movement away from the contemplative to the active life: simply staffing all the ministries to which priests and religious were committed took all the energy available. The combination of the council's positive affirmation of lay and active discipleship, and the collapse of the patriarchal structures that made the transmission of wisdom from the old to the young intelligible, weakened the entire framework of spiritual mentoring as it had previously existed.

The weakening of institutional structures was accompanied by real changes in the understanding of the spiritual life. Three are particularly noteworthy. The Catholic Charismatic Movement, which began in the late 1960s, privileged the immediacy of powerful spiritual experience: speaking in tongues, prophesying, healing. The gift of the Holy Spirit energized many Catholics, leading them to form intentional communities based on such experiences. The need for the "discernment of spirits" in such settings was obvious: enthusiasm could and did lead to a variety of unhealthy expressions—as it did in the ancient church at Corinth. But the lack of an established structure for mentorship meant that centuries of wisdom concerning the spiritual life were not readily available; leaders of groups were often only months or weeks longer "in the Spirit" than newcomers. The desert fathers and Cassian would have known, for example, that an initial powerful experience is valuable only if it subsequently leads to a disciplined path of asceticism and prayer—real growth takes place after "the honeymoon period." By way of contrast, twentieth-century charismatic communities avidly sought new conversions to the movement because the initial experience of neophytes renewed and invigorated those whose own gifts had grown less exciting. Rather than dig deeper, the tendency in charismatic groups was to stay at the level of the surface.

A second development was a conception of discipleship that drew on the activist strain in the Second Vatican Council, manifested especially among those committed to a liberation understanding of the gospel. There is much that is positive in this prophetic understanding: the good news is translated into a passionate concern for social justice, and the rule of God is expressed through liberating humans from the structures of oppression and sin that keep them captive. Here, a concern for interior transformation is seen as less important than an active and external engagement with movements of social justice. Participating in actions of justice is seen as a more serious commitment to God than a life of conventional piety. Taken to an extreme, however, such a view of discipleship can actually exclude attention to asceticism and prayer: they are dismissed as narcissistic self-centeredness instead of a commitment to ameliorating social systems.

A third challenge to the classic understanding of the spiritual life as a quest for perfection was posed by a variety of therapeutic approaches to spirituality. The triumph of a psychological approach can be seen in the abandonment of language about sin and salvation in favor of language about sickness and health, in the perception of asceticism and self-abnegation as neurotic manifestations of an unhealthy masochism, in an emphasis on growth in self-esteem rather than stages of humility, in pursuing tranquility and peace more than an agonistic struggle with the passions, in rejecting the dark night of the soul in favor of constant comfort. The point of meditation is now to provide a rest for the spirit in a hectic world; the point of fasting—or dieting—is to have a healthier lifestyle.

The combination of institutional collapse and conceptual erosion means that the classic form of mentoring in the spiritual life has almost disappeared within Catholicism. Two important spiritual writers of the late twentieth century illustrate the change. Although the Trappist monk Thomas Merton drew attention because of his "turn to the world" in his later years—embracing a variety of spiritual traditions and adopting a prophetic stance toward an idolatrous culture—he was nevertheless formed by the most traditional forms of spiritual mentorship within the monastery, and he passionately sought the path to perfection along classic lines. A student of the great mystics from the desert fathers through John of the Cross, his own spiritual writings (*Seeds of Contemplation* and *The New Man*) were fresh and engaging iterations of that long tradition. And he provided both fellow monks and a wide range of correspondents with spiritual counsel according to the same pattern. His engagement with modernity enlivened and broadened but did not fundamentally change his conviction that the point of life was the quest for holiness. He stood firmly within the long Catholic tradition of mentoring, despite—or perhaps because of—his prophetic stance toward contemporary culture. People became monks because of the example of Thomas Merton.

The profile of Henri Nouwen was quite different, although he was equally admired by many devotees for his popular spiritual writings. A priest and member of a religious order, he was not situated within a monastery, but led a life that can only be called itinerant: he moved frequently from one setting to another, sometimes occupying the role of a seminary professor, sometimes engaging an active social ministry (such as *l'Arche*), using the new experiences offered by those places as occasions for spiritual insight into his own spiritual journey. Although the classic shape of the spiritual life is still visible in many of his writings, his primary training in psychology deeply influenced his approach (*The Wounded Healer* or *Intimacy*). Despite a charismatic presence that drew many of his readers to seek personal contact with him, Nouwen's awareness of his own brokenness made him reluctant to occupy the traditional role of a spiritual guide who offers himself for imitation. And it is difficult to imagine what such imitation might look like. He is the prototype of contemporary Catholic spiritual writers (such as Kathleen Norris), whose presence to others is primarily literary and whose vision of the spiritual journey is less face to face and more freelance and idiosyncratic (that is, less institutionally located and mediated) than in past generations. Matthew Fox's "creation spirituality," for example, engages many classics of spirituality within the Catholic tradition, but places them within an ecumenical eclecticism and highly personal "spiritual movement" that only with considerable effort can be seen as continuous with the longer Catholic tradition of spiritual mentoring.

The Catholic tradition is both long and remarkably resilient. It would be foolish to declare dead its longstanding commitment to spiritual mentoring; the Holy Spirit is always capable of breathing new life into dead bones and of bringing into existence new expressions of old values. But when in the first quarter of the twenty-first century we consider the magnificence of the tradition as it once existed, as well as its recent state of disarray and confusion, it is difficult to imagine what a revitalized future might be.

CHAPTER 10

Mentoring New Generations of Latin@ Leaders

Cristian De La Rosa

It was a late Saturday afternoon in August in Boston. As I contemplated the piles of papers on my office desk, boxes of leftover materials, and musical instruments to be returned to local congregations in the area, I smiled at a text message from Coralis Feliciano, a college student: "Thank you for everything. . . . It was an amazing opportunity being able to work with the HYLA High School group and share my own experiences with them. I also leave inspired by them to do more in my community and my church. Also, HYLA college made me appreciate more the blessings I have in my life compared to many other people and I gained knowledge to go teach others. I'm more than thankful for this year at HYLA and I hope I can come back next year."

She was at the airport, ready to board her flight out of Boston and wanted to share with me her experience serving as part of the leadership team for the high school student group and her experience as a college student participant in one of the summer leadership convocations of the Hispanic Youth Leadership Academy (HYLA).[1] Though I was extremely tired and had a great deal of administrative follow-up work, Coralis's message helped me remember the importance of the summer leadership convocations in the life of the participants. I reread her text and answered with a grateful heart: "You are welcome. We look forward to having you as a student mentor next year."

---

1. Hispanic Youth Leadership Academy is a national leadership formation initiative with high school and college students. It is supported by the United Methodist Church in the United States in partnership with Methodist universities, seminaries, and United Methodist national program agencies. HYLA coordinates regional leadership convocations and follows a leadership development curriculum for students at the high school and college levels across the country during the summer time. See hylaumc.com for more information.

We had designed the HYLA summer leadership convocations so that seminary students, accompanied by seminary faculty and clergy, lead the convocations for college students; and college students, accompanied by seminary students, lead the convocations for high school students. This design intentionally creates space for leadership formation and practice, with facilitation and accompaniment as the two driving components for building relationships within and across generations of Latin@ students. I smiled again and found new energy thinking about this summer's five convocations. Each one gathered twenty to twenty-five young Latin@ leaders from local Spanish-speaking congregations. I recalled every seminary and college student who for the first time, like Coralis, had been part of a leadership team. They practiced their leadership by facilitating curriculum components and *acompañando/* accompanying the young participants from across the country.[2]

This chapter considers the importance of mentoring within faith-based leadership-formation initiatives for young Latin@ leaders by gleaning what we have learned from a decade of personal experience facilitating formation processes through HYLA and the Raices Latinas Leadership Institute (RLLI).[3] First, it explores the contemporary complexities faced by Latin@ high school and college students as they enter the world of academia and navigate racist institutional processes. Second, it considers the relationship between facilitating and accompaniment as key practices of mentoring with Latin@ students. The chapter concludes by considering contextual integrations of facilitating and accompaniment as practices of mentoring with Latin@ youth and young adults.

I consider this work to be an epistemological retrieval effort as a pastor-scholar who bridges the worlds of the academy, the church, and the community. This chapter's consideration of mentoring is rooted in a Wesleyan tradition in which Scripture, tradition, reason, and experience together form the methodological lens. HYLA and RLLI identify Latin@ students already involved in the ministries of local congregations. An important aspect for consideration, as invitations are extended for participation in the summer leadership convocations, is the demonstrated desire of students to engage in a leadership-formation process for the transformation of the world as

2. *Acompañando* is the Spanish word meaning "accompaniment." A later section of this chapter discusses its definition and use.

3. Raices Latinas Leadership Institute is an initiative that complements HYLA as it caters to upper-level college and graduate students. It is an interdenominational program sponsored by Boston University School of Theology and supported by the United Methodist Church. See hylaumc.com/raices-latinas-institute for more information.

Latin@ church leaders.[4] Therefore, mentoring in this particular context is considered to be a subversive evangelistic praxis outlined by Paolo Freire in *Pedagogy of the Oppressed* as "a collaborative knowledge production process that facilitates a critical consciousness-building effort (conscientization), as well as a reclaiming of one's humanity in the process."[5] For the purposes of this chapter, Latin@ students are defined as individuals of Latin American (Mestizo or indigenous) descent, of Spanish- or Portuguese-speaking heritage who live in the United States.

Contextual Realities of Latin@ Youth and Young Adults

In the first chapter of *Mentoring as Transformative Practice*, Sharon Fires-Britt and Jeanette Snider conclude that mentoring with women and underrepresented minorities (URM) in higher education "is a very complex process." They recognize from their own research "that increasingly the needs of URM are not easily met by standard mentoring approaches."[6] The complexity of mentoring with Latin@ youth and young adults, who constitute the fastest growing percentage of URMs in higher education, derives from complex contextual realities rooted in a history of a violent conquest of the Americas and the imperialistic imposition of Christianity through processes of colonization. Social institutions like the church and the academy seem to overlook

4. The Wesleyan quadrilateral refers to what John Wesley considered to be the four principal factors that illumine the interpretation and practice of faith: "For United Methodists, Scripture is considered the primary source and standard for Christian doctrine. Tradition is experience and the witness of development and growth of the faith through the past centuries and in many nations and cultures. Experience is the individual's understanding and appropriating of the faith in the light of his or her own life. Through reason the individual Christian brings to bear on the Christian faith discerning and cogent thought. These four elements taken together bring the individual Christian to a mature and fulfilling understanding of the Christian faith and the required response of worship and service" (umc.org/what-we-believe/wesleyan-quadrilateral). The mission of the United Methodist Church, as stated in its book of discipline §1.20, is "to make disciples of Jesus Christ for the transformation of the world"; available at umc.org/what-we-believe/section-1-the-churches.

5. Julie López Figueroa and Gloria M. Rodríguez, "Critical Mentoring Practices to Support Diverse Students in Higher Education: Chicana/Latina Faculty Perspectives," in *Mentoring as Transformative Practice: Supporting Student and Faculty Diversity*, ed. Caroline Turner (San Francisco: Jossey-Bass, 2015), 26.

6. Sharon Fires-Britt and Jeanette Snider, "Mentoring outside the Line: The Importance of Authenticity, Transparency, and Vulnerability in Effective Mentoring Relationships," in *Mentoring as Transformative Practice*, ed. Caroline Turner, 9.

that the bodies and identities of Latin@s emerged out of the physical rape of indigenous women, the violent occupation of indigenous territories, and the systematic erasure of cultures, religions, and languages native to the Americas.[7] In *Decolonizing Methodologies*, Linda Tuhiwai Smith notes that the colonizing process resulted in complex and fragmented realities for descendants of the colonized:

> As Fanon and later writers such as Nandy have claimed, imperialism and colonialism brought complete disorder to colonized peoples, disconnecting them from their histories, their landscapes, their languages, their social relations and their own ways of thinking, feeling and interacting with the world. It was a process of systematic fragmentation which can still be seen in the disciplinary carve-up of the indigenous world: bones, mummies and skulls to the museums, art work to private collectors, languages to linguists, "customs" to anthropologists, beliefs and behaviors to psychologists. . . . Fragmentation is not a phenomenon of postmodernism as many might claim. For indigenous peoples fragmentation has been the consequence of imperialism.[8]

As descendants of the colonized in the Americas, Latin@s live in a state of cultural tension and fragmentation that perpetuates a vulnerable existence of marginality as they enter the academy or attempt to participate in the leadership of church-related institutions. It is important to consider that Protestant Latin@s manage an additional kind of fragmentation, the product of a second encounter with Christianity. The first encounter occurred during the conquest of the Americas when Christianity was introduced by Roman Catholic priests who arrived with the Spanish *conquistadores*. In this traumatic introduction of Christianity to the Americas, the priests declared all indigenous religious practices to be idolatrous and all indigenous cultural traditions to be uncivilized. This violently imposed religion was yet to establish roots within the devastated surviving communities in the Americas when a second

7. David Carrasco, *Religions of Mesoamerica*, 2nd ed. (Long Grove, IL: Waveland, 2014), introduction and 151–74. Also see Luis Rivera Pagan, *A Violent Evangelism: The Political and Religious Conquest of the Americas* (Louisville: Westminster John Knox, 1991), for a historical perspective; and Walter Mignolo, *Local Histories/Global Designs: Coloniality, Subaltern Knowledges, and Border Thinking* (Princeton: Princeton University Press, 2012), for more on the impact of colonizing processes.

8. Linda Tuhiwai Smith, *Decolonizing Methodologies: Research and Indigenous Peoples* (New York: Zed, 2012), 28.

encounter occurred in the northern part of the Americas and moved south to Mexico. Christianity was reintroduced, against Roman Catholic practices and doctrines, as Protestantism.

Communities of Mexican descent in what is now the southwestern part of the United States were particularly impacted by the reintroduction of Christianity. Overnight, as the northern territories of Mexico became part of the United States, communities in this geographical area were pressured one more time to give up what was left of their indigenous culture. Protestant missionaries declared Our Lady of Guadalupe, a religious symbol and point of reference for popular religious practices in the Roman Catholic Church, to be an idol. They took away this last vestige of indigenous epistemology in the institutional church from those of Mexican descent who converted to Protestantism.[9] This traumatic second encounter with Christianity by those of Mexican descent is recounted by Chicana activist Gloria Anzaldúa:

> In the 1800s, Anglos migrated illegally into Texas, which was then part of Mexico, in greater and greater numbers and gradually drove the *Tejanos* (native Texans of Mexican descent) from their lands, committing all manner of atrocities against them. Their illegal invasion forced Mexico to fight a war to keep its Texas territory. The Battle of the Alamo, in which the Mexican forces vanquished the whites, became, for the whites, the symbol for the cowardly and villainous character of the Mexicans. It became (and still is) a symbol that legitimized the white imperialistic takeover. With the capture of Santa Anna later in 1836, Texas became a republic. *Tejanos* lost their land and, overnight, became the foreigners.[10]

9. Our Lady of Guadalupe emerged as the religious symbol from the encounter of the conquered peoples of the Americas (Mexico and what is now the southwest part of the United States) with Christianity. The image communicates new life and hope for Roman Catholics of Mexican descent. It is a powerful symbol even for some Protestant Mexicans and Mexican Americans because of what she represents culturally. The account of her apparition is recorded in classic Nahuatl in what is titled *Nican Mopoh*, a section of a text known as *Huei tlamahuicoltica* ("the great event"). See Lisa Sousa, Stafford Poole, James Lockhart, eds., *The Story of Guadalupe: Luis Laso de la Vega's Huei tlamahuiscoltica of 1649* (Stanford: Stanford University Press, 1998); Virgilio Elizondo, *Guadalupe: Mother of the New Creation* (Maryknoll, NY: Orbis, 1997); Timothy Matovina, *Guadalupe and Her Faithful: Latino Catholics in San Antonio, from Colonial Origins to the Present* (Baltimore: Johns Hopkins University Press, 2005); and Jeanette Rodriguez, *Our Lady of Guadalupe: Faith and Empowerment among Mexican-American Women* (Austin: University of Texas Press, 1994).

10. Gloria Anzaldúa, *Borderlands/La Frontera: The New Mestiza*, 3rd ed. (San Francisco: Aunt Lute Books, 2007), 28.

It is interesting to note that Christianity was reintroduced in this second encounter by Protestant missionaries who came into Texas with the *illegal Anglo migrants*. Under the ideological impetus of Manifest Destiny, these missionary efforts managed to embody a dominant discriminatory ethos toward those of Mexican descent. Official reports of Methodist and Presbyterian missionaries from 1836 to 1938 include blatant racist remarks as pretexts for retention of power and leadership in the newly established missions. "Even after Mexican and Mexican Americans converted to Protestantism, Anglo American missionaries deemed them incapable of managing their own institutions."[11] These racist attitudes, designed within the institutional church and promulgated within all social systems in the United States almost two centuries ago, still impact Latin@s today. In their experience as Chicana/Latina faculty, Julia L. Figueroa and Gloria M. Rodriguez draw from their own interactions with Latin@ students and explain the impact of institutional racism mediated through a meritocratic culture that "shapes practices, traditions, norms and language in higher education."[12] They consider several studies in higher education and recognize the operating ideology of meritocracy in relation to the socially embedded racist attitudes impacting students' formation. Figueroa and Rodriguez explain their understanding as follows:

> Meritocracy operates purportedly as an independent, neutral, and objective ideological vehicle for governing and educating college students. . . . Presumably, learning and teaching are dispensed through a color-blind approach where excellence is cast as race-neutral, individualistic success. . . . Entrenched within what is considered a "normal routine" . . . , however, reside unexamined attitudes and practices, which is where institutionalized racism remains invisible to many, unchanging. . . . Though not personally intended, institutionalized racism is far from incidental when meritocracy is one inherited, unchallenged element still operating within higher education.[13]

Latin@ students, like most students of color, struggle with the management of meritocracy, racism, and their own vulnerable positioning in academia. It becomes critical for mentors to understand this contextual reality

11. Paul Barton, "Inter-ethnic Relations between Mexican American and Anglo American Methodists in the US Southwest, 1836–1938," in *Protestantes/Protestants: Hispanic Christianity within Mainline Traditions*, ed. David Maldonado Jr. (Nashville: Abingdon, 1999), 69.

12. Figueroa and Rodríguez, "Critical Mentoring Practices," 24.

13. Figueroa and Rodríguez, "Critical Mentoring Practices," 24.

in academic settings, with equivalents in religious settings, which further problematize the already complicated circumstances of Latin@ students.

Facilitation and Accompaniment as Essential Practices in Mentoring

A mentoring relationship with young Latin@ church leaders begins with a consideration of their contextual realities and continues with taking seriously these leaders' own experiences. With that knowledge as a foundation, mentors facilitate these young leaders' formation processes and accompany their contextual practices. In light of the contextual realities of Latin@s, specifically the inherent limitations of their involvement in church leadership and their underrepresentation in academia, I suggest that mentoring Latin@ youth is a contextual evangelistic task of the pastor-scholar, a task that facilitates the youth's critical consciousness and access to new places and spaces. In the case of church leaders, the essential theological contextual practice is the choosing of life (Deut. 30:19). Mentors facilitate spaces and processes where Latin@s are able to recognize God's greatest gift (life) and "choose life" so that they and their families can survive and claim the fullness of life communicated in the gospel (John 10:10). I propose a relationship between facilitating and *acompañamiento*, as driving elements of mentoring, that needs to be permeated with a praxis of justice and deeply rooted in the essence of life.

Facilitating

The key practice of facilitating in mentoring Latin@s has to do with making accessible new geographical places and social spaces to find means of articulating their own problematized realities as well as the social conditions of their communities. For new places and spaces allow them to reconsider their present circumstances, share their understandings and experiences, learn their own history that is typically not made available through the educational systems, consider the Scriptures from their own perspectives and experiences, dialogue with others who resist injustice and practice the appropriation of hope for a better reality. Facilitating is an incremental process of forming leaders who will be able to resist epistemological erasure. The prophetic message of Hosea notes that "people are destroyed for lack of knowledge" (Hos. 4:6); access to new places and spaces provides opportunities for the retrieval of cultural knowledge. With time, this will form individuals and communities where Latin@s are able to practice their leadership skills and begin to ask questions.

As a mentor, I recognize that Latin@ high school students who graduate and make it to college learn to manage institutional power dynamics even if they are not consciously aware of the racist systemic designs. And I understand that Latin@ students who graduate from college and access graduate programs and church leadership beyond their local congregations become experts in the management of institutional processes. Most mentoring literature on Latin@ students attributes this management to resilience and the ability to solve problems, understanding at least two cultures with the ability to exist in both without prioritizing one over the other, and a sense of purpose nurtured by family and significant individuals in their lives who serve as role models and/or mentors.[14] Successful students of this type are able to glean what anchors their social location and what practices can facilitate cultural translation and contextual practices. They are able to tap into meaningful and relevant cultural resources to survive, live, and even thrive within racist institutional power dynamics in spite of their problematized realities.

Latin@s have survived the fragmentation of their indigenous cultures. Protestant Latin@s have survived the fragmentation of Christianity on this continent. Fragmentation is a way of life typically considered to be a disadvantage, a state of marginalization. However, it can also be considered an asset, a contextual resource for Latin@s in leadership. The management of fragmentation requires flexibility, adaptability, a constant state of cultural tension and flux, in order to survive and establish some kind of life-sustaining process. A mentor facilitates access to, and appropriation of, useful fragments that inform the conditions of all the descendants of the colonized and encourages a redeployment of such fragments as epistemological anchors for their humanity. Linda Tuhiwai Smith notes the importance of marginal spaces for the retrieval of such anchoring cultural resources:

> The problem is that constant efforts by governments, states, societies and institutions to deny the historical formations of such conditions have simultaneously denied our claims to humanity, to having a history, and to all

14. Andrew Garrod, Robert Kilkenny, and Cristina Gomez, eds., *Mi Voz, Mi Vida: Latino College Students Tell Their Life Stories* (New York: Cornell University Press, 2007), 2–9. See Eleazar S. Fernández, ed., *Teaching for a Culturally Diverse and Racially Just World* (Eugene, OR: Cascade, 2014); and Sue Grace and Phil Gravestock, *Inclusion and Diversity: Meeting the Needs of All Students* (New York: Routledge, 2009).

sense of hope. To acquiesce is to lose ourselves entirely and implicitly agree with all that has been said about us. To resist is to retrench in the margins, retrieve "what we were and remake ourselves." The past, our stories local and global, the present, our communities, cultures, languages and social practices—all may be spaces of marginalization, but they have also become spaces of resistance and hope.[15]

In order to consider meaningful and relevant mentoring approaches for new generations of Latin@ leadership, one must consider that identity-formation and cultural resources for these young leaders are rooted in indigenous epistemologies that are absent from most academic settings and preached against in most mainline religious institutions. Mentors facilitate retrieval of cultural and historical fragments about Mesoamerica that inform leadership-formation processes. For example, indigenous cultures of Mesoamerica had very complex pictographic and codex-based rhetoric that "required use of the entire body through choreography, recitation, chanting, and choral production."[16] The Aztec Empire used a complex pictographic Nahuatl language where each word had at least two contextually fluctuating conceptual meanings relating to time, physical space, and the divine-human relationship.[17]

As a mentor I consider that the indigenous cosmological complexity survived to be encoded in the Mestizo bodies of Latin@s. The practice of graffiti and other sophisticated art forms that visual artivists use, for example, have to do with the Mesoamerican writing systems.[18] In *Mestiz@ Scripts*, Damián Baca explains:

Mesoamerican writing is considered to be "semasiographic," a configuration of permanently recorded marks that signify thought, ideas, and

15. Smith, *Decolonizing Methodologies*, 4.

16. Damián Baca, *Mestiz@ Scripts, Digital Migrations, and the Territories of Writing* (New York: Palgrave Macmillan, 2008), 72.

17. Juan Diego was part of the Nahuatl people, one of the groups of indigenous peoples in the Americas at the time of the Spanish conquest. The Nahuatl language used *Flor y Canto* ("flower and song") as a style of communicating, a combination of flowers, dance, and music associated with divine presence. The Mesoamerican writing (means of communicating visually) involved sophisticated drawing and translating skills. See Baca, *Mestiz@ Scripts*, 72–73; and Davíd Carrasco, *Religions of Mesoamerica: Cosmovision and Ceremonial Centers* (Long Grove, IL: Waveland, 1990), 77–85.

18. Artivism is a compound of the words *art* and *activism*. It is used by different artists to identify their art as a form of activism.

imagery rather than visible speech. Notably, this writing practice fuses into a single symbolic account what for Western minds are separate and hierarchical concepts of annotation and illustration. While early Mexicans did designate some symbols to voice specific words, their larger graphic system did not correspond directly with spoken language. Because the symbols did not replicate any single linguistic system, speakers of *Nahuatl, Yucatecan, Mixtec, Zapotec,* and *Quiche Maya* had the advantage of translating the pictographs into their own respective tongue. Readers mediated a combination of naturalistic images, pictorial conventions, and abstract symbols that were recorded within an organized structure. By knowing the basic conventions and the meanings of the symbols and recognizing their arrangements, readers interpreted the pictographic messages. A precise reading order is not set, however, so that different readings and interpretations remain possible.[19]

Facilitating access to knowledge about the Mesoamerican worldview, information about historical processes in the Americas, and acquisition of tools for reading the particularities of their own contextual realities is an evangelistic task for those involved in church leadership formation with Latin@ youth. The implications of this knowledge are beyond the scope of this chapter. However, a question that I consider as a mentor of Nahuatl descent has to do with the possible limitations of Christianity to attend, in a meaningful and relevant manner, to identity-formation processes of Latin@s. The introduction of Christianity itself problematized the present reality of Latin@s, and Christian practices today are substantially permeated with racist attitudes. Most important is the recognition that my Nahuatl traditions extend to a time before the establishment of Christianity. In light of that, I wonder whether the traditions of Christianity and its contemporary practices can even facilitate identity-formation processes and transformative practices for Latin@s.

Acompañamiento

In his writing about Mexican migrant youth at Bosque High School, Enrique Sepúlveda points out that most educators fail to ask, "What do these transnational subjects know? What are their critiques of the new global order? What

19. Baca, *Mestiz@ Scripts,* 69.

are their needs and concerns?"[20] He explicates the importance of recognizing, in any accompanying process with students, that they are already learning and making their own interpretations about complex issues and situations outside the classroom.[21] As a mentor, I consider that most relevant cultural learning for Latin@ students happens outside the classroom, through collective experiences with each other and leadership in their communities. Their life experience, engagement with each other, and dialogue with community and church leadership are opportunities for the processing and contextualization of classroom theories and the appropriation of relevant knowledge and serve as platforms for the identification of useful institutional survival tools.

Powerful life experiences inform and motivate acquisition of new knowledge within formal institutional processes for Latin@ students. Once when I called my daughter when she was in her first year of undergraduate education, she answered the phone in a very soft voice. Concerned about the softness in her tone, I asked, "What are you doing?" She answered, "I am in the library complementing my education." She explained that she "did not believe" what was presented in one of her classes and she was looking for more information "to know for real." Conversations like this confirm that the practice of accompaniment in mentoring needs to be rooted in the basic Freirean understanding that individuals are not blank slates or empty containers waiting to be filled with selective information. Wise mentors realize that their mentees already have a wealth of knowledge, survival skills, and management tools gleaned in the process of their formation, long before the mentor shows up.[22]

Accompaniment as a practice of mentoring begins with this recognition of knowledge and skills that Latin@s already possess. In my own practice, this recognition communicates my respect for their being and wisdom. This recognition also demonstrates—right up front—my own intelligence. I regard this recognition as currency for mutual space, an invitation for the possibilities of dialogue, and a relevant mentoring relationship within institutional processes. In the spirit of the Canaanite woman in the gospel narrative who pushes Jesus and his disciples to pause and reconsider her and her child (Matt.

20. Enrique Sepúlveda III, "Toward a Pedagogy of Acompañamiento: Mexican Migrant Youth Writing from the Underside of Modernity," *Harvard Educational Review* 81.3 (Fall 2011): 551.

21. Patricia Sanchez, "Urban Immigrant Students: How Transnationalism Shapes Their World Learning," *Urban Review* 39.5 (2007): 489–517.

22. Paulo Freire was a world-renowned Brazilian educator who laid the ground for the critical importance of popular education and pedagogies of liberation.

15:21–28), I model the appropriation of space for reconsideration. The institutional process is interrupted, and I, as faculty with a space of privilege in the institution, facilitate the space for a reconsideration of possible cultural resources and life-giving spaces in academia. I asked one of my students to share with me a statement about mentoring. She called these facilitated spaces a safe haven: "Graduate school is challenging overall, but it comes with a distinct set of struggles for Latino/a students and other students of color. I see mentoring as a practice of *acompañamiento* that lightens the burden of these struggles. Here both mentor and mentee embark on a journey of support and accountability. An element I consider to be important in this pairing is the meaningful relationship that can stem from it. A successful mentorship creates a resourceful space of encouragement and relatability, sets clear and realistic goals, and can turn into a safe haven."[23]

In the curriculum design for HYLA and RLLI, the recognition of young leaders' already acquired wisdom is embedded in the strategic identification of Latin@ faculty and clergy who respect students' abilities, affirm their cultural traditions, and recognize their leadership and potential. Such faculty and clergy are recruited to serve as leaders for seminarians and other graduate students. The selected group of faculty and clergy then helps to identify graduate students who can join the leadership teams to lead and mentor college students. Graduate students in turn help identify and select the college students who become summer interns and lead and mentor high school students. Students acquire or refine their skills of facilitation and accompaniment both by experiencing them as participants and by practicing them while accompanied by those who have more experience. Everyone facilitates access to particular spaces and accompanies contextual leadership-formation practices within new and established relationships. According to Freire, these spaces become cultural spaces that support personal development, foster intellectual growth, and inspire collective organizing through what Sepúlveda calls "a pedagogy of *acompañamiento*."[24]

Acompañamiento in mentoring is more than walking with others, more than empathy. In *Caminemos con Jesus*, theologian Roberto S. Goizueta considers, from a Latin American liberation-theology perspective, the preferential option for the poor in relation to struggles for social justice. He notes that the act of *acompañamiento* includes being, feeling, and doing with another. This

---

23. Yara González-Justiniano (graduate student), personal interview by Cristian De La Rosa, Boston, May 26, 2016.

24. Sepúlveda, "Toward a Pedagogy of Acompañamiento," 552.

conceptualization involves a relationship with the "other" that "incorporates both the ethical-political and the aesthetic dimensions of human praxis" producing "communal action."[25] As he works toward a theology of accompaniment, he identifies the social, historical, ethical, and political dimensions of *acompañamiento* from a liberation perspective:

> To be in relationship with others and, therefore, to be a human person is to walk with others. The notion of "walking with" incorporates both the ethical-political and the aesthetic dimensions of human praxis. It is, first of all, a concrete, physical, historical act. The act of walking implies directionality: one walks in a particular direction. That directionality implies, in turn, an ethical-political content: implicit in the act of walking are the questions, "In which direction?" "How is the direction determined?" And "Who determines the direction?" These are ethical-political questions.[26]

Goizueta gleans from ethicist and Mujerista theologian Ada María Isasi-Díaz's conceptualization of solidarity and love of neighbor. She questions the interpretation of the gospel message "to love our neighbors" that leads to the practice of charity and points out "that love of neighbor is linked intrinsically and foremost to justice." The centrality of justice in the loving of our neighbor fosters agency—not charity—that identifies solidarity as a character virtue. In her elaboration of solidarity and the practice of love of neighbor in the twenty-first century, Isasi-Díaz concludes that solidarity is the new way of living out the gospel message: "It is an attitude and disposition that greatly influences how we act. As a virtue, solidarity becomes a way of life." Therefore, in light of more "than two-thirds of the people in the world liv[ing] under terrible oppressive conditions," we need to redefine love of neighbor and the demands this new interpretation and way of life place on us if we want to "continue to claim the centrality" of this gospel message.[27]

25. Roberto Goizueta, *Caminemos con Jesus* (Maryknoll, NY: Orbis, 1995), 206.

26. Goizueta, *Caminemos con Jesus*, 206.

27. Ada María Isasi-Díaz speaks about mutuality as a way toward solidarity as it is a strategy for equal interaction and dignity among people; see *Mujerista Theology* (Maryknoll, NY: Orbis, 1996), 100–102.

Conclusion

Latin@s are among the fastest growing underrepresented minority in higher education, and their participation in the church remains limited, particularly in mainline Protestant denominations. However, "Latinos are now the largest minority group in the United States, forty-two million individuals, or approximately 14 percent of the population. By 2050, the US Census estimates, one out of four individuals living in the United States will be of Latino heritage."[28] For that reason alone, we ought to pay attention to this significant population.

The realities and identities of Latin@s, who are descendants of the colonized in the Americas, are very complex. Institutions of higher education and the institutional church, particularly mainline Protestant denominations, need to consider that the formation processes and social agencies of Latin@s today are problematized by embedded racist institutional attitudes that emerged from the conquest and colonizing processes through which Christianity was introduced into the Americas. In light of this problematized and complex context, relevant designs of leadership-formation initiatives and mentoring programs begin with the recognition that Latin@s come to the table with significant knowledge and skills acquired through life experience. In this context, two components of mentoring that can be particularly helpful are facilitation and *acompañamiento*: facilitating places and spaces for Latin@s' epistemological retrieval of Mesoamerican cultural traditions that inform their identity formation and serve as resources in the management of fragmentation, and *acompañamiento* as solidarity that generates collective ethical and political praxis.

In the work of Enrique Sepúlveda with Mexican migrant youth at Bosque High School, these considerations are taken into account in the pedagogical approach rooted in a process of accompaniment. Combining the arts, cognitive skills, affective skills, and a reconceptualization of *acompañamiento* informed by Freire's pedagogical approaches and Goizueta's ethical-theological frameworks transformed the spaces for teaching and relationships with students at that school. Sepúlveda explains the practice of *acompañamiento* in relationship to students' agency and the facilitating work of faculty:

> *Acompañamiento* was an organic, hybrid cultural form and educational practice of adaptation and assistance born out of a deep sense of empathy, a place where people came together to dialogue on their most pressing concerns and to support each other as they made their way in their new

28. Garrod, Kilkenny, and Gomez, *Mi Voz, Mi Vida*, 1.

school and country. It emerged because fellow human beings were in need of community and deeper relationships. Far from being the passive receptors of global modernity, *acompañamiento* represents the creative acts of a people making space, creating place, and building community in an increasingly fragmented global world.[29]

In the experience of HYLA, facilitating and *acompañamiento* as the driving forces of mentoring practices can nurture generations of emerging Latin@ church leaders. HYLA's curriculum is contextual and includes identity formation, discernment of call, and preparation for higher education and church leadership. Participants find the space to consider pressing social issues relevant to their circumstances. The first generation of HYLA high school graduates facilitated the reorganizing of the national coordinating leadership team's work in 2011 and articulated a new mission. While in college and working with an equal number of high school students as part of a special convocation to evaluate and plan for the future of HYLA, they established new procedures and the following mission:

> We, the Hispanic★ Youth Leadership Academy (HYLA), are a coalition of United Methodist Youth/Young Adult student leaders. Our mission is to discern our call to ministry through the pursuit of higher education, awareness of social issues, spiritual and mental growth, and our awakening as leaders. We develop our leadership skills as we discover our passion through practice within The United Methodist Church and our individual communities. We unite together in solidarity through our common Latin@ experience and are committed to help the Pueblo Latino★★ regardless of legal status in order to transform the world.

★It is by the consensus of HYLA that we identify ourselves as Latin@s but continue to use the term Hispanic due to the historical formation of the academy and the use of this word to describe our community within society. In addition, we recognize that the name HYLA is well known and regarded within the UMC and in our communities.
★★ As articulated by the Real Academia Espanola, the masculine term Latino is inclusive of both Latino and Latina communities.
@2011 National leadership team of HYLA

This mission of HYLA addresses the needs and circumstances of the Latin@ communities and the particularities of young Latin@ leaders in the

29. Sepúlveda, "Toward a Pedagogy of Acompañamiento," 568.

church. It embodies the practices of facilitating and *acompañamiento* framed in this chapter and strongly demonstrates the agency of the students and their intentionality in bridging the church, the academy, and their communities through their leadership and commitment to transformation.

Mentoring initiatives with Latin@s are meaningful and relevant when they consider the importance of epistemological retrieval from Mesoamerican worldviews, when they respect and love the other as their neighbor, and when they build on the wisdom already in place. When these essential elements are overlooked or ignored in any formation process with Latin@s, established (and typically racist) institutional power dynamics and attitudes are strengthened and participants become complicit with oppressive powers in this world through institutional processes they are invited to transform.

CHAPTER 11

Mentoring Perspectives from East Asia

Kwok Pui-lan

When I was a doctoral student in Boston in the 1980s, womanist ethicist Dr. Katie Geneva Cannon gathered a small group of women of color to discuss our work and the issues we faced in church and academy. Coming as I did from Hong Kong, these meetings offered me incredible insights into American academic life and the reality of living as racial and ethnic minority in the United States. The cross-racial group became a supportive network and provided mentoring opportunities to learn about strategies for navigating racism in predominantly white institutions. Over the years, I was fortunate to have mentors who offered advice when I considered job prospects, applied for foundation grants, encountered difficulties in teaching, and dealt with racism in institutions. They also offered me effective models of mentoring.

Since becoming a seasoned scholar, I have had the privilege of mentoring Asian and Asian American students and junior scholars.[1] They are very diverse in terms of gender, ethnicity, language, culture, age, class, family background, and sexuality. Some of them have become established scholars and teachers and have collaborated with me on various projects. I have learned much from them, for I believe that mentoring always involves two-way traffic—both sides grow and benefit from the relationship.

---

1. I have been involved in Pacific, Asian, North American Asian Women in Theology and Ministry and the Asian Theological Summer Institute. I have also directed Asian and Asian American pre-tenure faculty workshops for the Wabash Center for Teaching and Learning.

Mentoring Asian and Asian American Students

Asian and Asian American students have vastly different life experiences, educational background, national and cultural identities, and reactions to teachers and mentors.[2] It is important to bear these differences in mind when mentoring them. Asian students identify themselves primarily with their country of origin, nationality, and cultural backgrounds. Many of them are highly motivated students and academic achievers in their home countries, which are the reasons why they are admitted to graduate schools in the United States. But once in the United States, they quickly find out that the American academic culture, defined by individualism, competition, and speaking up in class, is different from what they are used to. Many students struggle to express themselves in English, while adjusting to the American classroom. Some lose self-confidence because of the pressure to catch up and the poorer grades they receive compared to their grades at home.

Although the educational system has been changing in some Asian countries, the pedagogy is still largely teacher-centered, with lecturing the dominant mode of instruction. Education means the impact of knowledge, much like the banking model described by Paulo Freire.[3] Students are asked to regurgitate what they have learned from the lectures and textbooks and seldom encouraged to express their own ideas or viewpoints. Because of such schooling, Asian students often find it difficult to participate in US classroom discussion. Some of them have to translate what is being said into their own context before they can come up with adequate responses. It often takes them more time to think of what to say, and when they find the courage to speak, the discussion may have moved on to another topic. They also fear appearing foolish by making mistakes in public such as errors in grammar and pronunciation. The difficulty of speaking in public is compounded because of gender and class.

Those who have grown up in Confucian culture are taught to respect their teachers and elders as authority figures. Researchers show that some of

2. For a discussion of the differences between Asian and Asian North American students, see Rita Nakashima Brock et al., "Developing Teaching Materials and Instructional Strategies for Teaching Asian and Asian American/Canadian Women's Theologies in North America," Final Report of a Teaching and Learning in Theological Education Project submitted to the Association of Theological Schools (November 1999), 17–18. Available at www.panaawtm.org /presentations-papers-research.

3. Paulo Freire, "The 'Banking' Concept of Education," in *Ways of Reading: An Anthology for Writers*, ed. David Bartholomae and Anthony Petrosky, 8th ed. (Boston: St. Martin's, 2008), 242–54.

the characteristics of Asian culture (e.g., status hierarchy, emotional/verbal re-
strictions, and interdependence) may pose barriers in establishing mentoring
relationships with authority figures. Students who live in America but hold on
to Asian values might have difficulties in connecting with a mentoring figure
because of conflicting cultural expectations. Whereas Euro-Americans are socialized to express openly their needs and initiate relationships with authority
figures, Asian students are socialized to be more restrictive and deferential in
various ways. They may not take the initiative to form mentoring relationships,
and potential mentors, most of them Euro-Americans because of the lack of
Asian faculty members, may not be aware of the cultural differences and assume
that these students are not interested in forming mentoring relationships.[4]

Asian American students may or may not share these Asian values depending on their ethnicity, immigration history, socialization, and generational background. Unlike Asian students, Asian American students grow up
as racial and ethnic minorities and have very different life experiences. One
of the stereotypes about Asian Americans is that they are perpetual foreigners,
even though they were born in the United States and their families have been
in the United States for generations. Asian American students have to negotiate their hybrid identities of being Asian and American in a predominantly
white culture. Some of them insist that they are Americans and downplay
the connection with Asia in order to avoid the perpetual foreigner label.
Others want to reclaim their Asian identity and heritage as a way to coun-
teract racism in the United States, defined largely by black and white. But
they are not considered authentic Asians, because they may not speak Asian
languages fluently and have not been immersed in Asian cultures. However,
in the politics of US multiculturalism, they are expected to put their Asian
culture on display, such as introducing ethnic festivals, bringing ethnic foods,
and putting on ethnic costumes as symbolic representations of diversity.[5]

Asian Americans are stereotyped also as model minority, a myth that pits
Asian Americans against other racial and ethnic minority groups. As model
minority, Asian Americans are "singled out as a group that has successfully
assimilated into American society, becoming financially well off and achieving
the American Dream."[6] In school, they are seen as overachievers: hardwork-

4. Bell Liang et al., "Mentoring Asian and Euro-American College Women," *Journal of
Multicultural Counseling and Development* 34.3 (2006): 151–52.

5. Gale A. Yee, "'She Stood in Tears amid the Alien Corn': Ruth, the Perpetual Foreigner,
and Model Minority," in *Off the Menu: Asian and Asian North American Women's Religion and
Theology*, ed. Rita Nakashima Brock et al. (Louisville: Westminster John Knox, 2007), 45.

6. Yee, "'She Stood in Tears amid the Alien Corn,'" 50.

ing, cooperative, compliant, and not troublemakers. Their parents were stereo-typed as acting like tiger mothers: placing a high premium on their children's education and pushing them to succeed.[7] Such expectations have exerted a lot of pressure on Asian American students, who suffer from achievement stress. Because of the myth of model minority, teachers expect Asian Ameri-can students to do well and find support in their families and communities. As a result, Asian American students who fall outside the model-minority myth are doubly suspect, and their needs for support and mentoring may be overlooked.

Confucian Perspectives on Mentoring

In East Asia, the Confucian tradition has influenced teaching, learning, and mentoring for millennia. It was traditionally believed that Confucius had three thousand students, and he was a mentor to seventy-two disciples who belonged to his inner circle. Confucius's disciples and followers later compiled the *Analects* to preserve the teachings of the master, a book that has played a foundational role in understanding the Confucian tradition.[8] The *Analects* is a record of conversation between Confucius and his disciples within the context of a mentoring relationship. In the Confucius tradition, mentoring involves the development of the whole person: intellectual capacity, moral formation, interpersonal and communal relationships, and contribution to society. One does not exist as an autonomous individual, but exists in a network of relationships, extending from the family and the nation to the whole universe. A central focus of the Confucian tradition is self-cultivation (*xiushen*), which means a self-reflective understanding of the self.[9] Through the process of self-cultivation, a person develops his or her moral virtues and character and harmonizes his or her network of relationships. The key virtues of being a human are benevolence (*ren*), righteousness (*yi*), ritual propriety (*li*), and wisdom (*zhi*).

The *Analects* is in the form of conversation and dialogue. Confucius's teaching was not didactic, but conversational in style, and he used many con-crete examples. When he described his teaching, he used the word *hui*, which

7. Amy Chua's bestselling book *Battle Hymn of the Tiger Mother* (New York: Penguin, 2011) created a controversy on Chinese and American styles of parenting.

8. Confucius, *The Analects*, trans. D. C. Lau (New York: Penguin, 1998).

9. Tu Weiming, *Humanity and Self-Cultivation: Essays in Confucian Thought* (Boston: Cheng & Tsui, 1998).

means "by way of imparting light" or "throwing light." The term *xun*, which refers to teaching "by means of giving a lesson or a lecture," does not appear in the *Analects*. It is possible that Confucius was not disposed toward making long lectures or speaking in front of an audience.[10] Instead, his students would bring questions and problems to the master, but sometimes Confucius initiated questions. Within a mentoring relationship, Confucius would encourage active discussion of ethics in practice, with participants offering opinions and receiving correction or encouragement.[11] Confucius paid attention to the individual disciples, and his answers were tailored to their needs. A group of researchers said, "Taking both the knowledge level and personality traits of individual students into account, [Confucius] would often give different responses to the same question, or advise contrary courses of action for the same problem posed."[12] Thus, Confucius practiced individualized teaching and customized curriculum long before our time, as he mentored according to the disciples' potential.

The Confucian tradition emphasizes teaching and mentoring by example. In *The Courage to Teach*, Parker Palmer argues that it is the inner life and the integrity of the teacher, rather than teaching techniques or skills, that make teaching effective.[13] Confucian scholars would agree completely. The authority of a Confucian mentor is derived from "achieved authority," based on the knowledge, personal integrity, and quality of life of the mentor, in addition to "ascribed authority," based on the teacher's social status, rank, age, or gender.[14] The nurture of a moral person takes practice, and the Confucian virtue of wisdom (*zhi*) includes not only learning but also an ability to perceive situations accurately and make sound judgments.[15] A mentor who has the knowledge and can demonstrate how to apply it in concrete situations will become an effective role model for students.

Confucius established close and long-term relationships with students

10. Annping Chin, *The Authentic Confucius: A Life of Thought and Politics* (New York: Scribner, 2007), 147.

11. Peter R. Woods and David A. Lamond, "A Confucian Approach to Developing Ethical Self-Regulation in Management"; available at www98.griffith.edu.au/dspace/bitstream /handle/10072/40042/71443_1.pdf;jsessionid=B1DE1B0CC15EE5F91CE3740BB91D3F99? sequence=1 (accessed March 23, 2016).

12. Brock et al., "Developing Teaching Materials," 10.

13. Parker J. Palmer, *The Courage to Teach: Exploring the Inner Landscape of a Teacher's Life* (San Francisco: Jossey-Bass, 1998).

14. Brock et al., "Developing Teaching Materials," 10.

15. Woods and Lamond, "Confucian Approach," 3.

so that he could know them well and offer them sound advice. For example, Confucius was very close to his favorite student Yan Hui, who was thirty years his junior. Of all of Confucius's disciples, Yan Hui was most eager to learn, and Confucius praised him for his virtues. After Yan Hui died, Confucius was bereft and said no one could replace him, because Yan truly understood his teaching.[16] Following Confucius's example, other Confucian scholars set up academies and schools to teach students and pass on their wisdom. The teachers advised students not only about academic pursuits, but also about career advancement and personal issues. The mentees were grateful for the long-term support they received from their mentors.

The Confucian approach to mentoring has many good points, but it has also been criticized for fostering social hierarchy and blind obedience to authority figures. In the Confucian moral order, power and authority are defined by one's social status: the ruler has power over his subjects, the father has power over his son, and the husband has power over his wife. These dyad relationships are hierarchal, and not reciprocal. In a mentoring relationship, the mentee is expected to obey and follow the mentor. The Confucian respect for social order and authority figures has been used by repressive regimes in East Asia to justify their actions. But to Confucius's credit, he told his best students to hold their own under certain circumstances even at the risk of contradicting him. "When encountering matters that involve [the basic principles] of humanity," Confucius said, "do not yield even to your teacher."[17]

The Confucian tradition has also been criticized for its attitudes toward women. Since only men were accepted into Confucius's circle of students, women's lives and issues did not form part of this great teacher's curriculum. Traditionally, women were not given the same opportunities to study as men, and their social roles were limited. A woman's place was in the home, since the highest ideals for women were to be virtuous wives and good mothers. Modernization has brought dramatic changes to East Asian societies, and women's status has been much improved. However, women still do not enjoy equal status with men socially, economically, and politically.

16. Chin, *Authentic Confucius*, 73–74.
17. Chin, *Authentic Confucius*, 145.

Cultural Adaptation and Negotiation

Students who have grown up influenced by the Confucian tradition have a lot to adjust to in the American academic context. Much has been written on the silence of Asian and Asian American students in the classroom.[18] While a low level of English proficiency may force some Asian students to be silent in class, other cultural factors are at work. Students may lack the knowledge of American academic culture and of the dynamics of classroom requirements. They do not come from an educational system in which speaking and participating in class would earn a better grade. Some of them may even be socialized to think that one is not supposed to say too much and view negatively students who are too outspoken. American students frequently bring issues of their home, family members, and workplaces into the classroom. Many Asian and Asian American students would confide personal matters only to close friends and are reticent to bring them up in class. Asian students may also be concerned that American students have little knowledge of their context and may even harbor negative stereotypes of their culture. They are therefore hesitant to share what they know.[19]

The students' silence deprives them of opportunities to ask questions, clarify what has been said, and offer a different point of view. At the same time, their silence deprives the teacher and classmates of the opportunities to learn what they know. To remedy this, researcher Carol A. Tateishi suggests that the teachers can clarify their assumptions about learning and speaking in class, such as "oral language can be used to negotiate meaning, risk-taking in talk is valued, speaking in class increases engagement, and classroom dialogue deepens learning."[20] The teachers can create a range of communication channels and different modes of participation, including discussion, debate, analysis, and brainstorming. They need to create a classroom climate that

---

18. For example, Jun Liu, *Asian Students' Classroom Communication Patterns in U.S. Universities: An Emic Perspective* (Westport, CT: Ablex, 2001); Ikuko Nakane, "Negotiating Silence and Speech in the Classroom," *Multilingua* 24.1–2 (2005): 75–100; and Carol A. Tateishi, "Taking a Chance with Words: Why Are the Asian American Kids Silent in Class?," *Rethinking Schools* 22.2 (Winter 2007–8); available at rethinkingschools.org/archive/22_02/word222.shtml (accessed March 26, 2016).

19. Tateishi, "Taking a Chance with Words"; and Krishna Bista, "A First-person Explanation of Why Some International Students Are Silent in the U.S. Classroom," *Faculty Focus*; available at facultyfocus.com/articles/learning-styles/a-first-person-explanation-of-why-some-international-students-are-silent-in-the-u-s-classroom/ (accessed March 26, 2016).

20. Tateishi, "Taking a Chance with Words."

values students' contributions, such as the use of small groups with group leaders, so that students will feel less intimidated in speaking.

American higher education, especially at the graduate level, values highly creative and original thinking. But Asian students, because of their schooling, have not been encouraged to develop and articulate their own point of view. Even though these students have tried very hard, they may still receive lower grades in the United States than at home and feel disappointed. Noted cognitive scientist Howard E. Gardner studied creativity in cross-cultural contexts, drawing from the US educational tradition, his long study of creativity at Harvard, and what he saw in Chinese classrooms. He observed that in art education in China, students were required to imitate and model after famous painters in order to master the necessary skills. Only after they have practiced for a long time and acquired those skills would they be open to exploration and doing something new. This is directly opposite to the liberal, child-centered American educational philosophy, which encourages discovery and ingenuity. Gardner elaborates the cultural difference in the context of Confucian philosophy and the long history of the hierarchical ordering of Chinese society. But Gardner does not think the American system is necessarily better. He was trained to play the piano as a child and knows the importance of practice and acquiring skills. As someone who pioneers in the study of multiple intelligences, Gardner suggests a middle-of-the-road approach for American education, one that could benefit from greater emphasis on skills, while allowing for exploratory do-it-yourself behaviors that encourage individual cognitive styles and creativity.[21]

For Asian and Asian American students, this means that they have to develop their critical thinking and not just accept what the authorities have said. Students who come from conservative Christian backgrounds and believe in biblical authority find it difficult to critically reflect on their faith and ask questions. For some, asking questions would mean that they do not have enough faith. But Anselm defines theology as "faith seeking understanding," which affirms that critical thinking and reasoning are important intellectual tools. The word *critical* comes from the Greek word *krinein*, meaning "to separate; to choose; to decide; to judge; to interpret."[22] The term *critical*, Lucretia Yaghjian explains, "implies an interrogative, consciously reflective process

---

21. Howard E. Gardner, *To Open Minds: Chinese Clues to the Dilemma of Contemporary Education* (New York: Basic Books, 1989).

22. Lucretia B. Yaghjian, *Writing Theology Well: A Rhetoric for Theological and Biblical Writers* (New York: Continuum, 2006), 67.

that engages the writer and the reader in *analysis, evaluation,* and *critique* of the problem, text, or other subject matter addressed."[23] Critical thinking does not mean that one always disagrees with what is said or written, but one must examine the data, exercise judgment, and form one's own conclusions. In fact, Confucius encouraged his students to be inquisitive by asking questions and applying what they have learned to concrete cases. He even said that the students could contradict him in certain circumstances.

It takes courage to stake out one's position and be creative because it involves taking risks. In a society in which one is expected to conform to social norms, risk-taking may bring shame to oneself and one's family. China and Japan have been labeled shame societies, whereas American society is seen as a guilt society.[24] Paul G. Hiebert characterizes a shame society as follows:

> Shame is a reaction to other people's criticism, an acute personal chagrin at our failure to live up to our obligations and the expectations others have of us. In true shame oriented cultures, every person has a place and a duty in the society. One maintains self-respect, not by choosing what is good rather than what is evil, but by choosing what is expected of one.[25]

In a shame society, collectivity is more important than individuality, and there is tremendous pressure to follow the crowd. There is less incentive and encouragement to be original and to act outside the norm for fear of alienation and censorship.

Asian students are afraid of making mistakes or failing because they do not want to lose face, which means the loss of respect of others or the experience of public disgrace. Influenced by a shame culture, they often take criticism personally and suffer the hurt privately, instead of reaching out to seek help. I often encourage these students to see negative criticism not as targeting them as a person ("you are a bad person"), but as an evaluation of their performance ("your work needs improvement"). In this way, they can focus on improving the skills or crafts to be learned and not internalize the shame as if their personality is under attack. I share the experience that I had as a graduate student. One of my professors corrected the grammatical mistakes in my final paper in addition to giving feedback on the contents.

23. Yaghjian, *Writing Theology Well,* 67 (emphasis original).

24. This idea was popularized by Ruth Benedict, *The Chrysanthemum and the Sword: Patterns of Japanese Culture* (Boston: Houghton Mifflin, 1946). Her theory has been debated in scholarly circles.

25. Paul G. Hiebert, *Anthropological Insights for Missionaries* (Grand Rapids: Baker, 1985), 212.

At first, I was so ashamed of making those grammatical mistakes. But on second thought, I appreciated the time and effort the professor had devoted to my work. She showed that she cared for my learning and did not lower her standards and expectations because I was an international student. Since then, I have paid much more attention to the craft of writing and have consulted many books on writing well. Books on writing by Amy Tan, Anne Lamott, and Stephen King showed me writing is a craft to be learned, and it takes a lot of effort even for these established authors.[26] Just as in creating any art, the development of one's individual and unique writing voice needs much learning, practice, coaching, and openness to receiving feedback.[27]

Asian and Asian American students need different kinds of advice and support to survive and flourish. W. Anne Joh distinguishes between advising and mentoring and says that while these two functions are not mutually exclusive, they are also not synonymous. While an advisor is usually someone from the student's home institution, a mentor need not be because they perform different functions. She writes: "An advisor with cultural competency best serves the needs of students by negotiating and navigating their particular institutional culture and the specific requirements of their program. On the other hand, a mentor often offers more general support, critical feedback, and, significantly, contribution to the student's scholarly formation and self-identity."[28] Sometimes, a mentor can provide a much-needed outsider's perspective and encouragement when a student encounters problems working with the advisor or the home institution. It is difficult to find such a mentor who takes an active interest in the student's well-being, but some seasoned scholars are willing to invest in the next generation of Asian and Asian American scholars. They can be approached by recommendation or through professional guilds and social networks.

26. Amy Tan, *The Opposite of Fate: A Book of Musings* (New York: Putnam, 2003); Anne Lamott, *Bird by Bird: Some Instructions on Writing and Life* (New York: Pantheon, 1994); and Stephen King, *On Writing: A Memoir of the Craft* (New York: Scribner, 2000).

27. See my blogpost "Asian Theological Summer Institute"; available at kwokpuilan.blog spot.com/2013/06/asian-theological-summer-institute.html (accessed March 27, 2016).

28. W. Anne Joh, "Mentoring Models with Promise," American Academy of Religion; available at aarweb.org/publications/rsn-october-2013-mentoring-models-with-promise (accessed March 28, 2016).

Mentoring Asian and Asian American Faculty

The classroom is shaped by the culture of the larger society, and many students bring their racial and cultural stereotypes with them to class. Some have never had an Asian or Asian American faculty member teaching them. The cultural stereotypes or even fantasies are projected onto the racial body of the Asian and Asian American faculty person, even before he or she begins to teach. For example, Asian women are portrayed in the media as gentle, sexy, and lacking authority, while Asian men are portrayed as kung fu heroes or sidekicks to white American stars. Asian and Asian American faculty have to challenge these myths and stereotypes to gain credibility in their teaching. A group of educational researchers defines teacher credibility as a composite of character, sociability, composure, extroversion, and competence.[29] This definition underlines the differences in the conception of teacher credibility in American and East Asian cultures. In American culture, credibility includes the qualities of being sociable and relatable to students, whereas in East Asia, credibility is usually defined by the teacher's knowledge of the subject and competence. This means that even though Asian and Asian American faculty members may devote a lot of time to the contents of the subject, preteaching preparation, and organization of material, they cannot be effective and gain credibility without being conscious of and adjusting to the students' cultural expectations.

Successful teaching depends on the selection and application of appropriate pedagogies and procedures. Xue Lang Rong, a Chinese American professor in education, advises that teaching does not take place in a vacuum, and a teacher needs to pay attention to the sociocultural context of the institution. This includes "an awareness of the characteristics of the student population, recognition of a school's physical and human environment, an understanding of its academic programs, and a familiarity with the learning resources available at the university and in the community."[30] As an immigrant teacher from China, she shares her experience of learning to become a

29. J. S. McCroskey, W. Holdridge, and J. K. Toomb, "An Instrument for Measuring the Source Credibility of Basic Speech Communication Instructors," *Speech Teacher* 23 (1974): 26–33, cited in Chikako Akamatsu McLean, "Establishing Credibility in the Multicultural Classroom: When the Instructor Speaks with an Accent," in *Neither White nor Male: Female Faculty of Color*, ed. Katherine Grace Hendrix (San Francisco: Jossey-Bass, 2007), 17.

30. Xue Lang Rong, "Teaching with Differences and for Differences: Reflections of a Chinese American Teacher Educator," in *Women Faculty of Color in the White Classroom: Narratives on the Pedagogical Implications of Teacher Diversity*, ed. Lucila Vargas (New York: Peter Lang, 2002), 133.

more effective teacher in a predominantly white university as one of the few minority women faculty on campus when she was hired. She says that she refuses to let other people define her with ethnic identity, stereotypes, and misconceptions. During the first class of each semester, she would conscientiously communicate to her students her perceptions of her accent, ethnic identity, competency, teaching philosophy, and work ethic. She continues to clarify any confusion or issues about her background and experience when they emerge and believes that open communication benefits both the teacher and students. She has repeatedly sought out multiple mentors, especially during the pretenure period, for advice in teaching and even attending some of their classes to observe their teaching strategies. Over the years, she has become more comfortable with shifting from her old lecturing style to a more student-centered classroom interaction, which encourages peer learning and coaching.[31]

Studies repeatedly show that student evaluations of teaching are biased by the instructor's race and gender. Male students tend to give female instructors lower ratings in teaching and credibility than they give male instructors.[32] In a study of student evaluations of faculty teaching at the twenty-five highest ranked liberal arts colleges, racial minority teachers are evaluated more negatively than white faculty. Asian faculty received negative ratings relative to all other groups except black faculty.[33] One of the concerns of Asian and Asian American faculty is how to deal with students' course evaluations and their biases toward racial minority and female faculty. Negative course evaluations can affect contract renewal, tenure, or promotion, especially in institutions that weigh teaching more heavily than research. We need a multipronged approach to address this issue.

First, faculty can get feedback and input from students during the semester and respond to it. Teaching should be seen as an ongoing process and not an end product. Second, Asian and Asian American faculty should not internalize the shame after they receive negative course evaluations, but reach out to senior colleagues, administrators, and mentors to help interpret the evaluations and find ways to improve their teaching. This should be done before contract renewal or tenure review to lessen the pressure. Third, institu-

31. Rong, "Teaching with Differences," 137–39.

32. S. A. Barsow, "Student Evaluations of College Professors When Gender Matters," *Journal of Educational Psychology* 87 (1995): 656–65.

33. Landon D. Reid, "The Role of Perceived Race and Gender in the Evaluation of College Teaching on RateMyProfessors.com," *Journal of Diversity in Higher Education* 3 (2010): 137–52.

tions and administrations should provide adequate mentoring opportunities for new faculty members, especially racial minorities. They should be aware that increasing evidence shows that standard course evaluations are biased against faculty of color and women and should not let important personnel decisions be affected by potentially misleading and biased data. Fourth, the institution can incorporate other methods of evaluating teaching so that course evaluations are not weighed as the sole or primary means of evaluation. These other methods of evaluating courses and teaching include "peer observations of teaching, peer reviews of course materials, student interviews, self-appraisal, and teaching portfolios."[34]

In addition to teaching, scholarship and research and service to one's department, institution, and professional organization are factors for evaluation for reappointment, tenure, and promotion. From my observation, Asian and Asian American faculty spend a lot of time in teaching because they have high standards and expectations of themselves as teachers. Those whose mother tongue is not English work doubly hard in preparing for lessons and teaching material. The time devoted to teaching may cut into the time they have for research. Additionally, many of the junior colleagues are teaching in small colleges and schools far from large research institutions, without the resources and facilities necessary to do research. But teaching and research feed into one another, because continuing expansion of the knowledge in one's field makes one a better and more competent teacher. Research is not only for tenure and promotion, but for disciplining the mind and nurturing an active scholarly life, without which one can easily experience burnout.

As racial minority faculty, Asians and Asian Americans are called upon to provide a range of services for their departments and institutions. They can serve as racial minority representatives on committees, advisors to racial minority students, leaders of travel seminars to Asian countries, designers of service learning programs, and liaisons to the Asian and Asian American communities. Many faculty members find that they are overloaded and stretched from all sides. For example, they provide mentoring to racial minority students even when they are not their official advisors. The time spent on mentoring, such as meeting students outside the classroom and providing professional counseling, cannot be easily quantified and does not usually count toward the

34. Therese A. Huston, "Race and Gender Biases in Higher Education: Could Faculty Course Evaluations Impede Further Progress toward Parity?" *Seattle Journal for Social Justice* 4.2 (2006): 604; available at uis.edu/aeo/wp-content/uploads/sites/10/2014/09/Race-and-Gender-Bias-in-Higher-Education-Could-Faculty-Course-Ev.pdf (accessed March 28, 2016).

faculty member's workload. Thus, it is important to challenge the myth that only faculty of color can mentor students of color. All faculty should have equal responsibilities and commitment to recruiting and sustaining students of color, so that the faculty of color will not be overburdened.[35] Transracial or communal mentoring can also add to the students' experience.

In addition to the heavy workload, Asian and Asian American faculty often engage in activism and ministry within their own communities. These multiple roles and demands make the balance of work, family, and community very challenging. Some Asian and Asian American faculty have internalized the myth of the model minority and feel the pressure to work harder, to publish more, and to be highly involved in school affairs or community to gain respect and recognition. The demands are even greater for female faculty who are married and have children, because Asian mothers are still expected to take up the bulk of parenting. Women faculty cope with the situation by relying on extended family members and their spouses, making adaptations in routine, multitasking, seeking help from friends, and finding ways to decompress.[36] The academic tenure system does not work well for women because the pretenure period overlaps with child-rearing years. Institutions can offer more support to women faculty by being more flexible and adopting more effective maternity and parental leave policies. Asian women faculty also have to struggle for their rights and know the resources available. Instead of always putting others' needs first—family, workplace, community—they will do well to remember that self-care is not an indulgence, but a necessary means of survival for the long haul.

Asian and Asian American faculty sometimes encounter difficulties in relating to other racial and ethnic minority colleagues. Because of the history of slavery, some members of the black community perceive Asians as "voluntary immigrants" who come to the United States looking for economic, social, and political betterment. They resent that Asian immigrants come and take away jobs from native-born minorities. Seeing American racism in terms of black and white, they feel that they are the most oppressed group in society. In racial politics in higher education, issues faced by Asian and Asian Americans are often ignored, because they are seen as doing better than other minority groups. As a result of a long history of struggle against racism and

---

35. Joh, "Mentoring Models with Promise."

36. Several female faculty members discuss their coping strategies in Maike Ingrid Philipsen with Timothy Bostic, *Challenges of the Faculty Career for Women: Success and Sacrifice* (San Francisco: Jossey-Bass, 2008), 70–79.

the Civil Rights Movement, black Americans often adopt a more direct and confrontational tactic to fight discrimination. In contrast, Asian and Asian Americans shaped by their cultures value harmony and relationships over conflict and confrontation. This cultural difference may reinforce the perceptions that Asians and Asian Americans are less angry, less argumentative, and easier to work with. They are sometimes caught in between, asked to take sides, or called upon to be mediators for black and white racial conflicts. It is important to understand the history and cultural differences among the different racial and ethnic minority groups in order to struggle together in solidarity and to form alliances. The white dominant society often uses the divide-and-rule tactic so that racial and ethnic minorities will keep fighting each other. Oppression against one group means oppression for all. Open dialogue and acknowledgment of both differences and commonalities among different minority groups are important steps to move forward.

Conclusion

Mentoring is an important part of scholarly life and a meaningful way to give back to the scholarly community by supporting the next generation of scholars and teachers. Mentoring relationships bring fulfillment and joy when the mentees grow in their professional identity and become scholars contributing to their fields and professional guilds. Mentors of East Asian background need to create mentoring relationships in which the mentees can have the freedom to explore and grow, and mentors should not assume the position of authority figures. Successful mentoring relationships depend on many factors, such as personality, interpersonal relationships, knowledge, and experience. When a mentoring relationship does not work out, both the mentor and mentee should be honest and recognize it and remedy the situation or find a better fit. The mentor should have the mentee's best interest in mind and respect the mentee's choice and decision, even though they may contradict the mentor's. A good mentor provides guides and clues for the journey, but the mentee has to find his or her own path and take risks along the way.

PART 4

Generational Mentoring

Building Intentional, Demanding, Mutual Relationships for the Mentoring of Youth

Rodger Nishioka and Melva Lowry

Rodger:[1] Ted Uomoto was a greatly respected ruling elder serving on the session of the Japanese Presbyterian Church in Seattle. Gracious and kind, the Boeing engineer surprised me when he called my home and instead of wanting to talk with my father, the pastor of the church, he asked to speak with me. As the church school superintendent for that upcoming school year, he invited me to teach the middle school Sunday school class with him. I was a rising senior in high school. He had talked with my parents already, and both supported the idea, knowing that I had grown bored (and no doubt ornery since I knew the answers to all the world's questions as most rising seniors in high school do) with my own high school Sunday school class. When I asked Mr. Uomoto what that would mean, he said we would meet every week on Tuesday at the church in the late afternoon to go over the lesson for the next Sunday. We would pray and study the lesson together and then plan what and how we were going to teach. The invitation intrigued me and, truthfully, sounded much more interesting than sitting in my own class for the next year. I was ready to say a quick "yes," but Mr. Uomoto encouraged me to think about it, pray about it, talk with my parents and friends, and then give him an answer when I saw him at church on Sunday. When we met on Sunday, I agreed to be his assistant teacher for the next year, and what followed was my first significant experience of mentoring. For a full year, Mr. Uomoto and I met weekly to pray and study and plan and then teach each Sunday. I looked forward to our meetings as much as I looked forward to our teaching together.

---

1. Portions of this chapter written by only one author are set off from the text and labeled by the author's given name. Paragraphs that do not have an individual tag are jointly authored.

At first, Mr. Uomoto taught most of the hour, but by Christmas, we were sharing the time equally, and by the spring, I was teaching the majority of the hour. The next year, as a freshman in college, I taught the middle school class by myself with Mr. Uomoto checking in on me monthly.

In her important book *Big Questions, Worthy Dreams: Mentoring Young Adults in Their Search for Meaning, Purpose, and Faith*, Sharon Daloz Parks defines mentoring as "an intentional, mutually demanding, and meaningful relationship between two individuals, a young adult and an older, wiser figure who assists the younger person in learning the ways of life."[2] For the remainder of this chapter, we will use Parks's definition to further explore the different dimensions of mentoring youth.

Intentional

Everyone yearns to be recognized—to be truly seen. This is a particular need for youth today. It is stunning how many young people believe they are overlooked by most adults around them. Professor Chap Clark in his book *Hurt 2.0* makes the bold argument that for most adolescents in the twenty-first century, their experience of adults is one of abandonment. "There are at least two consequences," Clark writes, "of parental and adult abandonment. First, the adolescent journey is lengthened, because no one is available to help move the development process along. Second, adolescents know that they are essentially on their own." Whether it is the adolescent who is being driven (sometimes literally in the SUV) by well-meaning but misguided parents to succeed in school and sports and church and every other kind of activity or the youth whose parents no longer speak to them or care about them, both feel that who they are is neither recognized nor truly seen by adults in their life, and hence they feel abandoned.[3] As adults and leaders, it is not enough to simply try to understand the world of adolescents, but those who seek to be mentors of adolescents must engage them beyond the norms of their everyday life.

Faithful mentoring of adolescents begins with recognizing the young person, truly seeing them, and letting them know that you recognize and see them. It starts with naming them and explicitly telling them about the gifts

---

2. Sharon Daloz Parks, *Big Questions, Worthy Dreams* (San Francisco: Jossey-Bass, 2000), 127.
3. Chap Clark, *Hurt 2.0* (Grand Rapids: Baker, 2004), 53.

you see demonstrated through their actions. Time and again, young people are often surprised when an adult even knows their name let alone tells them that they saw how the young person helped that older adult put on her coat or helped put away the chairs and tables in the fellowship hall or read aloud the Scripture passage so beautifully in worship.

> *Melva:* I remember the first time I felt truly recognized by an adult. I had started writing poetry in elementary school (winning my mom two dozen roses in a local competition hosted by the newspaper) and by middle school had tried my hand in other writing competitions. In eighth grade my mom's coworker, Mr. Bennett, stopped me one afternoon and spoke about a poetry workshop for high schoolers that was being offered by the College of Charleston. Though I would be the youngest student in the class, he encouraged me to apply, stating he would write my recommendation letter. What struck me outside of this was that Mr. Bennett began by recalling a brief earlier conversation. He remembered how I told him about my interests in reading (he gave me a literature textbook of African American writers) and writing. He listened. He remembered! It turned out to be the best summer experience of my life. This began my understanding of what it meant to have someone not only see my gifts and talents, but to help me to see them in myself and to put these gifts and talents to work for others.

Consistent recognition develops further into the second dimension of being intentional in the mentoring of youth: support. Adults mentor young people when they champion the faithful gifts they see and the potential those gifts represent. Some scholars liken this role of adult mentors offering support to young people as the scaffolding that helps to build the structure. In building construction, scaffolding is crucial. It is constructed before the walls of the structure are built, and it surrounds the whole structure as, floor by floor, the building grows and emerges. Strong buildings need strong scaffolding. That is why support is such an important part of the intentionality needed in mentoring.

> *Rodger:* After a month of meeting with Mr. Uomoto, I remember asking him a question that had been on my mind for a while. "Mr. Uomoto," I asked, "why did you choose me to be your assistant teacher?" He smiled at my question and said, "Because I can see God has given you the gift of teaching, and I want to help you grow in that gift." In that simple yet

profound exchange, Mr. Uomoto conveyed that he both recognized and truly saw me *and* that he wanted to support me in growing into a calling that I had not yet even named for myself.

Good mentors not only offer support through consistent recognition and affirmation, they also offer support through providing tangible ways to practice and hone that potential.

Mutually Demanding

While recognition and support are crucial in the mentoring relationship with adolescents, another important characteristic is that the relationship be mutually demanding for both the adult and the young person. It is a delicate balancing act and likely one of the reasons that mentors need to bring the wisdom of life experience to the relationship. The truly healthy mentoring relationship is not simply one of recognition and support—it also includes making significant demands.

Professor Kenda Dean and Pastor Ron Foster, writing in the important youth ministry text *The Godbearing Life*, remind us that "affirmation in the absence of expectation does little for the faith development of adolescents." In fact, they argue, this pattern of affirming young people without expecting anything of them is one of the leading reasons that many young people find the church to be so boring and inconsequential.[4] If nothing is demanded of them, they expect little as a result.

Affirming and supporting adolescents in the midst of the many changes they are encountering in their lives is crucial. But as Dean and Foster so clearly and convincingly state, affirming and supporting must include challenge as well. Educators have long understood that for learning and growth to occur, support and challenge must balance one another. When support is strong and challenge is weak, there is very little if any incentive to change and to grow. It makes sense. If the young person feels supported and very few demands are made upon them, they will just exist in that pattern even if they are bored by it. But when challenge is too strong and support is weak, fear becomes the dominant characteristic, and paralysis often sets in for adolescents. Overwhelmed by the magnitude of the challenge with little to no

---

4. Kenda Dean and Ron Foster, *The Godbearing Life: The Art of Soul Tending for Youth Ministry* (Nashville: Upper Room, 2005), 54.

sense of support, the young person recedes into a self-protective posture, and little to no growth occurs. The indication of a healthy mentoring relationship between an adult and an adolescent is the balance of both support and challenge.

What is most telling in Parks's definition of the mentor is that challenges are not unidirectional, meaning they are not made only by the mentor and placed upon the youth. These demands and challenges are *mutual*. It is why entering into any mentoring relationship must be done with all seriousness and even caution. Not only must the mentor be able to assess if and when the young person is ready to face the demands of this mentoring relationship, the mentor himself or herself must also recognize when he or she is ready. The truth is that any mentoring relationship is bound to encounter unforeseen and unanticipated opportunities, ideas, and successes as well as dangers and risks for both persons. In this way, the mentoring relationship *is* truly mutually demanding. Yet while the relationship is mutually demanding and challenging, it is also mutually inspiring.

Something remarkable occurs when persons realize that they have accomplished some task or have grown in some way that they themselves did not or could not imagine alone. This inspirational result happens because of the consistent, intentional recognition and support and challenge inherent in the healthy and faithful mentoring relationship between the adult and the young person. In the midst of challenge, sometimes arduous and sometimes exhilarating, the mentoring relationship serves as a steady point of orientation beckoning both to God's imagined future.

Rodger: By the spring of my senior year after I had been teaching with Mr. Uomoto for the better part of eight months, at our usual Tuesday afternoon meeting, he told me that he could not be there for class on Sunday. He had to be out of town. This was to be the very first Sunday (in eight months!) that I would be alone. I asked if we shouldn't get some other adult to sit in, and Mr. Uomoto smiled and said, "No. You will do just fine. You are ready. You can teach on Sunday by yourself." I was not at all convinced, but Sunday came and, by God's grace, all went well. On the following Tuesday when we met yet again, he asked how everything went, and I told him I was surprised that the middle schoolers actually listened to me and cooperated for the most part. I remember Mr. Uomoto beaming and saying, "See, I told you it would be fine. Always remember, when God calls us to do it, God will be with us." Unaware at the time but fully cognizant now many years later, I realize that Mr. Uomoto was ushering me into a future that I had not imagined but surely that God, through Mr. Uomoto, had prepared for me.

Meaningful Relationship

It is important to note that parents can play a strong role mentoring their own children. It can be as simple as connecting their child to someone who can guide the youth further toward their gifts and interest. Just as the National Study of Youth and Religion concludes "that the best way for youth to become more serious about religious faith is for parents to become more serious about theirs,"[5] for youth to be serious about the gifts they have, it takes the parents to be serious and invested in their child.

Another key characteristic of mentoring youth according to Parks is that included within the intentional (both recognizing and supporting), mutually demanding framework is a meaningful relationship between the adult and the young person. By "meaningful relationship," Parks means that the adult mentor needs to "make sense" in terms of the young person's own experience. Parks goes on to further explain that the adult needs to be relatable to the young person. Specifically, the adult needs to be able to engage the young person in dialogue. This is one of the reasons that formally constructed or assigned mentoring relationships between adults and youth rarely work.

Melva: If it were not for my mother's own relationship with her coworker, Mr. Bennett, and trusting in his experience and character enough to introduce him to me and give us a chance to interact, I would not have had the opportunity to stretch myself during that summer poetry workshop. She could have easily just brought the information home and handed it off to me at the dinner table. Her willingness to be invested in my relationship with Mr. Bennett was the encouragement I needed. Giving me access to someone who could truly relate to my love of writing created new and different ways to learn about myself and find the right places to grow my talents. Providing space for our own relationship to develop allowed Mr. Bennett space to present to me the best outlets based on what he was learning about me on his own.

5. Kenda Creasy Dean, *Almost Christian: What the Faith of Our Teenagers Is Telling the American Church* (Oxford: University Press, 2010), 111.

The meaningful relationship happens best when it begins with an adult with whom the young person already has some regular contact. The consistency of this relationship, already established, allows for the mentoring relationship to grow more quickly.

Rodger: I already knew Mr. Uomoto after seeing him every Sunday at church for years. I knew he was an elder in the congregation. He and his wife were friends with my parents. I saw him leading in worship as the liturgist and had experienced him to be trustworthy and kind. Both of my parents clearly loved and respected him. Such consistency and constancy allowed our mentoring relationship to begin readily and easily.

Even so, the strongest and most durable mentoring relationships have some chemistry to them. Even in their intentionality, they are more organic and natural than systematized and mechanical. They ebb and flow even as they are mutually demanding and challenging. This kind of mentoring relationship obviously takes time.

Rodger: When I was a professor of Christian education specializing in youth and young adult ministry at Columbia Theological Seminary, I remember talking with a pastor whose congregation was involved in a search for a new youth ministry staff person. He relayed that they had been through three youth ministry staff persons in the past three years and the youth and their families and the whole congregation were frustrated. "We're going to start this whole search again," the pastor told me. "Clearly we have been doing something wrong. What should we be looking for first?" I recall telling him that on the first day of my basic youth ministry class, I tell my students that I can teach many things during the class, but I cannot teach two things. To be a faithful pastor in youth ministry, I need these adults to already possess two things. First, they need to truly love Jesus Christ and the body of Christ—the church. Second, they need to truly love young people. That's it. When I finished, the pastor gasped and said, "You know what, we don't have either of those things listed on our position description."

No significant mentoring relationship can happen without the adult genuinely possessing a love for Jesus Christ and Christ's church and a love for being with young people. You must start there.

Assists the Younger Person in Learning the Ways of Life

In an unpublished dissertation, Erika Knuth writes that the two aspects of a significant adult-youth relationship that contribute the most to faith formation that continues beyond the high school years are (1) that the adult engaged the student directly and consistently and (2) that the content of their conversations had to do with applying their faith concretely to everyday life.[6] Parks goes further when describing the importance of this characteristic in mentoring youth. "The task at hand," she writes, "is to search for ways to strengthen and confirm the still fragile young adult self and its integrity, while the young adult finds a place of participation, contribution, and significance in the world of adult work and relationships, freedoms, and responsibilities."[7]

The mentoring relationship for youth is not about a relationship with an adult for the sake of the relationship. At its core, the purpose of the mentoring relationship is to help shape young persons into adults who are able to live out their faith across all the spheres of their lives in ways that bring honor and glory to God and help adolescents grow as those created and redeemed and sustained by God. This is what makes the adult-youth mentoring relationship so significant and powerful to faith formation. At their best, mentors develop in youths a way of seeing the world that helps them live out their faith in meaningful ways. The adult mentors do this not only through demonstrating this in their own lives but also through the consistent use of action and reflection *with* the youths. This acting together then reflecting together creates a lifelong pattern of living out an abiding faith in Jesus Christ and participation in the church as the body of Christ. It is a way of living, but specifically it is also a way of honing a set of skills or disciplines that sets forth a lifelong pattern.

This leads us to a discussion of a term that is rising in adult-youth mentoring: apprenticeship.

Rodger: In a focus group of young adult leaders in the church recently, I asked one twenty-something young man how he grew to be a leader in his home congregation. His answer was quick: "I was apprenticed," he told me. When I asked him to explain what that meant, he said his home

---

6. Erika Knuth, "Intergenerational Connections and Faith Development in Adolescence" (unpublished dissertation, Fuller Theological Seminary Graduate School of Psychology, 2010), 17.

7. Parks, *Big Questions*, 131.

congregation had an apprenticeship process where interested youth were asked to identify an older church leader they respected and would like to emulate. For him, it was one of the pillars of the church—an older gentleman whom this young man had long admired for his vibrant faith and upfront leadership skills. "He just seemed to be able to talk about his faith and doubts so genuinely," the young man told me. "I always admired that and wanted to be able to do that." So over the course of several months, the two met together and the older adult taught the younger man how to speak out loud about his faith.

This is a helpful example of an apprenticeship, so named originally from the various trades and crafts of earlier days. Traditionally, apprenticeships are more skills based. A young person was chosen as an apprentice to a skilled worker. The young person would initially observe and watch the skilled craftsperson and then eventually be invited to practice incrementally and hone the various skills needed to become an expert at that craft. This often took many years. While apprenticeship was initially restricted to the various trades, lately corporations are identifying the specific skills needed for leadership (listening, analyzing, communicating, resolving conflicts, team building, problem solving, etc.) and selecting promising young adults who, like the early apprentices, begin by observing and watching successful business people ply these skills, then emulating them with constant supervision and evaluation. Once young adults have successfully mastered one skill, they move on to the next skill, eventually building a repertoire of abilities they will use in the future.

Timothy the Apprentice

The discussion of mentoring vs. apprenticeship leads us to look anew at the relationship between the apostle Paul and Timothy. Born and raised in the Roman colony Lystra to a Greek gentile father and a Jewish–Christian mother (Eunice), Timothy most likely met the apostle Paul on his first missionary journey. When Paul visited Lystra again, Timothy was already recognized by the Christian communities there as a potential leader. He was already seen and being supported by his congregation of nurture. Paul was clearly impressed and recognized gifts in Timothy, so with the support and blessing of his mother and grandmother (Lois), Paul invited Timothy to accompany him and circumcised him and ordained him. Timothy accompanied Paul to the end of Paul's life. References to Timothy are numerous throughout Paul's writings. The two began churches together in Philippi, Thessalonica, and Berea. Timothy was left by Paul to care for those new Christian communities and later rejoined Paul in Athens. It is clear that Paul believed Timothy was well qualified to lead. Paul sent Timothy to Thessalonica and brought him from Ephesus through Macedonia to Corinth. Timothy is mentioned in six letter greetings (2 Corinthians, Philippians, Colossians, 1 and 2 Thessalonians, and Philemon) and named by Paul as his own "beloved and faithful child in the Lord" (1 Cor. 4:17). Paul commends Timothy for his loyalty as one who follows Paul's teaching and his way of life through persecution and suffering. Bible scholar Thomas Oden writes: "No one was a more constant companion of Paul than was Timothy, in a close and long relationship that lasted about two decades."[8]

Clearly, as Paul's ministry on his missionary journeys continued to grow and expand, what may have begun as a mentoring relationship between the apostle and Timothy changed to an apprenticeship. Over the years, Timothy observed and emulated Paul's preaching and writing and teaching. He learned how to lead in the midst of conflict and persecution. He learned how to work with fledgling communities that were struggling, and he discovered ways to uphold and correct them. All of these apostleship skills were taught to Timothy during his years of working under Paul so that eventually, after working beside Paul for two years in Ephesus, he was entrusted with the responsibility of being the pastor of the congregation. This is the ultimate sign of the apprentice. After years of learning a trade, the apprentice eventually begins work on his or her own. Later, as an expert, she or he would take on another apprentice, and the cycle would continue.

Mentoring Communities

In an important further development of mentoring, Parks adds to her definition of mentoring by discussing the role of mentoring communities. After discussing the importance of the adult as mentor, she then explores the role of the community as mentor. "Because we are social beings," she writes, "if each new generation is to contribute to the ongoing creation and renewal of life and culture, young adults need more than to be challenged individually.... They need to know they will not be alone—or alone with 'just my

---

8. Thomas C. Oden, *First and Second Timothy and Titus*, Interpretation Bible Commentary (Louisville: Westminster John Knox, 1989), 5.

mentor.'"[9] Parks's claim is true. Youth are *social* creatures. One of the marks of the adolescent journey is the rise of the influence of peers and the community as a whole.

Those who seek to be mentors with youth must place that relationship within the whole of a community that recognizes and supports both the adult mentor and the youth who is being mentored and holds them both accountable. This accountability prevents the two from insularity and the relationship from the distortion that can come from isolation. Parks presents a vision of the mentor and the young adult in the midst of a broader mentoring environment. She names this as a context in which a "new, more adequate imagination of life and work and faith can be composed and anchored."[10] Mentoring communities in this twenty-first century take more effort than in the past. And though much of the mentoring experiences we discuss take the form and fashion of traditional face-to-face interaction, there is a space for technology in the building of a mentoring community and establishing a mentoring relationship. In fact, because we allow technology to do much of the work in teaching, parenting, and developing of our youth, it is important for the mentor to assist the youth on how properly to use technology as a tool to engage a larger community. Doug Pagitt writes in his book *Church in the Inventive Age* that we are "moving into a culture of creativity" and that this "creativity has altered the way we think about ourselves" and how we express who we are to the world.[11] Helping youth navigate how to be expressive and engage their faith more deeply on a global platform assists them in the creative process. It gives them another space and ability to learn what it means to have authority within and outside of the space they create.

In the book *Networked: The New Social Operating System*, Lee Raine and Barry Wellman speak to the changing nature of relationships, especially the role of confidantes. They say critics of technology believe that "community is falling apart because internet use has led people to lose contact with authentic in-person relationships."[12] Though the role of a mentor is more than being a confidante or a friend on social media, this aspect of a confidante in the mentor relationship is crucial. Let us be clear that the role of confidante is not to keep something from the parents or guardians of youths, but rather

---

9. Parks, *Big Questions*, 134.

10. Parks, *Big Questions*, 135.

11. Doug Pagitt, *Church in the Inventive Age* (Minneapolis: Sparkhouse, 2010), 28–29.

12. Lee Raine and Barry Wellman, *Networked: The New Social Operating System* (Cambridge: MIT Press, 2012), 118.

to build enough trust between both parents and adolescents so they know someone is really listening to their needs. In this inventive age, the mentor role as confidante allows young persons to be expressive as active participants in the relationship.

We are still learning what this new age of technology means to life over-all. Bringing the practicality of traditional mentoring relationships into the space of creativity and invention helps show the need for balance to today's adolescent. There is need for both collaboration and learning.

These mentoring communities then work to broaden the perspective and view of both the mentor and the youth. They form what Parks terms a "network of belonging" that offers a spacious home for growth. This home is characterized by asking "big enough questions"—questions that are worthy of pursuit for one's whole life. The home offers direct encounters with the "other" so that identity is not simply confirmed but is transformed. Mentoring communities enable the young person to engage in broader dialogue and to develop habits of the mind that include both appreciative inquiry (questioning that begins from a posture of delight and wonder) as well as critical inquiry (questioning that begins from a posture of deficit and deconstruction). And finally, mentoring communities engage both the youth and the mentor with the power of imagery—actual images and visions—of truth and suffering and hope and joy. In fact, Parks says that mentoring communities owe it to young persons to consistently show them images of their best and most positive selves as creations in God's own image, images of the other as both similar and different, and images of the world that are signs of life as well as death. While the mentor can offer these images in a one-on-one relationship with a young person, she argues, it is best and most powerful for the mentoring community to offer these images. We argue that the best place for these images to be shown is in the one moment that draws all of us together—in the worship of God.

Worthy Dreams

For Parks, the power and the role of the adult-youth mentoring relationship is clear. It is through the intentional, mutually demanding, and meaningful relationship of the adult and youth that the young person discovers a way to live and thrive in the world. Even further, it is when that relationship is nested in a mentoring community that it best grows and thrives so that young people dream worthy dreams.

Rodger: Ten years after my mentoring year with Mr. Uomoto, our whole congregation was devastated by the news that he had been diagnosed with pancreatic cancer. After a struggle through various kinds of treatments, Mr. Uomoto died, survived by his wife and two sons. By then, I had graduated from college and was teaching in a public middle school in Seattle. Years later, after seminary and graduate school, I found myself in a classroom teaching at Columbia Theological Seminary. In my introduction to Christian education class, as part of a ritual early in the semester, I invite students to recall a teacher who left a lasting imprint on them. I invite students to write the name of that teacher on a stone and to come to the center of the class and gently drop that stone in a large bowl of water, watching the ripples emanate from that action and imagining those ripples transcending the limits of the bowl and moving out to the whole of God's creation. And each time I do that, I write the name of "Ted Uomoto" on my stone and drop it in the bowl. I can see the ripples. I can see them through someone who named in me the Holy Spirit's gift of teaching and in a real and life-giving way demonstrated to me what that means. The ripples continue still. Thanks be to God.

Melva: About three years after my summer experience, my mother got a call one evening that Mr. Bennett had died suddenly. We had moved from Charleston, SC, to Augusta, GA, and so the news stung deeply. In fact, my mom and I had just discussed a need to reach out to Mr. Bennett, who had recently lost his father to a heart attack. It reminded me that time is not promised and that it is important to thank those who give life to your dreams. Though I never was able to thank Mr. Bennett or share with him the many writings I have done over the years, I know he is present and still encouraging me. Even in this opportunity to coauthor this chapter with another mentor from my youth, I can give credit to the courage I gained under Mr. Bennett's mentorship. To trust the voice I hear through my writing has stayed with me as I learn and express God's presence in my life. I have stated before that I knew I would write a book; and the chance to add my voice to a chapter in this book is a great start to the larger dream!

When we pause to look back over our lives, hopefully we can all recall a person or persons who gave of their time, experiences, and talents during a crucial point in our development that we still lean on today. Such a person or persons saw something that we were not yet able to see for ourselves and created the environment so that other distractions did not hinder what it was God gave them to instill inside. From these relationships grew courage, creativity, self-awareness, and most importantly faith. These relationships created space for creativity, enlarged our community and networks, and gave definition to dreams hidden in the gray area of the mind. So whether we can fully articulate the relationship or immediately recognize a key interaction or two with the person, it is clear that mentorship is crucial in helping our young people grow and develop to shape the church and the world for the glory of God.

CHAPTER 13

Mentoring toward a Humane Disposition, Attitude, and Imagination

Douglas Ottati and Elizabeth Hinson-Hasty

This is one time it makes sense to begin by considering a word and its history. Mentor, when capitalized, is a friend of King Odysseus in the *Odyssey* who is entrusted with the education of the king's son, Telemachus. Edward Tenner, an associate at the Lemelson Center for the Study of Invention and Innovation at the National Museum of American History, credits François Fénelon with bringing the character of the teacher Mentor into Western consciousness as "the archetype of a wise and benevolent counselor" in his *Les Aventures de Télémaque* published in 1699.[1] So does the *Oxford English Dictionary*, which claims the part played by Mentor is made more prominent in Fénelon's romance than it is in Homer.[2]

Both Tenner and the OED also suggest that, during the eighteenth and nineteenth centuries, educated people were expected to be familiar with the classical allusion to Mentor as Telemachus's teacher or tutor. For example, Lord Chesterfield wrote a letter to his son in 1750, which refers to "the friendly care and assistance of your Mentor."[3] Until recently, then, the word *mentor* referred to a trusted counselor, friend, guide, wise person, or teacher; and had *mentoring*—the gerund or past participle—emerged earlier, it would simply have named "a deeply personal and broadly educational relationship."

---

1. Edward Tenner, "The Pitfalls of Academic Mentorships," *Chronicle of Higher Education* 50.49 (August 13, 2004); available at ebscohost.com.
   2. *The Compact Edition of the Oxford English Dictionary* (Oxford: Oxford University Press, 1971), 1771.
   3. *Compact Edition of the Oxford English Dictionary*, 1771.

More Recent Usage

Tenner tells us that, during the 1970s, the term *mentor* began to acquire more definite meanings. An article by Yale psychologist Daniel J. Levinson published in *The Christian Century* in 1977 was based in research conducted on middle-aged adults. Levinson claimed that the mentor-mentee relationship is a "peer or older brother" relationship rather than a "father to a son" relationship. Mentors, in his understanding, imparted wisdom—sponsoring, criticizing, and bestowing their blessing on ventures undertaken by their mentees.

Also in 1977, sociologist Harriet Zuckerman published *Scientific Elite: Nobel Laureates in the U.S.*, a book that emphasized the importance of graduate supervision for setting American Nobel laureates on their way. Zuckerman noted that women laureates in particular "lagged in recognition and promotion"[4] due to fewer opportunities for productive mentoring relationships. Two articles by Gerard Roche published by *Harvard Business Review* in 1978 and 1979, says Tenner, mark the emergence of a literature about mentoring in corporations. Roche, then president and CEO of Heidrick and Struggles, says "his company's survey of recently hired business leaders" indicates that many "had had mentors, and that those with mentors took greater pleasure in their careers."[5]

The meanings of *mentor* and *mentoring* continued to develop along these same lines. For example, "Mentoring Millennials," an article published in 2010 in *Harvard Business Review*, notes that employees born between 1977 and 1997 want companies to furnish "a road map to success," and among other things, it also describes how "anonymous mentoring" can take place online.[6] Businessdictionary.com defines mentoring as an "employee training system in which a senior or more experienced individual (the mentor) is assigned to act as an advisor, counselor, or guide to a junior or trainee."[7] The University of Washington Graduate School touts benefits of mentoring. "A mentor," it says, "is more than an adviser. A mentor provides you with wisdom, technical knowledge, assistance, support, empathy and respect throughout, and often beyond your graduate career. Mentoring helps students understand how their ambitions fit into a graduate education, department life, and career

4. Tenner, "Pitfalls of Academic Mentorships."
5. Tenner, "Pitfalls of Academic Mentorships."
6. Jeanne C. Meister and Karie Willyerd, "Mentoring Millennials"; available at https://hbr.org/2010/05/mentoring-millennials (accessed June 8, 2016).
7. "Mentoring: Definition"; available at businessdictionary.com/definition/mentoring.html (accessed June 8, 2016).

choices."[8] Additional literature for colleges, universities, and theological schools explores the goal of increasing diversity through curriculum reform and also by nurturing faculty of color, women, minority students, and first-generation college students. Interestingly, however, even when these institutions resist the simple equation of advising and mentoring with career counseling, accrediting agencies often introduce corporate management models by emphasizing clear goals, outcomes, and assessment processes.

In recent years, statements about mentoring have proliferated. Thus, a 2015 article in *Harvard Business Review* argues that "CEOs Need Mentors Too" if they are to continually "upgrade their game," and that, when CEOs get mentoring support, "good outcomes follow."[9] The embedded assumption here is that mentoring will give professionals a competitive edge in their careers. A list of "9 Famous Mentor-Mentee Duos You Should Meet" includes Barbara Walters and Oprah Winfrey, Ezra Pound and T. S. Eliot, and Bing Crosby and Frank Sinatra.[10] A feature article in *Nature: International Weekly Journal of Science* claims that "having a good mentor early in your career can mean the difference between success and failure in any field" and then explores what makes a good mentor, for example, enthusiasm, appreciating individual differences, inspiration, and optimism.[11] A press release from the Carolina Panthers of the National Football League says a recently acquired veteran cornerback, Robert McClain, is competing for a position but also mentoring recently drafted rookies.[12] One internet list of quotations to inspire your own mentoring program includes Proverbs 27:17: "Iron sharpens iron, and one man sharpens another" (English Standard Version).[13] A second list includes the following from Mother Teresa: "Do not wait for leaders, do it alone, person to person."[14]

8. "UW Graduate School: Mentoring"; available at grad.uw.edu/for students-and-post -docs/core-programs/ (accessed June 8, 2016).

9. Suzanne de Janasz and Maury Peipert, "CEOs Need Mentors Too"; available at hbr .org/2015/04/ceos-need-mentors-too (accessed June 9, 2016).

10. "9 Famous Mentor-Mentee Duos You Should Meet"; available on mmlafleur.com /mdash/9-famous-mentor-mentee-duos (accessed June 9, 2016).

11. Adrian Lee, Carina Dennis, and Philip Campbell, "Nature's Guide for Mentors"; available at http://www.nature.com/nature/journal/v447/n7146/full/447791a.html.

12. Bryan Strickland, "McClain Mentoring, Competing at CB"; available at http://www .panthers.com/news/article-2/McClain-mentoring-competing-at-CB/30854fbc-1fc6-47b7 -b49f-854fea836762 (accessed June 9, 2016).

13. Available at https://www.geteverwise.com/mentoring/from-oprah-to-churchill-20 -inspiring-mentoring-quotes/.

14. "Mentoring Quotes"; available at risingoak.org/pages.asp?pageid=86992.

Toward an Alternative Idea

The authors of this chapter are theologians who want to hold out for a broader and deeper idea of mentoring-toward-a-humane-disposition-attitude-and-imagination-in-the-midst-of-life's-many-roles-and-demands. We are led to this perspective in part by a Christian humanist tradition with roots in John Calvin, a Protestant who linked true knowledge of self with knowledge of God and who also regarded the arts and sciences as God's good gifts.[15] The activity we call mentoring (or else something very much like it) has been critical for liberal arts education as well as for theological education. Certainly, it can be connected with instruction in various subject matters and practices, but it primarily has to do with existential self-knowledge and with a broader context of commitments. It concerns the building of character and sensibility and the cultivating of human imagination for the sake of a deeper life and a wider community more so than technical training in a given subject or solely for individual or commercial success.

From this perspective, much contemporary usage seems reductive. Sharon Daloz Parks, the commentator on faith development, business ethics, and leadership, made an observation nearly thirty years ago that still rings true today: "We are haunted by the awareness that we are vulnerable to mirroring instead of mentoring our society at this time in our culture's history."[16] "Mirroring" simply reflects the dominant norms and values of our society without thinking critically about their origin or their impact upon individuals, institutions, society, and culture. The hypnotic force of the commercial market in the contemporary United States encourages us to use the terms *mentor* and *mentoring* in ways that become synonymous with *coaching* or *training* for successful careers and building one's own personal success and wealth often at the expense of a larger community. A utilitarian commercial mentality comes to the fore that risks losing the integrity of life by abstracting one, comparatively self-serving goal, purpose, or task from the welter of interdependent relationships and responsibilities in which we live and move.

Within the theological frame of reference that we favor, a more appropriate view of mentoring will build on the earlier and more classical picture. Mentoring names a deeply personal and broadly educational relationship that

15. John Calvin, *Institutes of the Christian Religion*, trans. Ford Lewis Battles, ed. John T. McNeill (Philadelphia: Westminster, 1960), vol. 1, pp. 274–75.

16. Sharon Daloz Parks, "Social Vision and Moral Courage: Mentoring a New Generation," *Cross Currents* (Fall 1990): 357.

often takes place at a critical and formative time in the life of the mentee. Perhaps this will be a time that is also especially significant with reference to an important life-defining role, skill, or activity. Thus, mentoring may be intertwined with preparation for a specific profession, such as medicine, teaching, or ministry, or a with specific activity, such as managing an office or playing soccer, but it just as easily may have to do with a more general preparation for other aspects of life. It can involve the transmission of specific facts and skills, but we should also emphasize that the relationship takes place at points when the mentee is conscious that her attitude toward her future is coalescing and coming into focus. Most deeply and fundamentally, then, mentoring has to do with the formation of a disposition, style, or stance in life.

Two Early Mentors

Elizabeth:[17] Much of my understanding of mentoring was formed early on, long before I knew that I wanted to become a professor. Fleta and Ossie Marsh, my father's aunt and uncle, were two of my most important early mentors. They lived on a small farm near Sullivan, Missouri, a town just about fifty miles outside St. Louis. They raised a few dairy cows, cultivated a garden large enough to supply a bit more than the food they needed to sustain themselves, and canned enough fruits and vegetables during the summer months to eat well through the winter. They always made sure that they grew and canned enough to share with others.

I took the five-hour drive with my family from our home in Louisville to Aunt Fleta and Uncle Ossie's farm at least once, sometimes twice a year, when I was a child. As the youngest of two and with a brother more than five years older, I usually came in dead last in all of the family competitions, from the car games we made up to make the time pass more quickly to sporting events and game nights.

When we visited in the summer, Uncle Ossie usually planned a fishing trip to Meramec Springs State Park. The springs there are well stocked with trout. He took great care to make sure that I was included, especially when I was quite young, by teaching me how to choose the right bait, where to look for the best strategic locations to catch a big fish, string a fishing rod, attach the hook, cast, and then reel the fish in.

17. Portions of this chapter written by only one author are set off from the text and labeled by the author's given name. Sections that do not have an individual tag are jointly authored.

I seldom caught the biggest fish. But there were a few occasions where Uncle Ossie made sure that I caught the biggest fish. You can imagine that my success disrupted the family competition. It took a few visits to Meramec Springs along with time to grow in size and awareness that my fishing skills were not quite as good as I thought. Several of the times when I caught the biggest fish as a little girl, Uncle Ossie had actually replaced the small fish pulling my line with a much larger one when I was not looking.

In looking back on this experience, Uncle Ossie was doing much more than just making me feel good. He was watching out for the youngest, most vulnerable member of the family, ensuring everyone's inclusion, nurturing my confidence, and encouraging a stronger sense of community. In retrospect, I learned more from the intent of his actions than I ever did about fishing. Neither he nor Aunt Fleta talked a lot about their commitments or disposition toward life; nor did they seem to need to do so. They simply lived them. One of the most important ways they lived them was by taking in my father and his brother when their mother could no longer afford to feed her sons during the Great Depression.

Mentoring Relationships Remembered and Reinterpreted

Douglas: Mentoring relationships are deeply personal and connected with particular contexts and life events. While they often intertwine with the preparation of the mentee for a particular line of responsibility or a calling, they frequently also have a broader significance. And this is why they are remembered and reinterpreted again and again through the prism of the mentee's ongoing life and activities.

So, for example, my undergraduate English professor at the University of Pennsylvania, Benjamin F. Fisher IV, meant a great deal to me when he made the world of Charles Dickens come alive in his classes and then also took the time to interact outside of classes. He not only showed me rare manuscripts in the Firestone Library at Princeton and had me and other students to his home for dinner; he also talked over whether I should join a fraternity. (I did not.) But he means some additional things to me now as I enter my fortieth year of teaching. Or as another example (and despite the recent insistence that the relationship of mentor and mentee be sharply distinguished from all things parental), my relationship with my parents, Fernando and Alberta, stands out. My sense of how they cared for me and my brothers meant something more and also a bit different to me once I had children of my own.

There is, of course, nothing at all unusual in this. Similar relationships are likely to have been critical for the sort of person you have become. But please note: the specific roles and lines of activity, important as they are, do not exhaust the broader meaning of these relationships. That is because mentoring relationships such as these also intertwine with and point toward something more fundamental and far-reaching. Thus, while the roles of professor and student certainly ground my relationship with Benjamin Fisher, and while I use texts by Dickens in my classes to this day, the meaning of the relationship to me (as well as my appreciation for Dickens) also has to do with considerably more than technical training in English literature or in how to be a successful teacher. It points to a kind of faithfulness that ought to permeate other activities and roles as well.

Allow me a more extended illustration. Years ago, I worked with a man named Herb at the Rustic Cabin Esso Station on Route 9W in New Jersey near the George Washington Bridge. Herb was from Jersey City and had worked in gas stations for a long time. He was balding, married, had two daughters, and vacationed for one week each summer with his family in Atlantic City (before casinos). As I picture him now, he must have been in his fifties.

We worked together on some afternoon shifts to 11 pm. I arrived directly from school at 4 pm, whereas Herb began at 2 pm. We pumped gas and serviced cars through rush hour, but then, after the other attendants had gone home, unless we were swamped, Herb would not let me take care of another car until I had done my homework. After that, I took care of most of the cars. I learned a lot about how to be a gas station attendant from Herb, for example, how to fix a flat and the proper way to clean up oil-soaked concrete floors, but that really was not the half of it.

The station did a brisk business because gas was cheaper on our side of the bridge than in Manhattan. In warm weather, drivers in air-conditioned cars would sometimes pull up to the pumps, leave their windows shut, and signal with a "thumbs up" that they wanted you to fill the tank. If one did, and if you were an enterprising young man interested in a little extra cash, you might have tried the gas cap scam. Here is how it worked.

After receiving the signal to "fill'er up," you would walk back and open the small door to the tank, being careful to note what the driver could and could not see in his mirrors. You would then take a look at the gas cap, and if it was in good shape (i.e., not corroded), you would put it in your pocket and continue servicing the car (e.g., checking the oil and wiping the windshield). When you were done, you would tell the driver you noticed that his gas cap was missing, but not to worry because you could keep the gas from splashing out by stuffing a rag where the cap used to be. The driver might say "that's fine," in which case you became the proud owner of an extra gas cap. But there was a good chance that the customer, thinking you were about to turn his Buick into a Molotov cocktail (which, incidentally, you were not) would ask whether he could buy a replacement. You would say the station has some caps for sale, and that you could check to see if we have the right one in stock. Then you would walk back into the office, take the cap from your pocket, polish it, put it into a new box, return to the customer, and sell him his own gas cap for approximately $3.50 (which, in 1967 was twice your hourly wage).

One evening, I asked Herb, who gave me time to do homework because he figured that way I might not end up working in a gas station forever, why I had never seen him do the scam. He said because he did not do that kind of stuff. He also said that, even if some customers are not the nicest or the greatest, when they pull in for gas, they trust you to be honest, the same way you trust people when you buy a sandwich at the diner. "So, Doug, you need to ask yourself: Do you want to be the sort of person other people can trust or not?"

Well, that is why I never tried the scam. It is also a reason why I knew even then that Herb was not just teaching me how to be a gas station attendant. He was advising me about a sensibility, stance, and commitment in the midst of many activities, roles, and interdependent interrelations. Theologically speaking, he was instructing me in how to live in a manner that is faithful to others and indeed also to the wider enterprise of participating in God's world. There are covenantal and christological resonances here, for example, love of God and neighbor, true communion with God in community with others, but for the moment, I simply note that Herb also modeled a sense of personal meaning and worth. Maybe just how you act as a gas station attendant one Friday night on Route 9W is not the sort of thing on which the fates of nations, empires, or even successful careers turn. But what you do is sufficiently important to do it right and to do it well. And, to do it right and well is, in fact, to be responsible to the wider community in which you participate, or, in short, to be a responsible human being.

Institutions of Higher Education

In our therapeutic age, it is worth emphasizing that mentoring relationships like those described above ordinarily take place within specific institutional contexts, for example, family, business, or school. They are structured by an institution, its patterns, roles, history, and ethos. Because most of the mentoring relationships we have experienced have taken place in colleges, universities, and seminaries, here we offer some extended comments about mentoring relationships in the setting of educational institutions.

Colleagues

Some of these relationships are between colleagues. Consider these examples:

Douglas: Charles Swezey, an older and more experienced professor in the department of theology and ethics, took me under his wing when, at age twenty-seven and having never before set foot in the South and having never attended a denominational seminary, I began teaching at Union Theological Seminary in Virginia. Swezey taught me how to read a virtually foreign culture, and, as we taught the introductory course in Christian ethics together, he also had a strong influence on my approach to teaching.

Elizabeth: My first teaching job was at St. Andrews Presbyterian College. St. Andrews had a unique approach to mentoring in that it occurred through team-teaching in the CORE curriculum where faculty members met to determine their common interests in planning and teaching courses and then collaborated on a team to plan a multidisciplinary course. The first course I taught was CORE 400 Contemporary World Issues with Larry Schultz, a political scientist. Quite naturally, Schultz became a mentor for me as we planned the course together and created times for students taking their individual sections of the class to attend common lectures. We had the opportunity to respond to each other according to our individual expertise. It was a growing experience that continues to shape my teaching pedagogy even today.

Professors and Students

Most often, however, mentoring relationships at institutions of higher education are refracted through the roles of professor and student. Professor-student relationships differ in part according to whether the mentor is the mentee's doctoral advisor, seminary professor, or undergraduate teacher. In the first instance, the mentor ordinarily has a significant degree of power over the mentee's future, and the mentee herself may be preparing to be a professor. In the second, she may be preparing to minister in congregations, and in the third she may be verging on the challenges, joys, and responsibilities of adulthood and also exploring a number of callings and vocational possibilities. Again, it seems important to note that, in the first two instances, students are training for professions whose basic task it is to hand on and interpret values, traditions, and practices. That is, they are preparing for institutional roles that will encourage them to become mentors, and so they are sometimes especially sensitized to qualities that render some professors as trusted guides and advisors.

In most educational institutions, curricula and classes frame a critical setting. Opportunities for mentoring relationships between professors and undergraduates are affected by class sizes, whether or not students write senior theses at the direction of a single professor, and other curricular matters. Residential and commuting patterns on a particular campus also enter in, as do regular institutional activities, such as chapel services and athletic events. Again, the school's particular history and setting also contribute to its social atmosphere, and this in turn shapes or sculpts the specific sorts of mentoring relationships that occur. So, for example, the ethos of City College of New York, with its history of educating students tuition-free from the varied immigrant, ethnic, and religious communities of a specific city, differs markedly from the atmosphere of Davidson College, a small, high-tuition, liberal arts college outside Charlotte, NC, that was founded by Presbyterians, draws students from around the country, and fields Division 1 athletic teams. The ethos of Bellarmine University, which under the leadership of President Joseph J. McGowan from 1990 to 2015 was defined as an independent Catholic university, is different still. Bellarmine was founded relatively recently, in 1950, and began as an all-male diocesan liberal arts college with a strong focus for faculty on teaching. Today, the student body is coed and diverse, and the institution emphasizes growing programs in all colleges of the university, especially on the graduate level.

Academic advising also furnishes a possible setting for mentoring relationships between faculty and students, though formal advising systems where undergraduates are assigned more or less randomly to particular faculty have fallen on hard times. For one thing, students who look upon advising as a practical aid for negotiating institutional structures and expectations, how to register for courses, which courses they may prefer, how to monitor their progress toward their degrees, often are not much interested in formal advising. Especially at smaller residential institutions, they find out much of what they want to know from other students and from the professors with whom they are taking classes. Almost regardless of an institution's size, however, PhD faculty members tend to think their primary task is to give advice about studies in their particular area of expertise. Partly to counterbalance this idea, administrators try to strengthen pre-major advising systems. Unfortunately, the results frequently reflect management models favored by accrediting agencies that stress clear goals, outcomes, and assessment processes, but fail to encourage less quantifiable dimensions of mentoring relationships. Indeed, taken as a whole, these factors tend to obscure what is arguably "the most important job of the advisor, even the academic advisor," namely, "to help students understand themselves and take responsibility for their decisions" and to free them to make choices that may be "at odds with the expectations others have for them."[18]

Critical Issues

At this juncture, we should also raise some critical points. First, though meaningful mentoring relationships may emerge anyway, their emergence can be helped when potential mentors reflect upon and endeavor to read and interpret the sorts of institutions, structured roles, and patterns in which they operate. What characteristic occasions for formative personal interactions and advising does your particular institution furnish? Second, meaningful mentoring relationships require unstructured time for conversations as well as occasions for self-reflection on the part of the mentor and mentee. And these cannot be fully assessed according to particular rubrics applied to definite outcomes that materialize before graduation or sometimes even years later.

In our obsessively meritocratic educational culture, the unstructured time needed for self-reflection and meaningful conversation without assessment is

18. Harry R. Lewis, *Excellence without a Soul: How a Great University Forgot Education* (New York: Public Affairs, 2006), 99–100.

becoming increasingly difficult to come by. An institution that wants to encourage meaningful mentoring relationships needs to ask how it can organize itself in order to make available to people the needed time. Administrators beware! A school that saddles professors with egregious teaching loads and committee assignments, packs students' schedules with extracurricular activities and internships, and demands that faculty devise assessment techniques for every conceivable outcome organizes itself in a manner that retards self-reflection and the emergence of mentoring relationships between faculty and students.

Moreover, the problem does not simply begin with the schedules and expectations at colleges and universities. As William Deresiewicz points out, elite college admission offices today demand an extraordinary combination of academic achievements (e.g., advanced placement courses, science and engineering fairs, and high standardized test scores) and activities (e.g., travel, volunteer community service, and wilderness expeditions) that leaves little time for anything other than resume building. Students who attend elite colleges and universities generally are formed by this pattern already in high school and middle school, if not earlier. And, of course, their parents often encourage it. Indeed, Deresiewicz speaks of a system of elite education that manufactures students who are driven, but also anxious, "with little intellectual curiosity and a stunted sense of purpose," addicted to compulsive achievement, and largely headed toward careers in only two related areas: consulting firms and banks.[19]

The point we wish to stress here, however, is simply that the general pattern is especially damaging to self-reflection and to education in the humanities. This is because studying novels, patterns of family life in different cultures, historical religious practices and ideas, and so on does more than merely convey information. It also fosters the human imagination and presents the lived experiences of and proposals for human self-understandings made by authors and communities, proposals that students should be encouraged to ponder, consider, and compare with their own.[20] This is one reason why we call these studies humanities—they have to do with being human—and it is also a reason why the humanities help people to inhabit the world and participate in it self-critically, sensitively, and humanely.

19. William Deresiewicz, *Excellent Sheep: The Miseducation of the American Elite and the Way to a Meaningful Life* (New York: Free Press, 2014), 3, 10, 15–20.

20. Willem Drees, *Naked Apes or Techno Sapiens? The Relevance of Human Humanities* (Tilburg University, 2015).

Will liberal arts colleges continue to find ways to educate humanely in a meritocratic age of commerce and therapy that worships success? Can they hold out for and devise a different approach, a timely education to competence, character, and wisdom? That is a genuinely difficult question to answer, especially since these colleges find it increasingly difficult to make the case for (we resist the temptation to say market) their distinctive educational mission. But in any case, a step in the right direction would be to offer an alternative vision of mentoring, one driven not by commercially defined success and/ or meritocratic obsession, so much as by a wisdom that supports a humane disposition, attitude, and imagination in the midst of the many roles and demands of life together.

Mentoring through General Education Courses

Elizabeth: Like most Catholic colleges and universities, Bellarmine requires two general education courses in theology. I have learned in eleven years of teaching there how important this requirement is for creating the space for formative personal interactions with students and to cultivate not only knowledge but wisdom, wonder, and imagination for our common life. Of course, the impact these courses have upon students varies depending upon their own interests and investment in religion, but frequently the courses open up the students to new ideas about their own sense of meaning and purpose in the world.

One student who comes to my mind I met during my second or third year of teaching at Bellarmine. I will call her Emma (not her real name). The first required course in theology is called THEO 200 Ultimate Questions and introduces students to the various disciplines of theology as well as questions of meaning, purpose, justice, peace, equality, and fairness.

Emma was raised in an extremely conservative Catholic family and anticipated that the class would focus on the catechism. As a Presbyterian, I did not have the compass early on in my teaching at a Catholic institution to navigate all of the differences between the denominational traditions. More important for this story, when I introduce justice, equality, and fairness, one of the sets of readings I always include is a survey of the writings of feminist and womanist theologians such as Katie Cannon, Elizabeth Johnson, Judith Plaskow, Rosemary Radford Ruether, and Sallie McFague. Women's experiences are the lens through which we examine questions of justice worldwide. Emma had never encountered feminist theological arguments before, and during the class she really resisted them. I figured that I was not making much of an impact on Emma.

About five years after Emma graduated I received an email from her that talked about the importance of the class in her formation. She explained that the feminist theologians we read and talked about challenged her at the time and also created the cognitive dissonance she needed to see the marginalization of women around the world. At the time she wrote the email she was in medical school and planned to be an ob-gyn. Emma set a goal for herself to travel at some point to Africa to work in a women's hospital helping women with fistula damage, and she was seeking my advice. We have had even richer conversations since she emailed me.

Mentoring Lends Orientation, Direction, and Meaning to Life's Activities

To return to a basic point, mentoring connects with vocation and calling as something that lends orientation, direction, and meaning to life's activities. Quite often, it is a relationship that looks forward to particular activities and professions, for example, ministry and teaching. But, as is sometimes especially clear in the context of undergraduate or general education, it also approaches questions less circumscribed by specific roles, jobs, and professions. Who am I? What sort of person am I becoming? How shall I live meaningfully and responsibly?

In the context of an education that raises questions such as these, a mentor surely may offer verbal and specific instructions that have real intellectual content, for example, about the literary forms and themes in the book of Ecclesiastes and in Camus's *The Plague*. But just as important as what she says is her demeanor and/or what she does, how she structures her course, and other nonverbal communication. For, by her demeanor and her actions, she may show or demonstrate her integral commitments to the broad educational enterprise at hand, and thus also her sense for the importance of the mentee's formation as a person. And here we come across a kind of *assurance* or *reassurance* of meaning and worth, a sense that it makes a difference who the mentee becomes, and a demonstration on the part of the mentor that, in the business of human relations, there is something more and something different at stake than merely a commitment to personal achievement and success.

These reflections also recall one of the points in the earlier story about

Herb. Perhaps this is why good humanities education and good theological training are fundamentally subversive of merely commercial educational paradigms. Questions about who one is becoming and how one may live meaningfully have to do with wisdom rather than merely the comprehension of facts. And, they are endemic to education in the humanities, where we reflect upon the depth of human experiences and relationships and/or pictures of the human presented in diverse works of literature and art, social structures, cultural patterns, religious texts, rituals, and beliefs. Indeed, at some level, each of these meets us as a proposal or a suggestion for how to live.[21] And, of course, similar questions may also be featured in religious and theological training because they are part and parcel of inhabiting a religious tradition. How shall we be human in a religious and/or Christian sense? How shall we be Christian or religious humanly or humanely?[22]

Reflections on Mentors as the Primary Text

Elizabeth: Doug Oldenberg, president emeritus of Columbia Seminary, once said that the best and most effective teachers will become aware that "you are the primary text." In other words, a teacher's authenticity will matter to students or others with whom you work. Oldenburg was likely making a reference to the writing of essayist Louis Menand. Menand appealed to the philosophy of John Dewey who underscored the importance of professors as role models. "People learn, Dewey insisted, socially. . . . For those of us who are teachers, it isn't what we teach that instills virtue; it's how we teach. We are the books our students read most closely."[23]

When I was completing my Master of Divinity degree at Louisville Seminary, I served as the student pastor at Jeffersontown Presbyterian Church. I chose that placement because at that time a woman named Jane Krauss-Jackson served as pastor of the congregation. Krauss-Jackson had a reputation for authenticity, collaborative leadership style, commitments to justice, and work with the session of the church to make decisions by consensus rather than voting. Her leadership was very effective in a

---

21. Drees, *Naked Apes.*

22. These are perhaps the sorts of questions we expect to see raised by Christian humanists whether in the tradition of John Calvin, who linked true knowledge of self with true knowledge of God and regarded the arts and sciences as God's gifts, or in the tradition of the great twentieth-century Roman Catholic Jacques Maritain.

23. As quoted by Lewis, *Excellence without a Soul,* 102.

small congregation, which is where women are most likely to serve in my denomination.

At first I approached my work there as I would any program by creating a detailed, well-organized plan so that I could be efficient in my delivery of it. During one of our regular weekly meetings together Jane interrupted my planning of a program for the church with this question: "Where is God in all of that?" For a few moments I was not sure what to say. Jane's question cut right through my first approach to the task of working in the church and enabled me to realize it was a ministry instead. Most of the real work happens during the interruptions because you are not just dealing with a plan or vision to accomplish a strategic mission. You are dealing with people who inevitably have messy lives. Jane taught me well that it matters how mentors and pastors respond to the reality of the messiness and unruliness we inevitably confront in our lives. This is very true with teaching as well.

On Teaching and Paying It Forward

In this chapter, we have explored mentoring relationships, frequently focusing attention on their ordinarily taking place at a critical time in the life of the mentee as she or he prepares for her or his future. But of course the personal relationship also takes place at a particular time in the life of the mentor, who is almost always someone else's mentee. What needs to be said at the end is that the mentor will have a sense—and one that often becomes increasingly apparent over time—that her personal debt to her mentors can never be either entirely or directly repaid. In the final analysis, one honors and remembers one's mentors, one expresses devotion to their care and to their instructive devotion to their causes, by paying it forward to one's own students and mentees. To be a mentee or a mentor is to contribute to a valued historical line or tradition of those who kept the faith, those who remained convinced that the sorts of persons we become matters and makes a difference.

CHAPTER 14

Cross-Generational Mentoring

Theodore J. Wardlaw and Camille Cook Murray

It Is a Calling (You Cannot Pick Your Mentee)

Camille: Jim Collins in *Good to Great* says that great leaders often talk about being lucky. Their luck plays a role in their success. In church-speak we call this providence. Providence means that in unknown ways God's hand gently guides and shepherds us. In ministry, we find "luck" when our paths cross with people who become our mentors. Mentors shape our education and personal development more than almost any textbook, seminary class, or continuing education retreat. Finding a good mentor really can be providential. For me, this was most certainly true. It was in my second year of seminary when I crossed paths with a person who would become my mentor. Fred Anderson was the well-known and respected pastor of Madison Avenue Presbyterian Church in New York City. He was a towering figure with vast knowledge, experience, and gravitas. I was a seminary intern whose only certainty about ministry was that I knew far too little about it.

Over my two years as Fred's intern, I gained clarity about my own call to ministry. I learned the ins and outs of church polity and politics. I witnessed the joys and burdens of pastoral care. When I graduated from seminary and finished my service at Madison Avenue, I had a solid model for congregational ministry from which I have been drawing ever since. Since my ordination in 2006, I have called Fred dozens of times for career advice, ministry ideas, and simple encouragement. He mentors me still to this day.

Not everyone is so lucky as to find a mentor in seminary but if we are on the lookout, there are good people out there who are ready and able to walk alongside us in the various chapters of our ministry or life calling.

Ted: I agree that there is a definite providential element to mentoring and to being mentored. In this sense, there is something deeply biblical about mentoring as a calling. Young Samuel—essentially an acolyte and errand boy in the temple during a time when "the word of the LORD was rare" and "there was no frequent vision"—is asleep on his mat and hears his name called out in the night. He goes repeatedly to Eli the priest, and Eli first assures him that it was not he who was calling Samuel. Then, amazingly, as dissipated, out-of-gas, and as near as he is to the end of an exhausted priestly tradition, old Eli nonetheless gets it; and when Samuel once more hears his name being called in the night, Eli interprets to Samuel that it is God's voice, not his own, calling Samuel (1 Sam. 3).

An unlikely presence, Eli was Samuel's mentor in that moment of calling. Scripture is full of such helpful interpreters who, however flawed they may be, show up—as does Eli, providentially—at critical moments of vocational discernment. They remind us that mentoring in this sense is a holy thing, not always neatly plotted out in advance; and that what is often at stake in our conversations with our own Elis is an encounter with our own destiny and vocation in the eyes of God.

Like Camille, I am indebted to certain very powerful mentors in my life. Surely my father was an important mentor to me, modeling to me across earlier years of my life innumerable lessons in the school of character. He was a gentleman, raised on a family farm that formed generations of my ancestors; and he modeled for me an elemental grace and goodness toward others that was a far more desirable thing than the merely external measurables of success that are so often bottom lines in our culture. He had a gold watch—a Hamilton "Railway Special," complete with a gold chain, that he wore in the watch pocket of his pleated trousers—that I now keep in a glass display case on a dresser in my bedroom. That watch reminds me of my father, long deceased, and of the essentials of his impact upon me.

Another fundamentally important mentor to me was Dean Thompson, one of the editors of this book, with whom I served for a full year as a seminary intern in a parish in the coalfields of West Virginia. In that watershed year, he showed me a transformational vision of ministry that is not just priestly but also prophetic; and through his witness I began to hear more profoundly the voice of God speaking into the hardships, injustices, and inequities of life. I am certain that my ministry would have taken a more constricted shape had I not, in that crucial and formative year, encountered Dean's mentorship. Moreover, that one formative year in a working relationship with Dean morphed into a lifelong friendship (and cross-generational mentoring) in which each of us has regularly called upon the other for help or advice in a critical moment. There have been other Elis as well. A number of them, as I consider their relative seniority, have been father figures: compensating in part, I am sure, for my father dying when I was seventeen. They have been shepherds for me at various junctures.

Some of my mentors have been people who have preceded my own lifetime, who have spoken to me, through books or poetry or essays, from the annals of history. One of them was H. Richard Niebuhr, perhaps the most important and substantive American theologian of the twentieth century, whom I never met but whose writings I devoured as a graduate student at Yale Divinity School.

And some of my Elis have been younger than me. Which brings us to our second hint when it comes to mentoring and being mentored.

Seek Mutuality

Ted: Across my years of parish ministry, and now in this long season in which I have served as a seminary president, I have discovered that it is not a given that mentors must always be more senior, more experienced, and more titled figures. In my twenty-three years of parish life, serving with a total of eight associate pastors, and numerous gifted staff members and lay leaders; and now in my fourteenth year of serving with a large cadre of staff, cabinet, faculty, and students in my work at Austin Presbyterian Theological Seminary, I have chosen, and have been chosen by, at least a handful or more of mentors from younger generations.

These relationships have depended upon a climate of mutuality and have not developed overnight. Indeed, they would not have developed at all had there been the assumption of a rigid hierarchy at the root of our work together. For a mentor-mentee relationship to develop, there has to be a certain amount of comfortable space in which to risk conversations in which the primary topic is one's identity and not just one's position description. If a head of staff is so wrapped up in (or, perhaps, too insecure to set aside) the entitlement of being the boss—and therefore closed off to the possibility that there are things that he or she can learn from an intern, associate pastor, support staff person, music director, Christian-formation director, or maybe just about anybody—then, sadly, space for mutuality around some dimension of the pastoral life is not likely to happen. The mutuality at the root of mentoring permits the exploration of matters related to one's *being* and not just matters related to one's *performance.*

Moreover, I believe that such mutuality is more possible when there is a shared area of vocational passion. I have a passion for preaching—especially preaching as framed within the larger context of worship and the cycles of the liturgical year—and, as that passion has been shared by several colleagues with whom I have worked, fruitful examples of mutual mentoring across generational or hierarchical divides have developed and have often become longstanding friendships. I have learned a lot more about thoughtful preaching—enriched as it can be not just by faithful exegesis but by the contemporary resources of art, literature, and poetry—from Agnes Norfleet and Kim Clayton, two former colleagues in ministry at Central Presbyterian Church in Atlanta, than they ever learned from me. In this and so many other ways, they long ago became mentors as well as cherished friends.

Similarly, a few students, cabinet colleagues, and faculty members at Austin Seminary have met me in some other such space of mutuality and shared interest, and over and over again I have been their debtor. If one can set aside one's ego, or one's nagging need to be in a top-down relationship with colleagues, the blessing of mentoring or being mentored often just happens—like a gift, not a plan. Tom Tewell, a Presbyterian minister who has worked for years with the Atlanta-based Macedonian Ministry, tells me, "You do not decide you're going to be someone's mentor—*they* decide." Moreover, he says, "Sometimes you do not know you are a mentor." In the group work at the heart of the Macedonian experience, Tom observes that it is often through the mutual work of framing and asking good questions, and listening and probing and caring, and praying for one another that "everybody becomes mentors, and everybody becomes mentees."

Camille: Gallup's *Strength Finders* research emphasizes that all of us have unique skills and combinations of gifts. Everyone is gifted, everyone is valuable. The church affirms the same in our belief that each of us is created in the image of God. Each of us is equipped for service. Each of us is called into ministry. If Gallup affirms it and the gospel preaches it, then it must be true. These affirmations turn hierarchical models of ministry on their heads. It is not just the old who are wise, not just the powerful who should be heard, not just the seminary educated who should be respected. Younger generations of clergy are more comfortable with linear leadership structures and more collegial models for ministerial teams. They have less need for the supposed clarity that top-down leadership models provide.

With flatter structures, there is new openness with many more possibilities for who can serve in the mentor role. Mentors could be younger than us, less experienced, our peers in ministry, in different professions entirely, from a different faith tradition, or outside our normal social circles. Many, regardless of who they are, have gifts and insights to bring to the table to thereby empower them to mentor others.

The ministerial team at the church I serve in Washington, DC, operates without a great need for hierarchy. There is a high level of trust between colleagues, and there is space for open dialogue between us. We understand that we have the same end goal in mind but come at it with different ideas, experiences, and strengths. We each have become stronger individually by learning from one another. I see my role, as the head of staff, not simply to mentor and shape others but to create an environment that calls forth the best in each of us. This means my being open to receiving feedback from members of the team and their being able to trust that they will have feedback from me when it is needed. This means we have to use our individual strengths for the good of the team. This means we have to hold each other accountable. In these ways, there is significant mutuality. While we have different job descriptions and strengths to bring to the table, we all have something to contribute, teach, and give to the team. This model of ministry means we must at times be the mentor and then trade chairs and be mentored by that same person. Mutuality in mentorship relationships requires humility and trust from both parties. In these relationships we open ourselves to authentic growth.

I also frequently point to the NEXT Church movement within the Presbyterian Church (USA) as a splendid example of seeking mutuality in an intergenerational context. The movement is asking important questions about what God is calling the church to become. With this conversation, all voices of the denomination are being lifted up and given a seat at the table. In many ways, members of the old guard are asking the question but also recognize that they might not be the ones who will answer it. Those with years of experience in ministry are setting up the platform, funding much of the work, and then stepping back so that others might lead. In this way, younger and more diverse leaders are being empowered through the NEXT Church movement to discern God's call for the church.

NEXT Church is working to create a space where young and old will learn from each other in order to address many challenges and opportunities for the twenty-first-century church. This movement maintains great gratitude

for the current church, its past, and strong traditions. Yet, it is also enthusiastically curious and open to what is next for the church. It is a model for
how the church can mentor both young and old toward greater faithfulness
and fruitfulness.

Be Intentional

Ted: Thankfully, I am less likely to do this now, but earlier in my journey as a
dad, and with all the best motives, I would schedule special time with one or
another of our two daughters—say, when they were home from college for the
holidays, or when at other times I wanted to make sure that "this or that special
conversation about life" took place. The problem, as I gradually discovered,
was that the conversation was always (a) an appointment, (b) an appointment
based on my own availability, and (c) a source of some combination of anxiety
and irritation because it was so heavily structured. So, predictably, when time
came for that conversation, my daughters heard whatever I had to say with the
same openness that I associate with hearing fingernails dragged across a chalk-
board. I used to think that such careful attention to being a dad and scheduling
such conversations was a great example of "being intentional." My wife—a
psychologist who is far wiser than I will ever be—compared such artificiality
to that parental fiction that goes by the name "quality time." "You can't expect to successfully *schedule* a meaningful conversation," she said to me; "they
happen in the natural course of time spent together." She also shared that one
of the most effective settings in which rich conversations with your children
just *happen* is when you are all otherwise engaged in some other meaningful
activity. A driving trip to visit grandparents. An afternoon in the kitchen bak-
ing together. A time of need or vulnerability and a plaintive request, "Can we
talk?" In other words, parental intentionality is not simply getting a "special
conversation" on the calendar. It is more a matter of successfully *being there* in
so many of the other family moments—not just the scheduled ones.

What I learned from the passive resistance of my daughters is a lesson
that also applies to effective mentoring. Being intentional as a mentor means
practicing a certain presence that has to do with more than just showing up
for a routinized conversation scheduled on the calendar. Such conversations
can be helpful when two colleagues are checking off a to-do list. Maybe they
even help with the logging of a certain necessary amount of time needed to
build a relationship toward the moment when mentorship becomes visible.
But that moment cannot often be neatly scheduled or identified in advance.

Camille: Ted's insights remind me of an example one of my seminary professors gave us of being intentionally available during a pastoral care course. He said that each week on Wednesday he would pack a lunch and go out to the seminary chapel steps. For forty-five minutes a week he came out of his office to sit, eat, and generally look "not busy." He said his most fruitful counseling happened in those times when students would see him and sit down on a step and talk to him about what was going on in their lives and hearts. They might not have been willing to catch him after class or make an appointment to see him. But if he seemed so fancy free as to be enjoying a sandwich outside, then maybe he would not mind if they bothered him with their worries. This professor was, of course, as busy as the rest of the school but practiced being intentionally open and available to mentor and counsel the students. It is easier sometimes to just look busy and keep moving—dashing through coffee hour, arriving late to every meeting, keeping your laptop always open with an invisible sign reading "I am too busy." Mentoring requires a trust where others believe they are important to you and you have time for them.

A block away from the church I serve sits a very large and prominent Episcopal church. The rector had been in the neighborhood for over twenty years and knew the community and the challenges of ministry better than anyone else. When I arrived in Georgetown he walked over to my office and introduced himself and offered help if he could ever be useful to me. There was no rivalry or pretense, just a colleague in ministry being a good neighbor. A few months later, when a situation unique to the community arose, I called him to see if I could pop over. Throughout the next few years he became a wonderful sounding board for me, offering wise counsel, supportive friendship, and encouraging words. He made an effort to welcome me and be available to me whenever I called to ask for his time. He has since retired from the parish, but we remain in touch, and I count him as a mentor. He never would have become one if he had not been very clear that he was available and had stuck his neck out to be a good neighbor to me.

Sometimes It Is Just a Conversation

Camille: With my preaching group "The Moveable Feast," the mentor-mentee relationships are amorphous. The group is united largely by its common love for preaching the gospel of Jesus Christ. Beyond that, age, experience, region, and job titles differentiate us from one another. Each January the group spends a week together with a biblical scholar, with members sharing papers on scriptural passages. There are formal teaching moments in the structure of the group. Beyond those presentations the teaching becomes less formal. Around the table, the group tells tales, shares experiences, and catches up on the year gone by. I remember a conversation about the "dumbest things ever done in ministry." Seminary presidents and well-known preachers were one-upping each other with their best bloopers or rookie errors. The stories proved to be remarkable lessons to one another in what to do and what *never* to do in ministry.

In conversation and in friendship, these colleagues mentor one another. We share best practices, provide comfort in trying seasons, and make meaningful connections in ministry. The most important part of the time together is less about the time with the scholar and the biblical studies and more about the relationships being developed. Finding a group of cross-generational peers can provide opportunities to be in the mentor-mentee relationship. It does not always need to be a formalized one-on-one relationship. We often learn more from each other when we simply walk alongside others who share similar hopes, passions, and struggles.

Ted: I, too, am a member of "The Moveable Feast" and, like Camille, have found it to be the most significant colleague group I have ever experienced. The work that draws both older and younger members like us back each year is a shared passion for biblical preaching within the framework of the rhythms of the lectionary. But what we have also discovered in common across the years are strong ecclesial commitments that knit us together within the particular communion to which we all belong and whose churches we serve. This additional passion lies at the root, I suspect, of the conversations that turn around ministry. We share the same denominational polity and also share deep concern for the health and future of specific church councils and parishes; and thus the particulars of our various ministry settings and challenges are often well enough known for us to quickly be able to stand on the same playing field in our conversations. In our more casual times together, these conversations happen everywhere—around supper tables where a group is sharing wisdom or frustrations or good advice, or in quiet corridors where two people are sharing more privately regarding this or that pastoral blessing or challenge. And then, across the year when we are apart, group emails crackle with problem-solving conversations; or two persons speak on the phone regarding fears or struggles confessed and consoled. Over and over again, we have found ourselves in the company of great leaders!

None of the relationships within this cohort began with the overt agenda of mentees in search of mentors. They began instead with conversations. Conversations, to be sure, initially around preaching, and then deeper conversations around everything else at play within the universe of ministerial practice. The elements that make these conversations successful include, as Tom Tewell shared with me, framing and asking good questions, listening carefully as follow-up questions are formulated, observing well, probing thoughtfully, and, of course, caring.

My own experience in this and other cohorts reminds me, over and over again, that I could not practice my pastoral vocation without the trust, confidence and vulnerability that is possible in a group of competent intergenerational peers willing to be in bound conversations with one another.

Make Cross-Generation Work in Your Favor

Ted: A few years ago, while my older daughter was still in college, I had occasion to spend a couple of days visiting her on her campus. One night, I took her and eight of her friends to supper at a nearby restaurant. It was a great opportunity to listen, mainly, to what they were studying and thinking and preparing for. One was moving toward medical school, another was preparing for graduate work in civil engineering, and another was going to Los Angeles after graduation to try her wings at acting. It was a heady crowd around that table, and, during a lull in the conversation, I said something stupid. "I feel so fortunate tonight," I glowed, "to be in the company of the leaders of tomorrow!" My daughter said after a moment, "No offense, Dad, but you're currently spending time with the leaders of *today*."

If I did not know that then, I certainly know it now. My daughter's generation—the same generation that in the main is being prepared for the future by the seminary I serve—is a breathtaking collection of young adults. They are certainly preparing for the future, but they are also in profound ways creating that future now. If there was ever really a time in which a generation of young adults waited patiently for a retiring generation to finally hand them the keys, that time is gone. The mentee-mentor relationships in a time like this are necessarily fluid, and, to my delight (and sometimes chagrin), I observe the leadership roles shifting back and forth. Young mentees in my life sometimes surprise and delight me by becoming my mentors, and not necessarily because we negotiated it in advance.

Camille: When I was pregnant with my daughter, a college student in my church bought a fancy baby carrier for me to strap my daughter on my chest and parade around town. The note accompanying the gift said, "The rule is you must carry your baby onto the Georgetown University campus once a week. Nothing makes us happier than to see real people and *babies!*" Since I live only a block from the campus it was not hard to follow the rules. But the message was clear: when you are isolated from people of different ages and stages of life, it can feel very contrived and claustrophobic. The church is slowly learning this lesson.

"Intergenerational" is a buzzword these days in the church: intergenerational youth ministry, intergenerational mission trips, intergenerational Bible studies, intergenerational worship services. What we had identified is a need for mentoring to happen between the younger and the older. The church wants to learn from the faith and experiences of those who are in a different generation than their own. Former models would say we should segregate children, youth, young adults, singles, young mothers, men, retirees, housebound, and so on. Isolate the groups and then give them activities based on their interests. But now we are trying to figure out how to mix up those groups intentionally. Our older adults are now telling faith stories to our youth group. Our children are partnered with adults to serve the homeless. Shepherds are assigned to our young adults to mentor them in the church. We have much to learn from those who are younger and those who are older. The church can be one place where we help bridge the generation gap and enrich each other's lives because of it.

Pay It Forward

Camille: Paul writes in Philippians: "Brothers and sisters, join in imitating me, and observe those who live according to the example you have in us" (Phil. 3:17). In his letter to his friends, Paul is playing the role of mentor and teacher in the faith. And he is also asking them to play that role for one another; asking them to build each other up, grow strong in the faith, imitate each other in prayer, fast, give alms, and forgive; asking them to be companions for each other as Christ called his disciples to be for one another.

The truth is we actually need role models and mentors in the faith. We need people to strive to imitate. We need examples to look up to when we are learning the ropes. We have Christ himself, of course, but we need others to help make sense of this faith when the rubber meets the road. I have a list of people whom I try to imitate in faith. If you have heard me preach for very long you will have become familiar with these characters. Augustine for his very human wrestlings. William Barclay for his poetic way of making faith come to life. Dennis Olson for his wise and caring heart. My Catholic grandmother for her devotion. Ernie Campbell for his preaching. Fred Anderson, Frederick Buechner, Julian of Norwich, and the list goes on. These people of faith have given me glimpses for how to go about life as a Christian. If I did not have them—I would not be here.

When we mentor someone else we are not doing so because we have all of the answers or have perfected our doctrine. We do so because we are part of a cloud of witnesses, the communion of saints, the body of Christ. The joys of community are that we can learn from one another, be inspired by one another, correct one another, and forgive one another.

Mother Teresa, when asked about her holiness or saintliness, always answered in a matter-of-fact way that holiness is a necessity in life—and explained that it is not the luxury of a few, such as those who take the course of religious life, but is "a simple duty of all. Holiness is for everyone."

Perhaps that is a good reminder. Holiness is for everyone. We are all striving toward Christ's higher calling. And our odds of moving forward are much higher if we have people to look up to and imitate in the faith. As members of the body of Christ, other people are depending on us to help them find the way and mentor them as disciples. What a holy calling, indeed.

Ted: An effective ministry is well-nigh impossible if it is practiced in isolation. The minister who never reaches out for help, and never responds to someone asking for it, is disregarding a fundamental context for ministry—community—and that person's ministry is destined to fail. But the miracle of mentoring is that it has the power to expand throughout the community of time. In this regard, I love the image of the mustard seed that is found in Mark's Gospel. "When sown upon the ground," the mustard seed "is the smallest of all the seeds on earth"; yet, "it grows up and becomes the greatest of all shrubs, and puts forth large branches, so that the birds of the air can make nests in its shade" (Mark 4:30–32).

Fred Craddock once told of how Martin Luther King Jr.—the man most of us would say was the undisputed father of the Civil Rights Movement—never claimed that for himself. Instead, said Craddock, Dr. King bestowed that honor upon his father, Martin Luther King Sr. Sometime before his own death, Daddy King said that the real father of the Civil Rights Movement was the African American preacher who baptized him—a man named Paschal. But the Reverend Mr. Paschal said before he died that the real father of the Civil Rights Movement was a white Georgia legislator named Robert

Alston—a man who, long before civil rights became a public issue, proposed legislation calling for fair and humane treatment of African American convicts—and was shot and killed for it. But it was Alston who paid for Paschal to go to seminary; and Paschal baptized Daddy King; and Daddy King was the father of Martin Luther King Jr.; and through such a conveying of blessing from one person to another, a mustard seed grew into a tree, and birds of the air made nests in its shade.

This mystery is at the root of all ministry. Because generations before us have done the same thing—throwing seed that takes root and grows into something big—we, too, so germinated, proliferate in this time. We dig and we plant, and something grows up and people bless one another because of the seed that we throw. It is as if the gates of Eden are opened—even restored!—and we are allowed back in to live together in oneness. It is as if we remember that we were born for this: born to be a blessing, and to bless, and to be blessed. It is as if there is no moment, and no occasion, when living in such a way is not appropriate.

Afterword

Martin E. Marty

A Personal Word

When searching in my personal library for literature on mentoring and finding little, I retrieved Gilbert Highet's little classic *The Art of Teaching*. I had inscribed it "To Dad—a 'birthday card' to a master of the art—from a student. Marty 2/5/55." In 1959 I dedicated my first book to him as my "first and best teacher." My brother, historian Myron Marty, has used similar language to acknowledge our father, a Lutheran elementary school principal. Later, during my decade as a pastor, I was mentored by two senior pastors and then, in graduate school, was mentored by two historians and well taught by others. End of personal references. This book is not by me or about me, but about its accomplished writers and scholars and a subject dear to them and me.

I am breaking the rules of forewording books by intruding personally on the work of the authors, who had specific assignments. But, then, this is an afterword, so a momentary relaxation of authorial etiquette can, I hope, be forgiven. And doing so is here an immediate reference to a main theme observable to all readers of this book: it is impossible to speak properly about mentoring in entirely impersonal and theoretical terms. Mentoring is and is about a profound personal dimension of scholarly and pastoral work, as I shall soon note further.

Back to Gilbert Highet, who got crowded off the page after a one-line reference, but whose book could well serve as a companion volume to any book on mentoring. The distinguished Columbia teacher, who was in his prime when I was a student, wisely, in his preface, defended his thesis that "teaching is an art, not a science. It seems to me very dangerous to apply the aims and methods of science to human beings as individuals. . . . Teaching involves emotions," as, of course does mentoring.

Such a contention, if accepted, does not license scholars or other professionals to adopt stances that at least implicitly beg, "Let me tell you about myself." You have just met a diverse group of authors who did not beg for attention, but who responded, when invited, to share with readers their creative and mature understandings of the art of mentoring, and I shall henceforth give attention only to them.

There is no purpose in simply repeating, even in summary, what readers have read. Instead, I will engage in what I call "the act of noticing," in order to lift out and skein together a number of accents that readers can take with them and integrate into their own practice of mentoring or their experience of being, or having been, mentored. While the first several chapters in conclusion are not the first chapters in the table of contents, several on theology serve well as opening chapters, for they have opened the book for readers who bring various interests. Most of the authors pursue vocations in theological schools or departments, which sets them apart from most academic professionals in a largely secular culture.

"Say Something Theological"

Theology, in the broadest sense, first: I think of a time when my then colleague James M. Gustafson was introduced on a television program. The host, flipping through the data in his biographical sketch said, "I see that you are a theologian. So, say something theological." Some years later, when Gustafson was introduced for the University of Chicago's most prestigious in-house lecture and thus multidisciplinary audience, he titled his lecture "Say Something Theological." Which he did. So, now, we have asked our authors to say something theological. This they did, in a variety of genres and corollary disciplines.

Thus in the chapter by **Thomas Currie** on theological perspectives we read a comment by student Eberhard Bethge about theologian Dietrich Bonhoeffer's mentoring in an underground theological school in Nazi Germany. Bonhoeffer had worked out a course of study and prayer that, according to Bethge, forced students to "discover resources within themselves which they had never previously suspected." That quotation reinforces what Currie identifies and discerns as a key element in mentoring: theologians and pastors in this context, he writes, are "rendered open to being mentored, learning to ask questions they had not considered important before, even discovering questions that question their own firmly held certainties."

While tucking away the concept *discovery* and noticing also the word *open* for future mentoring reference, I also note that when Currie "says something theological" by reference to Jesus Christ (who aids in the task of what Currie calls "unlearning") he connects mentors in this tradition to the prophetic work of Christ. This unlearning helps in the formation of ministers, a task for which Eugene Peterson is quoted as being the task of "cleaning out the barn, mucking out stalls, spreading manure, pulling weeds," all messy business, as much mentoring, indeed, can be. And when mentoring is finished? It is not. In Currie's chapter, as in some others, there is talk of "becoming" a mentor, not "being one."

A second setting for mentoring discussed in this book, pastoral ministry, according to **Thomas Long**, is the pulpit. Unmentored leaders, or congregations of unmentored preachers, may approach their vocations drably and prosaically, when all along they ought to become increasingly endowed with what Long precariously calls "magic." Until one thinks about the unlearning of which Currie speaks, ministers are likely to find even the furniture they use working against them. The pulpit? When it is lofted above a congregation, as it so often has been in the history of architecture and piety, it suggests and sometimes (but only sometimes) it "preaches" an artificial authority. This is not the intimacy that almost all preaching should suggest—unless one is to preach a Sermon on the Mount to thousands.

Long's model for apostolic mentoring appears in a biblical quotation that does not find the author descending from a pulpit but working his magic through a letter, in this case from mentor Paul. "Now you have observed my teaching, my conduct, my aim in life, my faith, my patience, my love, my steadfastness, my persecutions and suffering. . . . But as for you, continue in what you have learned and firmly believed, knowing from whom you learned it, and how from childhood you have known the sacred writings that are able to instruct you for salvation through faith in Jesus Christ" (2 Tim. 3:10–15). Long reinforces the point for us: "It is all there in these verses, the essence of good mentoring: the mentor's life, in all of its majesty and all of its pain, . . . offered as a model." We are dedicated here to noticing what we might not have discovered without a mentor. This one is now hard to miss. It opens the reader or the one being mentored to magic.

Theological Mentoring in Ethics

To **Rebekah Miles**, the interviewer would not have had to say, "Say something theological," because Miles, professionally tabbed an ethicist, cannot say anything about mentoring in a Christian context without speaking of theology. She helps keep the plot of all this clear by drawing a line between theological mentoring and ordinary mentoring. She knows there is nothing ordinary in this field and finds that mentoring comes in diverse contexts. For her, the culturally common talk of mentoring today usually comes in the context of modern corporate life. That life is not, in her book, necessarily evil or wrong or weak. It simply is different and calls forth other models to advance mentoring in the world of commerce, industry, and career success.

Easy to miss, until we are called to be alert to context, is Miles's stress on the disadvantage to mentoring in the context of unmoored life, which thrives when there is not a shared worldview. Rather than leave a vacuum, unanchored and unmonitored mentoring tends to lapse instead into materialist versions. Instead of mentoring people in roles that advance only their own way, theologians mentor in the company of fellow believers who do share some measure of worldview, prompted by Jesus, and so they learn to give priority to the needs of others. Such mentoring is enhanced by the shared worldview that is prominent in and advanced by the company of fellow believers who would pursue justice together.

Mentoring in Relation to Traditions and Texts

Whether as individuals or in company, those who mentor and who are mentored need and find that they converge on traditions and texts. By "texts" I mean everything from ancient Scriptures through patriotic songs to formal guides to positive actions. In the Christian (and Jewish) traditions, there is no question but that a basic text must be used to bridge the generations. In present-day cultures, these are still what we might call privileged texts, but there is now so much evident diversity within and among the families of faith that the privilege is complicated and sometimes compromised by the presence of alternative ways of guiding and being guided. Still, it is likely that in present-day cultures, while textual traditions overlap, one may dominate in each.

For ancient Hebrews and the Christians who inherit scriptural texts, one title leaps out at the reader: the Torah. It is given absolute authority, because Yahweh is, in the end, its author and authorizer. Still, as **Walter Brueg-**

gemann makes clear, receiving a text as uniquely privileged does not by itself solve all the problems that come with mentoring and being mentored across generations. We who have by now read this chapter in the context of this whole book and who have been influenced by Professor Brueggemann recognize that one cannot simply point to Torah (and the whole "Old Testament") and assume that there are no questions to be asked.

Instead, Brueggemann uses language about the need for imagination and a leap of faith as one ponders what the text meant in ancient Israel and means today. He quotes James L. Crenshaw on the book of Proverbs and its insights about bringing up the young. The text promotes fresh discoveries "stated in succinct form," which "are presented as statements demanding assent because they represent a consensus. Such sayings need not be argued or defended; they just are." In what we think of today as a democratic age and when we are suspicious of patriarchal counsel ("listen, my son"), there will be many questions to ask.

To demonstrate some of the variety of potential and actual responses with Torah, we get several examples from within the text, and they are well worth revisiting by those who will be ready to leap and picture ways to imagine a variety of theoretical and practical outcomes. Here the "child of the Torah" becomes a mentor via his or her response to the text and speaks to the "children" (of any age) who would put the wisdom of the book into action today. One last time let me reinforce the awareness that, "Brueggemann being Brueggemann" as a mentor at this point, readers will be given the chance to learn to deal with contradictions, paradoxes, dilemmas, and more. Things can go wrong in such a tradition and in lives of persons and communities that live by it: "Mentoring may be wise, but it is not always prudent."

All this leads to the way a daughter community of children of Torah receives and wrestles with another set of texts in what we call the New Testament, as probed by **David Bartlett**. He deals with mentoring perspectives that, again, are privileged distinctively, now in Christian communities. Readers are not likely to forget the author's comment on limitations in the concept of mentoring. Mentoring belongs to what Dietrich Bonhoeffer spoke of as the "penultimates," and they have to give way to ultimates or the Ultimate. Bartlett, like so many of the authors in this book, offers a succinct and memorable sentence: "To put it too glibly, John's Gospel would have a very different christological climax if when he saw the risen Lord, Thomas cried out, 'My Mentor!' rather than what he does say: 'My Lord and my God!'" But Bartlett, in the spirit of Bonhoeffer, does not let that distinction lead to distraction, and so he turns due attention to mentorship.

To make his cases about mentoring, Bartlett turns to the letters of Paul, which he has long treated expertly and maturely. We profit from his familiarity with the letters, as he opens them to us as we seek to grow in our mentoring abilities. Right off, he turns to something hard to miss in Paul, but easy to overlook in many writings on mentoring in our time: he deals with and acknowledges the work of companions and fellow workers. Paul did not claim and put to work all his savvy in isolation. We do not have much evidence as to *how* Paul worked with the younger people whom he credited, but we can profit from what he wrote as a result of his work and dialogue with those who followed him.

Unsentimentally, Bartlett points out that, while the relationships signal mutuality and partnership, Paul is clearly the senior partner and acknowledges the way they carry on his work. And their relationship is special because it is prayed for. In the Christian context, no one should have responsibility for the growth of another unless all the dealings are marked by prayer, writes Bartlett. Yes, the notion of being prayer partners may be a cliché of our time, but Paul invokes it with thoughtful and demonstrative intent. Lest any reader think that Paul was utterly nondirective, leaving the one being mentored to be on his own and free to select his way at random, as it were, we have been brought up short by Bartlett's reminder that Jesus's prescribed rites of worship are commands. But Jesus also does not step back from the process. Astonishingly, while not abandoning his role as revealed Lord, he is also a friend and considers his well-mentored disciples to be friends to each other and to him.

A Tonal Chapter on Mentoring and Being Mentored

In the chapter by **Douglas Ottati** and **Elizabeth Hinson-Hasty** we readers get to profit from a dialogue between colleagues who have had a teacher-student relationship and now are both mentors and mentees, now interacting. The two were very clear about what they wanted their chapter to accomplish, and they phrase it in a hyphenated connection of almost record-breaking length. They promoted the idea of "mentoring-toward-a-humane-disposition-attitude-and-imagination-in-the-midst-of-life's-many-roles-and-demands." One hopes that the input of such an off-putting phrase does not alienate readers, because it summarizes vital themes in mentoring, and these the authors expound in graspable personal stories.

The reader rescues from one "tonal" chapter the idea of the "humane," in an era when much reductive talk about mentoring prevails, and the idea of "imagination," which they and other authors here regard as key in the world of mentoring. In their chapter we are made freshly aware that imaginative mentoring is calling-specific and colored by institutional location. Ottati reaches to the role of a gas station attendant to make his point, and Hinson-Hasty counsels awareness of the many dimensions that institutions, such as particular kinds of academies, impose on teachers and how these affect the disposition of everyone who participates in the life of such institutions. They show how to live with and then transcend the limits of academies that reduce their endeavors to résumé-building as a promise for students.

Circling back to a stress in an earlier chapter on the role of texts in shaping mentorships, this chapter served us well with a quotation from Doug Oldenburg, president emeritus of Columbia Theological Seminary, who urges teachers to regard themselves in a particular way: "You are the primary text"! They will be read as such by students. Those texts will often have explicit implications for those who seek to work in theological contexts. They will be asking, "Where is God in all of this?" This chapter begins to suggest how everyone who shares a calling and life with spiritually profound mentors will begin to find answers in the midst of what Hinson-Hasty calls "messy lives."

Now, Particular Contexts for Mentoring and Being Mentored

Luke Timothy Johnson provides a chapter typical of a second kind of essay. I might describe the first as general or generic approaches by Christians to mentoring. From here on I shall comment on insights and discoveries that the authors make or what I discern in a category that I call "particular." That shift does not mean that these chapters will not remain of interest to all potential readers. Thus, it is not that non-East Asians, non-Latin@s, and non-young will have found nothing of import for them because particular readerships are featured. Those who may seem outside the company of those particularly addressed will have certainly learned much about human varieties, transportable practical advice, and material of urgent interest in our era of ecumenism and globalism, when educated people will not hide from the stranger and, as Christians, will be highly motivated to learn all they can about the other.

So the essay by Johnson, who expounds on the realities of Roman Catholic mentoring, might be called the only "denominationally focused" chapter, recalling that Methodist, Baptist, or Orthodox Christians were not singled out in chapters. The accent on Catholicism needs little defense, in part because of the church's reach and scope and influence, seen through what different non–Catholics at different times regarded negatively or positively, and that they inherited or borrowed from in often unrecognized ways.

Here is a shocker that hits the reader well into the chapter: Johnson calls attention to most of what he detailed in the Roman Catholic tradition being treated in the past tense and belonging to the past. How can it be relevant among living traditions? Before that statement, the reader can hardly have been dissuaded from continuing to read because he or she can plunder what it contains for what can be put to use elsewhere. What's left? Before dealing with that, I recommend a rereading for the rich texture of particulars. Which other essay spoke of mentoring as a pursuit of sanctity? Yet sanctity was what the Catholic search was all about. Much formal mentoring before modern times was designed for life in monastic orders. It operated in contexts and with texts that were called "rules." Spiritual directors had taken direction and were to impart it. No longer does this situation prevail, at least not in classic senses.

This chapter brought home a realization that drastic changes in cultural contexts affect mentoring. What happened in the Catholic instance? Johnson points to the jostling that the Second Vatican Council gave to religious orders, to the attitudes to clerical and lay vocations, to the turn from mentoring of individuals in community, with the loss, for many, of the purpose of the former communities. Johnson's contrast between the ethos of two near contemporaries, Thomas Merton and Henri Nouwen, here illustrates the difference. Johnson ends with an honest confession that he cannot discern what new spiritual direction would and should look like. Perhaps he has simply left us with questions that have to be and are being taken up also in non-Roman Catholic communities.

Contexts Framed by Gender, Sex, and Race

All the authors imply or spell out that all mentoring is specific to the individual being mentored, usually in the context of the community that provides many values, positive and negative, that shape and are shaped by those who make it up. Most readers will assume that denominations represent choice, because even if one is born within one and is nurtured or hampered in it for years, the member can escape an inherited denominational tie, at no matter what cost. The same is not the case with matters of race—though one can, with strenuous effort, "pass"—and gender or sex. **Cynthia Rigby** and **Katie Cannon** take up the challenge associated with mentoring women. While they focus on the more than half of the Christian community, and though they are aware of centuries of women mentoring and being mentored, they are also aware that focus on and literature about women is lacking and that attention to the subject now in the twenty-first century is urgent.

Readers in many cases may have come to Rigby's chapter with expectations that, given its title, it would be about women mentoring women, and that would be it. Instead, the author may have startled such readers, especially newcomers to the scene, by shunning all concepts of exclusion. Instead, several times she stresses that feminist mentoring is "everybody's business," and she means it. Not for a moment does she represent what many would regard as ossified and retrograde: the notion of exclusion, that males are unwelcome as mentors and not integral to her thesis. No, she means it, though her "everybody" also does not for a line minimize the place of women in the mentoring transaction. I confess that I would have brought low expectations to the chapter because (a) I am a male and (b) I have pretty well figured out what mentoring should be.

Instead, Rigby comes up with a concept that one cannot easily evade or forget: feminist mentoring means "co-mentoring," something that all teachers and other leaders must learn. This means that they must recognize the built-in barriers to co-mentoring, such as patriarchalism, which is an oppressive force whether recognized or not. As a learner among learners, I was helped by her resort to a biblical instance for starters: Jesus as a feminist mentor. After she defines what is meant and draws upon Jesus's dealing with disciples Mary and Martha—biblical grounding being basic in so many chapters—she asks readers to realize that Jesus, Lord of all, is committed to "mutuality," not expressions of condescending lordship.

Rigby leaves no wiggle room for any who would evade the responsibilities of co-mentoring for any reason, including resort to patriarchal expression or, on the other hand, assign it to the tired zone of "women's work." Instead, "any and all who believe half the population should be equal to the other half, which should be all of us," are to—dare I interpret this way?—"co-grow" in mentoring. I hope that readers who traverse the terrain of all these chapters will return to this and others like it, to mine them for what is opened to them in "everybody's business."

Not so fast! So might some readers understand Cannon to be urging. She associates racial identity with sexual interests as she moves from feminist to womanist approaches to mentoring. She would have readers of this book and those who teach in spiritual zones associated with it not think that what Rigby discerned and promoted as mutuality or coactivity, whether it be mentoring or anything else, should be soft and cushy. Mentors are to be sensitive, but that does not mean that they are to operate as devotees of the soft, the sentimental, the compromising. And why? Because victims of oppression and people at the margins are especially capable of discerning, describing, and countering the patriarchal, economic, and, yes, religious structures that war against the soul.

While she is not called to and does not define much of what is meant by "soul," we readers can see that she recognizes soul when she sees it, and wars against whatever obscures or diminishes or oppresses soul. Her insight quickens her to advise "ministers, doctoral candidates, and undergraduate students" to be alert to and grow in "embodied mediated knowledge," which she defines and defends in some memorable detail. Hers is therefore a critique of "the notion of abstract, objective, detached, dispassionate, contemplative, mathematically calculated, spectator knowledge," which she sees as pervasive in the academy, including when religion is the focus in it. I would like to think that a case can be made for such, but not when mentoring is the focus.

Throughout, Cannon's goal is to mentor in such a way that mentees follow "the soul-wrestling invitation [she] extend[s] to all—*to do the work your soul must have*." That work will be informed in her case with explorations of the long roots of soul-expression and nurture visible in the glimpses we have of soul-work in Africa, among slaves in this hemisphere, endured under racial segregation, and other schemes of oppression. Her development of this approach to "soul" and "work" bears rereading by anyone committed to "embodied mediated knowledge" in cultural contexts of many sorts. May we also interpret all this in the light of what we have learned from Professor Rigby: that all this is "everybody's business."

In my reordering of the chapters for the correlative approach employed in this afterword, it is fitting to observe similar mentorial concerns displayed by Cannon in her stress on African peoples and people, especially women, and to follow **Alton Pollard**. No one need argue with Pollard's locating of his subjects as being "on the margins": understanding this is a given, it comes with the territory and history. The African American in America is the classic subject demanding embodied mediated knowledge, in his case, in relation to mentoring.

Pollard takes readers back to the intimate contexts in which informal and formal mentoring occur, such as "the extended family network inclusive of church and community," which he experienced as he was growing up and which he cherishes still. His focus on spiritual leader Howard Thurman serves well to demonstrate the good effects of mentoring in this context. We read of Grandma Nancy, who worked as undesignated mentor when Thurman's mother could not be present because she worked outside the home. She was "for [Howard] the transformative power of religion, challenging the hegemony of white racism and the religious parochialism of their local Black church, and creating her own hermeneutics of resistance and recovery." Pollard's necessarily brief portrayal of Thurman being mentored makes strong points about the value of modeling in religion and resistance.

In Thurman's case, as in so many others, there is an informal textual reference to provide a base. In this instance, it was in the preaching within Black churches. "My roots are deep in the throbbing reality of the Negro idiom and from it I draw a measure of inspiration and vitality." His next sentence is aphoristic and deserves the expounding he supplies: "I know that a person must be at home somewhere before they can be at home anywhere." At-homeness was vital in forming a necessary counternarrative and mode of existence for him, since oppression remains, as Pollard concludes: "To date not even the most resilient of Black counternarratives and resourceful challenges to the nation's racial calculus and animus has succeeded in making oppression a relic of the past." He quotes the reminder of Angela Davis—"freedom is a constant struggle"—and the need for mentoring to pursue it remains urgent.

If some questioned the value for *all* communities in the stories of *some*, in this case of people at the margins, a rereading of essays like Pollard's helps make the case. Names like those of murdered Emmett Till and the killing of Trayvon Martin serve Pollard well to rouse readers to being motivated to see through eyes of those on the margins more of what goes on in the presumed center. That center, again in Pollard's reading, makes mentoring difficult because of cultural trends that war against agencies that can foster mentoring. To face the situation, African American men will have to "embrace women's struggles as their own." Back to Rigby's counseling about realistic mentoring: it is "everybody's business."

Speaking about such mutuality, **Cristian De La Rosa** draws on the concept even when not explicitly referring to it as she concentrates on the person, the worth, and the goal of the mentored Latino/Latina = Latin@. Her chapter "considers the importance of mentoring within faith-based leadership-formation initiatives for young Latin@ leaders by gleaning" what she and others learned in a specific pedagogical program. It is perhaps the most specific of any of the chapters, but as open as so many others to discoveries and discernments that are translatable to other circumstances. The concern is over contemporary complexities that young Latin@ high schoolers face as they prepare for higher academia. Readers will also remember the specificity of her discussion of mentoring in a Wesleyan tradition. It is text-based and life-based in the quadrilateral of Scripture, tradition, reason, and experience.

She does not forget the ethnonational contexts of descendants of the colonized in the Americas. This positions them in intense versions of what other mentors discuss on these pages: they experience a "vulnerable existence of marginality" as they enter the academy to prepare for ministry in church-related institutions. The colonial context had been Catholic, but these Latin@s have another source of fragmentation, as they are Protestants, whose ancestors' religion was considered pagan and later, when they became Christian, were denounced as Catholics. One hopes that readers developed understanding, empathy, and resolve to identify with these "vulnerables" and would join their mentors in trying to be of support. Her discussion of the role of the buffeted Virgin of Guadalupe in all this is especially informative.

An afterword is by nature a summary gleaning, and readers may well take from this chapter both the concepts of facilitation and accompaniment, which point to "making accessible new geographical places and social spaces" in the emergent culture. Lest any non-Latin@ American readers take all this casually as an interesting tour of a marginal people, the author serves notice: get ready to take this into consideration in future concepts of mentoring. Statistics are on her side: Latin@s are now the largest minority group in the United States, as politicians everywhere have been beginning to learn, and by 2050 one of four people living in the United States will be of Latin@ heritage. "Facilitation and *acompañamiento*" will mark the Latin@s and leave a mark on other communities.

Continuing in that vein, East Asian people appear on the scene afresh. **Kwok Pui-lan** works with young Americans who have Asian and Asian American backgrounds and also have had "vastly different life experiences, educational background, national and cultural identities, and reactions to teachers and mentors." Admitted to American graduate schools, they often need a different kind of mentoring experience than those others, confused as they are by American academic culture, as it is "defined by individualism, competition, and speaking up in class." These are all perceived in opposition to the communal education in which one does not speak up, but expects lectures. Most Asians are used to courses in which there is an impartation of knowledge that they are expected to regurgitate. They are surprised to see how ready American students are to question and challenge their teachers, and this tradition and ethos calls for a different kind of mentoring than one experiences in non-Asian settings.

Paradoxically, Asian students may often suffer because they are regarded by many as model Americans who have assimilated well. Because of stereotypes that frame them, many of them suffer from what the author calls "achievement stress." They do well when teachers adapt to them and mentor by example. Such depends on the integrity of the teacher. Here is a leap in perceptions: the Asian American mentee appears in a context that is "directly opposite to the liberal, child-centered American educational philosophy, which encourages discovery and ingenuity," the very elements that authors and this "afterworder" pursue. No chapter in this book matches this Asian American "Confucian-inspired" culture in presenting challenges and complexities. The diversity helps prevent synthesists from too readily concocting an all-purpose, all-culture approach to mentoring.

Generational Complexities

While people in their eighties and even more are capable of being mentored and, of course, mentoring, in most mentoring relationships, even when they are not in patriarchal settings, the younger and, especially, the young will be the focus. They represent the future of the communities, whether of families, churches, academies, or nations, and have made their appearances in many of the chapters we have been reading. Still, they merit not isolation but special focus, and they received it in two chapters, the one dealing with intergenerational mentoring and the other focusing on youth as such.

Theodore Wardlaw and **Camille Cook Murray**, separated by twenty-eight years of age, engage in explicit conversations, even as most chapters revealed experiences drawn from implicit and remembered conversations. This whole book has been more devoted to conversation than to argument, to dialogue than to declaration. Argument is designed to settle things, while conversation is poised to raise questions and promote further inquiry and development. So we listen to the two authors of this conversational chapter, which reflects ministerial vocations but, as both participants make clear, its scope is not limited to professional ministers.

Inevitably, since they were talking about ministry, Ted Wardlaw speaks as a seminary president and Camille Cook Murray as a graduate and ordinand of ten years before they had engaged in this conversation. Not surprisingly, they converged on and began with the role of the calling to mentorship and wrestled with the questions of luck, accident, and contingency. Being Presbyterians, they are at home with and not ill at ease when speaking of God's providence in calling and mentoring relations.

If speaking so clearly of providence will seem surprising to many readers, Wardlaw immediately resorts to biblical models, juxtaposed with others, including his father, from the contemporary scene. (I am not embarrassed to point to Wardlaw's mention of Dean Thompson, an editor of this book, as a mentor: his career and his initiative in editing this book certainly certify him as a candidate!)

Wardlaw quickly elaborates on what he learned about mentoring, and stresses, as do one or two other authors in this book, mutuality. He believes it develops as both participants in the mentoring relationship share a vocational passion. It provides a zone where both can develop without constant reflecting on what mentoring means. He even quotes Pastor Tom Tewell who, grounding his work in his passion, says, "Sometimes you do not know you are a mentor." Wardlaw and Murray agree with others in this symposium: shared passion for mentoring and mutuality counter any impulses to rely on hierarchy and liberate those involved as mentor and mentee.

Following these themes is their injunction and conversation inspirer: that what transpires should be intentional. While the casual and accidental transmission of knowledge and experience is vital, arranging for formal transmission has a special value in a world of the random and confusing settings of vocations. Murray appropriately refers to a mentor who gave his seminary students an awareness that he was "intentionally available" during a seminary course. Not everything in class was rote and routine. All this occurs in contexts of collegiality and colleagueship based on trust, without which positive mentorship cannot develop. And the development occurs intergenerationally among the most forcefully and assertively mentored people. This point is sealed by Wardlaw's notice and recall of how Martin Luther King Jr. always reminded all who paid attention to him that Martin Luther King Sr. was the mentor who helped shape the life and ministry of his son.

This summary and reflection on noticed and noteworthy themes in this book does not do justice to a feature in the vocations of most mentees: they are young, and their youth calls for the special attention that **Rodger Nishioka** and **Melva Lowry** spotlight. In most chapters the author or authors diagnose the particular problems to be addressed or the barriers to effective mentoring. In the case of youth, Nishioka and Lowry regard their subjects not as representatives of living cultures that they embody, but as people who experience isolation or abandonment within a culture that surrounds them. That being the case in so many instances, the young do not naturally reach out to those who have gone ahead of them in the culture, but feel themselves isolated and alone. They occupy and embody youth culture.

When that is the case, developing mentor relationships is especially difficult, because people on their own need models and guides, but are not always at ease with adults who could complement them and journey with them. The authors, undeterred, throw out a lifeline to connect with them, suggesting that young people can begin to become open to mentoring if they feel themselves to be recognized. Constant recognition opens the young to becoming ready to experience support. This recognition can, in the Christian framework of these chapters, lead to the perception of theological dimensions. It is delightfully startling to read that Mr. Uomoto, Nishioka's teacher and a lay and volunteer Christian, had an answer when asked why he chose Nishioka to be his assistant as a teacher: "Because I can see God has given you the gift of teaching, and I want to help you grow in that gift." That was a high-risk answer, but it was perceptive and to the point for the mentoring relation.

The authors do not believe that being gifted and chosen are ends in themselves, bases for mollycoddling: instead, the supported youth is to experience demands, but these make sense only if—and here is that word again!—the demanding is mutual. They quote a youth ministry text that has a message for mentors of the young: "Affirmation in the absence of expectation does little for the faith development of adolescents." They begin to develop a meaningful relation across the boundaries of their years and their different roles. Then the mentored one will be assisted in "learning the way of life." And for that there appears a word rarely if ever mentioned in the other chapters in the book: *apprenticeship*, which in many relations and vocations tends to accent skills.

Throughout these chapters I was impressed at how at ease the authors were to observe and comment on models from the shared text, the Scriptures. Here it is Timothy who is asked to step up for examination. But even here, in another takeaway theme for all chapters and relationships: this apprenticeship is not a lonely technical skill development; it happens in the mentoring communities to which mentor and apprentice have access and on which they draw. In a useful phrase borrowed from a text by Sharon Daloz Parks, this is a "network of belonging," a valuable asset for any young person being mentored. All of these accents about young people can serve by analogy to all the other situations, counsels, and settings: in all cases, with Christian mentoring in focus, the end in view is what matters—growth in a new way of life that is promising to all. That is what this book has been about.

Contributors

David L. Bartlett was the J. Edward and Ruth Cox Lantz Professor Emeritus of Christian Communication, Yale Divinity School, New Haven, CT, and Distinguished Professor Emeritus of New Testament, Columbia Theological Seminary, Decatur, GA. He was an ordained American Baptist minister and served as pastor in congregations in Minnesota, Illinois, and California, as coeditor of *Feasting on the Word*, and as author of numerous monographs, including his 2001 Beecher lectures published as *What's Good about This News? Preaching from the Gospels and Galatians*.

Walter Brueggemann is the William Marcellus McPheeters Professor Emeritus of Old Testament, Columbia Theological Seminary, Decatur, GA. He is an ordained minister in the United Church of Christ and for decades has been among the most sought-after lecturers and preachers in the US. He is the author of over one hundred books along with numerous scholarly articles, including the 1989 Beecher lectures, *Finally Comes the Poet: Daring Speech for Proclamation*, the monumental *Theology of the Old Testament: Testimony, Dispute, Advocacy*, as well as many volumes focusing on the Psalms and the life of prayer.

Katie G. Cannon is the Annie Scales Rogers Professor of Christian Ethics, Union Presbyterian Seminary, Richmond, VA. She is arguably the "dean" among American womanist scholars and leaders. A nationally sought-after lecturer, she is a widely read prophetic author whose books include *Black Womanist Ethics* and *Katie's Cannon: Womanism and the Soul of the Black Community*. Her self-described mission is "to help people understand what it means to live as a moral agent," while confronted daily by "racism, classism and sexism." She was the first African American woman to be ordained as a Presbyterian minister.

Thomas W. Currie is professor of theology emeritus, Union Presbyterian Seminary. He was the organizing dean of Union's Charlotte, NC, campus, where he served for thirteen years. An ordained minister in the Presbyterian Church (USA), he had pastorates in Brenham, TX, and Kerrville, TX. His numerous articles, sermons, and meditations have focused on theology, Bible, ministry, spiritual disciplines, and church leadership. His books include *The Joy of Ministry, Bread for the Journey,* and *Searching for Truth: Confessing Christ in an Uncertain World.*

Cristian De La Rosa is the clinical assistant professor of contextual theology and practice and director of Contextual Education and Community Partnerships at Boston University School of Theology. She is an ordained elder with the New England Conference of the United Methodist Church and national director of the Hispanic Youth Leadership Academy (HYLA) and Raices Latinas Leadership Institute (RLLI). Among her research interests is the Hispanic/Latino community and its religious history.

Jill Duffield is the editor and publisher of *The Presbyterian Outlook,* an independent publication of the Presbyterian Church (USA), her denomination of ministerial ordination. She has served both large and small congregations and is the author of published curricula and numerous articles, editorials, and sermons. Duffield was the 2015 recipient of the Associated Church Press James Solheim Award for Editorial Courage. She is a frequent preacher and teacher at retreats, churches, educational institutions, and conference centers throughout the US.

Elizabeth Hinson-Hasty is professor of theology and chair of the Department of Theology, Bellarmine University, Louisville, KY. She is an ordained minister in the Presbyterian Church (USA) and is one of the emerging new theological leaders in the church. She is keenly interested in the intersection of faith and public life and an active participant in interfaith dialogue. Among her published works are *Dorothy Day for Armchair Theologians* and *Beyond the Social Maze: Exploring the Theological Ethics of Vida Dutton Scudder.*

Luke Timothy Johnson is the Robert W. Woodruff Professor Emeritus of New Testament and Christian Origins at Candler School of Theology and a senior fellow at the Center for the Study of Law and Religion at Emory University, Atlanta, GA. A former Benedictine monk and priest, he has written more than thirty books, including *The Writings of the New Testament: An Interpretation*, which is used worldwide in seminaries and religion departments. Johnson's research concerns encompass the Jewish and Greco-Roman contexts of early Christianity (particularly moral discourse), Luke-Acts, the Pastoral Epistles, and the Epistle of James.

Kwok Pui-lan is the William F. Cole Professor Emerita of Christian Theology and Spirituality, Episcopal Divinity School, Cambridge, MA. The author or editor of twenty books in English and Chinese, she is a cofounder of the network Pacific, Asian, North American Asian Women in Theology and Ministry. She is a past president of the American Academy of Religion and has lectured across the US and in Asia and Europe. Her publications include *Introducing Asian Feminist Theology*, *Postcolonial Imagination and Feminist Theology*, and *Discovering the Bible in the Non-Biblical World*.

Thomas G. Long is the Bandy Professor Emeritus of Preaching and director of the Early Career Pastoral Leadership Program, Candler School of Theology, Emory University, Atlanta, GA. He is an ordained minister in the Presbyterian Church (USA) and for the last four decades has been among the most sought-after preachers in the US. He is a preeminent homiletician whose textbook *The Witness of Preaching* is widely used and whose *The Good Funeral: Death, Grief, and the Community of Care* has provided a rich resource for pastors and people alike. His 2006 Beecher lectures were published as *Preaching from Memory to Hope*.

Melva Lowry is completing a dual degree program (Master of Divinity and Master of Arts in Practical Theology) focused on Christian leadership and nonprofit management at Columbia Theological Seminary in Decatur, GA. She previously earned a Master of Arts degree focused on discipleship development, from McCormick Theological Seminary, Chicago, IL, and is ready for new adventures in mentoring and leadership.

Martin E. Marty is the Fairfax M. Cone Distinguished Professor Emeritus of the University of Chicago Divinity School, where he taught from 1963 to 1998. For a decade earlier he had been grounded in Lutheran parish ministry. He was a columnist for and senior editor at *The Christian Century* for decades after 1956. He is a preeminent interpreter of religion and culture. Author of more than sixty books and coauthor, coeditor, or contributor to hundreds of books and more than 5,000 articles, Marty has served on two US Presidential Commissions and has received eighty honorary doctorates. His *Righteous Empire* (1970) won the National Book Award.

Rebekah Miles is professor of ethics and practical theology and director of the graduate program in religious studies, Perkins School of Theology, Southern Methodist University, Dallas, TX. She is the author, coauthor, or editor of six books, which include *The Bonds of Freedom: Feminist Theology and Christian Realism, When the One You Love Is Gone,* and *The Pastor as Moral Guide.* An ordained United Methodist minister, Miles represents the sixth generation in her family to live in Methodist parsonages. Among her works in progress is an introduction to Christian ethics.

D. Cameron Murchison is dean of faculty emeritus and professor of ministry emeritus, Columbia Theological Seminary, Decatur, GA, and has served pastorates in Virginia and Tennessee.

Camille Cook Murray has served since 2010 as pastor of the historic Georgetown Presbyterian Church (founded in 1780) in the heart of Washington, DC. After graduating from Princeton Theological Seminary, where she is currently a trustee, she received the Parish Pulpit Fellowship, taking her to the United Kingdom for studies and service. She previously served congregations in London, Oxford, Johannesburg, and New York City. She holds a master of theology degree from Oxford University and is a former president and current trustee at the Reformed Institute.

Rodger Nishioka is director of adult educational ministries at Village Presbyterian Church in Prairie Village, KS, and the former Benton Family Associate Professor of Christian Education at Columbia Theological Seminary, Decatur, GA. For many years he has provided unique insights into youth and young adult ministry, being widely sought as a conference speaker. As a preeminent leader in the field, he is the author of a series of books, including *Rooted in Love, The Roots of Who We Are,* and *Sowing the Seeds.*

Douglas Ottati is the Craig Family Distinguished Professor of Reformed Theology and Justice, Davidson College, Davidson, NC, having previously taught at Union Presbyterian Seminary. A gifted teacher and mentor of students, he is the co–general editor of the multivolume series The Library of

Theological Ethics, as well as the author of several monographs, including *Reforming Protestantism: Christian Commitment in Today's World* and *Hopeful Realism: Recovering the Poetry of Theology.*

Alton B. Pollard III is professor of religion and culture and former dean at Howard University Divinity School, Washington, DC. He has lectured, consulted, and preached throughout the US and Africa. He is consulting editor for the multivolume *Papers of Howard Thurman*, coeditor of *The Black Church Studies Reader*, and the author of *Mysticism and Social Change* and *Helpers for a Healing Community: A Pastoral Care Manual for HIV/AIDS in Africa.* An ordained Baptist minister, Pollard currently serves as associate minister at Covenant Baptist United Church of Christ in Washington, DC.

Cynthia L. Rigby is the W. C. Brown Professor of Theology, Austin Presbyterian Theological Seminary. An ordained minister in the Presbyterian Church (USA), she is committed to placing Reformed theologies in conversation with theologies of liberation, especially feminist theologies. She is co-chair of the Christian Systematic Theology Section of the American Academy of Religion. A dynamic and engaging speaker, Rigby is highly sought after by churches, academic gatherings, and conferences. Her books include *Holding Faith: A Practical Introduction to Christian Doctrine.* She is one of the general editors of Connections, a lectionary commentary series to be published by Westminster John Knox Press.

Dean K. Thompson is president emeritus and professor of ministry emeritus, Louisville Presbyterian Theological Seminary, and has served pastorates in West Virginia, Texas, and California.

Theodore J. Wardlaw is president and professor of homiletics, Austin Presbyterian Theological Seminary, Austin, TX. An eminent institutional leader, preacher, and pastor in the Presbyterian Church (USA), he served as pastor of Central Presbyterian Church, Atlanta, GA, from 1991 to 2002. He has also served congregations in New York, Texas, and Tennessee. He has taught and served as a trustee at several theological institutions and the Montreat Conference Center. He is the author of numerous articles on Bible, theology, preaching, and pastoral leadership.

Index